Industrial Economy of India

Industrial Economy of India

A. Sankaran
M. Ravichandran

SERIALS PUBLICATIONS
NEW DELHI (INDIA)

First Published - 2010

ISBN: 978-81-8387-364-2

Published by

SERIALS PUBLICATIONS
4830/24, Prahlad Street, Ansari Road
Darya Ganj, New Delhi-110002 (India)
Phone : 23245225 Fax : 91-11-23272135
E-mail: serials@satyam.net.in

CONTENTS

PREFACE

This book is the outcome of the research work conducted in the Department of Economics, Bharathidasan University, Tiruchirappalli. Industrial economics is one of the most important branches of the discipline of economics. This branch has been growing over the period through contributions made by several researchers in various parts of the country. However, research works in the recent past are scanty. Therefore it is necessary to bring out research studies in the form of a book with updation, which may serve as reference material for students and research scholars as well.

Authentic data from the Annual Survey of Industry were used, besides the valuable insights gained from the industrial experts. While presenting an analytical and critical account of theories, reviews and interpretation, care has been taken to treat the subject matter systematically and lucidly so that an average student can easily understand the content of this book.

This book comprises five chapters, among them, Chapter one comprises of meaning, objectives, methodology, hypothesis and limitations. Second chapter contains the summary of international, national and state level studies on industrial economy on growth, structural change, productivity and critical remarks. The third chapter is a short profile of industrial economy, the fourth chapter encompasse a detailed analysis and discussion of industrial economy using various statistics, information and analytical tools in different dimensions-growth structure and productivity trend. The final fifth chapter brings forth the quintessence of the study including summary, findings and conclusion. Information on classification on industries is included under appendix and hope that this book will be a useful companion for all the academic groups.

A. Sankaran
M. Ravichandran

ABBREVIATIONS

AAGR	=	Annual Average Growth Rate.
ABI	=	Agro-Based Industries.
AG	=	Annual Growth.
ASI	=	Annual Survey of Industries.
BG	=	Basic Goods.
CBI	=	Chemical Based Industries.
CDG	=	Consumer Durable Goods
CG	=	Capital Goods
CGR	=	Compound growth rate
CI	=	Capital Inputs.
CIF	=	Chief Inspector of Factories.
CMIE	=	Centre for Monitoring Indian Economy.
CNDG	=	Consumer Non-Durable Goods.
CP	=	Capital Productivity.
CSO	=	Central Statistical Organization.
DEAR	=	Department of Evaluation and Applied research
EPW	=	Economic and Political Weekly.
FC	=	Fixed Capital.
GDP	=	Gross Domestic Product.
GVA	=	Gross Value Added.
GVO	=	Gross Value of Output.
HDR	=	Human Development Report.
IBC	=	Input Based Classification.

ICICI	=	Industrial Credit Investment Corporation of India.
IDBI	=	The Industrial Development Bank of India
IDR	=	India Development Report.
IFCI	=	Industrial Finance Corporation of India
IIP	=	Index of Industrial Production.
ILO	=	International Labour Organization.
IMG	=	Inter Mediate Goods
LI	=	Labour Inputs.
LP	=	Labour Productivity.
MBI	=	Metal-Based Industries.
MVA	=	Manufacturing Value Added
NA	=	Not Available.
NAS	=	National Accounts Statistics.
NDP	=	Net Domestic Product.
NEC	=	Not Elsewhere Classified.
NIC	=	National Industrial Classification.
NNP	=	Net National Product.
NSIC	=	National Small Industries Corporation.
NSS	=	National Sample Survey.
OCDE	=	Organization for Economic Co-operation and Development.
PC	=	Percentage Share.
RBI	=	Reserve Bank of India.
SSI	=	Small Scale Industries.
TFI	=	Total Factor Inputs.
UBC	=	Use Based Classification.
WPI	=	Wholesale Price Index.

CHAPTER 1

INTRODUCTION

Real progress must ultimately depend on industrialization
–Jawaharlal Nehru

Every economy in this world has to undergo some perceptible transformation in its road to development. Broadly speaking, the pattern of development is indicated by the declining share of primary sector, growing importance of the secondary sector and subsequently the tertiary sector (Clark, 1960, Kuznets, 1972). "England, Japan, Russia and United States had different type of economic development over different periods of time and yet they all experienced one thing in common – the proportion of population engaged in agriculture declined and an increasing proportion got engaged in modern industrial production" (Kour, 1982). But occasionally, the tertiary sector is getting prominence even before the industrial sector is sufficiently developed.

The industrialization, what Kuznet called 'modern economic growth' (Kuznet, 1966) is a multi dimensional process. *In the literature of Marx* industrialization is defined as the establishment and development of the production of the means of production. It refers to the completion of the industrial revolution and the transfer of the economy to industrial methods of production. (Cf. Shirokov, 1973).

Industrialization is a sine quo non of economic development (GOI, 1980). The World Bank report rightly remarked that Industrialization is viewed as almost synonymous with development (World Bank, 1995), and it eventually leads to enhanced per capita income and standard of living through spread effect (Chenery et.al, 1986).

CHARACTERISTICS OF INDUSTRIALIZATION

There are some essential characteristics for an unambiguous industrialization process. Those are, first, the proportion of the national income derived from manufacturing activities and from secondary sector in general goes up, except perhaps for cyclical interruptions. Secondly, the proportion of the working population engaged in manufacturing and secondary sector in general also shows an uptrend. While, these two ratios are increasing, the income per head of the population also goes up except again for temporary interruptions (Cf. Datta. 1952, Kuznets, 1966, 1971, Sutcliffe, 1971). The other characteristics that are often associated with industrialization, include a narrowing and ultimate closing of the gap between productivity per head in the secondary sector and in the primary sector (that is, agriculture, forestry and fishing), frequent changes in the style of production, the fashioning of new products, increase in the proportion of population living in towns, changes in the relative ratios of expenditure on capital formation and consumption (Bagchi, 1987).

One of the distinguishing characteristics of industrialization process is the structural change that it brings about within the industrial sector (intra-sectoral) and between the sectors (inter-sectoral). The quality of industrialization largely depends upon the magnitude and pattern of the structural changes. The structural changes are defined (generally) as changes in the relative weight of the significant components of the aggregative indicators of the economy, such as national product and expenditure, exports and imports, population and the labour force. (Ishikawa, 1987).

The structural analysis of the industrial development is an essential aspect of development studies. The economic development of the state, or of any region, is, in other words the process of structural transformation, that is, "the changing proportional contributions of the major sectors-agriculture, industry and services–to aggregate product, and their changing share in labour force and other productive forces. Three shifts in productive structure associated with modern economic growth are... First, the movement away from agriculture (in favour of manufacturing activity) usually referred to as industrialization, second, the change in structure within industry proper, and particularly in manufacturing; and finally shifts in the structure of service sector" (Kuznets, 1966). The sequence of structural changes in the industry sector differs from region to region, from period to period ccording to the differences in the endowment of natural resources and in the strategy adopted in harnessing them. The magnitude and the structure of industrial development are largely influenced by the socio-cultural conditions and the political-economic ideologies. Industrialization is an effort in which the underdeveloped countries place a major role of finding a solution to their problems of poverty, insecurity, overpopulation and ending their newly realized backwardness in the modern world (Murray D, & D.Bryce, 1960). The effects of industrialization on the economy viz, productivity, occupational structure, the composition of the industrial output, national income and foreign trade and the structure of demand in the country-constitute the criterion to assess whether the economy is industrially advanced or not.

SIGNIFICANCE

The significance of industrial development and structural changes have been well expressed by an approach conducted by Fisher (1939), Clark (1940), Kuznets(1957-64) and Chenerry and Syrquin (1975) using inter country cross-section data for selected countries. They concluded that there are statistically certain universal relationship between economic growth and structural changes(Cf. Shigeru Ishikawa, 1987).

Similarly, the significance of structural changes in an economy is stressed by Simon Kuznets(1966). "The industrial structure of national output and productive resources is a key aspect of an economy in the process of growth because it permits us to observe the impact of advance in technological knowledge, the differential response of demand to increased productive capacity and rise in per capita income and the shifts in the size and location of groups in society associated with the different industries". The development of industry has been accompanied by wide spread changes in the whole way of life. It affects profoundly, the family structure socio-cultural values, social stratification, educational systems, economic pattern and the whole life. Many of the developing countries have experienced that; industrialization plays a dominant role in bringing about social and economic changes (Mohammed Peer, 1993). The chronic problems of developing countries are poverty and unemployment. Rapid industrialization is the best remedy suggested for the melody of unemployment and poverty. Industrial sector of an economy saves foreign exchange, raises output per head and creates investment capital much faster than any other sector possibly can. It is of practical significance to identify the important sources of structural changes in the manufacturing sector in order to regulate the pattern of industrialization in the proper direction. The study of patterns of industrial growth may be of much help in identifying and developing industrially backward regions and helps to understand the degree of industrialization.

The tendency of structural pattern of industrial development in Tamil Nadu resembles the industrially advanced states of Peninsular Indian unions such as Gujarat, Maharashtra and West Bengal and that of the developed Western countries of USA, UK and USSR. In this context, an attempt has been made to assess the rate and degree of structural shifts in Tamil Nadu. This study aims at assessing the structural changes viz., the economy of Tamil Nadu as a whole i.e., the changes in the relative shares of different sectors such as primary, secondary and tertiary. The composition of the industrial sector comprises of changes in the relative shares of different type of industries in terms of number of industries, productive capital, employment, value of output and value added.

STATEMENT OF THE PROBLEM

The economy of India has had undergone perceptible changes in its development since Independence. To develop the industrial economy, several measures have been adopted by the government. In particular, on 24th July 1991 in the industrial economy, licensing was unleashed for all the enterprises (except for a short list), the door was opened to free flow of capital, technology and labour, and the importance of the public sector was reduced. As almost a lapse of one and a half decade, it is the right time to discern the implications of the reform and performance of manufacturing sector in India in general and in Tamil Nadu in particular. Moreover, not much intensive research has been made in this state in recent decades and no work is comparatively (pre and post reform) made in this state. Hence, an attempt was made to analyze the following objectives:

(1) to highlight the economic traits of different types of industries and their relative role in the structural changes.

(2) to ascertain the changing trends in the industrial productivity of the state and the magnitude of industrial growth in the state since 1980.

(3) to understand the effect of New Industrial Policy on the industrial economy of Tamil Nadu.

As part of the work, some tentative propositions were made for empirical verification.

(1) There has been broad spectrum of industrial diversification, with a bias on chemical and its related industries in the recent period in terms of value added.

(2) The capital investment in the factory sector has grown much faster than that of employment leading to rising capital intensity.

(3) There is no significant difference between pre and post liberalization periods, with respect to growth of total factor productivity.

(4) The output growth of agro-based industries has no significant difference between the pre and post reform periods.

METHODOLOGY

This work is based upon the data collected under the scheme of Annual Survey of Industries (ASI), the Government of India and the Central Statistical Organization [CSO] have brought out the summary results of the Annual Survey of Industries. The C.S.O has been bringing out summary results of the A.S.I for the entire factory sector comprising both the census and non-census sector. The survey covers all the factories registered under the factory Act. 1948.

Industry wise data have been collected at two-digit level. There are 18 industry groups found in the two-digit level (see appendix), which have been rationalized by into 15. Similar grouping was done by Balakrishnan & Suresh Babu (2003) at all India level. For the purpose of analysing the structure of industries, industrial data at three-digit level were collected.

ASI follows a definite pattern of the use-based and input based classifications. Under the context of use-based classification, the industries are grouped into basic, capital, intermediate, consumer durable and non-consumer durable goods. Under the input based classification, the industries are grouped as agro based, metal based and chemical based.

Ahluwalia (1991), Unni, Lalitha and Uma Rani (2001), Das (2004), Khan (1980), Statistical Survey of the Indian Economy (1984), Chaudhuri (1989), and Tawari (1988), classified the three digit level data for India and Bharathan (1980), Shanthi (1981), Singh (1977), DEAR (1986) and very recently Vijayalakshmi (1994) have classified the three digit level data for Tamil Nadu. These classifications widely differ from one another.

The Reserve Bank of India gives a list of industries that fall within each category mentioned above. In the absence of concrete information about the specific uses to which the product of each industry in Tamil Nadu are put to, it becomes necessary to follow the precedent set by the R.B.I rather than make any attempt to formulate a new classification. In the case of a few industries, where the RBI list do not give any guidance, the index to the classification system as given by Ahluwalia (1985) has been referred.

This research is undertaken to examine the pattern and dimension of structural changes in the industrial development of Tamil Nadu over the period 1980-81-2003-2004 (24 years). However, due to non-availability of the data, this study is restricted upto 1999-2000. To understand the effect of new industrial policy on the industrial economy of Tamil Nadu, this period has been subdivided into pre-liberalization (1980-81 to 1990-91) and post-liberalization (1991-92 to 1999-2000).

To obtain fruitful results, the relevant statistical tools such as the percentage shares, annual average growth rate, annual compound growth rate, trend analysis, correlation, Partial factor productivity, Solow's Index of Total Factor Productivity, 't' test and H.H Index are computed. Side by side, the fixed capital per factory, fixed capital per employee, value of output per factory, value of output per employee, value added per factory and value added per employee are also calculated.

In addition to basic industrial statistics of Tamil Nadu, population census, Reserve Bank of India Bulletins, basic statistics relating to Indian Economy, Tamil Nadu an Economy Appraisal, and other published reports of various ministries of Government of India and Tamil Nadu are other sources of data for this study.

Even though, an attempt is made to analyse the structural change in the entire economy of Tamil Nadu with respect to income, the main concentration of this study is on registered manufacturing sector of the industrial economy of Tamil Nadu (which mentioned in the Figure 1). The industrial sector consists of three broad sub-sectors: (i) manufacturing, (ii) Construction and (iii) electricity, gas and water supply.

The manufacturing sub-sectors with a value added share of about 80 per cent in the industrial sector has two broad subdivisions: (a) the factory sector, referred to as registered or organized manufacturing sector, consisting of all manufacturing enterprises registered under the Indian Factory Act of 1947, and (b) non-factory sector or unregistered manufacturing sector consisting of all manufacturing enterprises which are not registered under the Indian Factory Act.

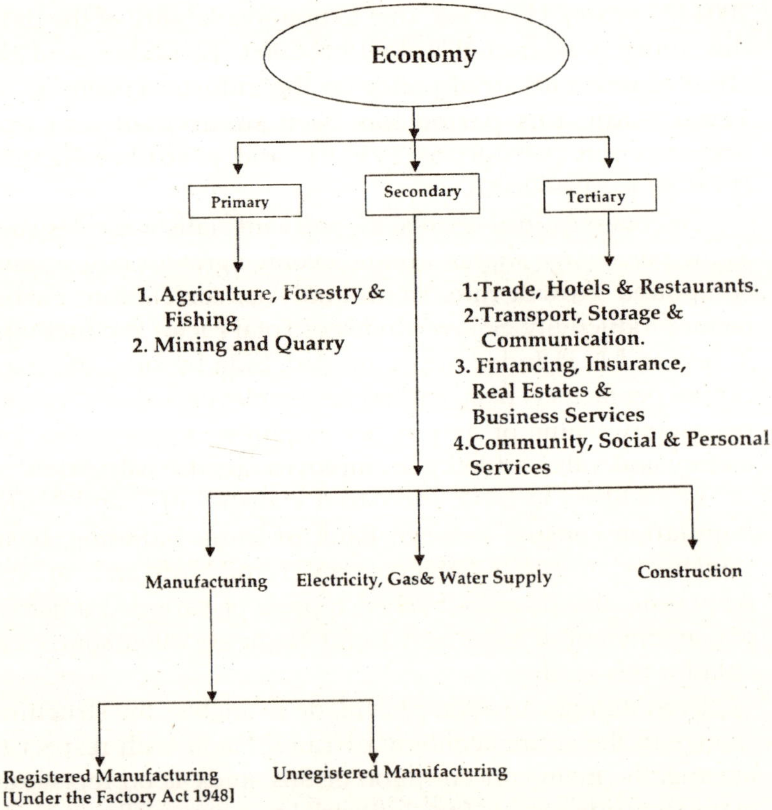

Figure 1: Role of Registered Manufacturing Sector

In Tamil Nadu, the registered manufacturing sector alone contributes 72 per cent in the total income of industrial sector and it accounted nearly 14 per cent in the net state domestic product.

LIMITATIONS

(1) The New Industrial Classification (1998-99) deals with 5 digit data, while the earlier classification deals with 3 digit data. Detailed distribution of each and every group of industry is given in the New Industrial Classification whereas; such classification is not available in the earlier classification. To make a meaningful comparison, some of the industrial units of a group are clubbed together.

(2) Current ASI data (after 2003-04) on the industrial economy of Tamil Nadu is not available and it takes a minimum of three years to publish all the characteristics features of all the groups of industries in Tamil Nadu.

(3) No year-to-year uniformity in industrial classification was observed. This nature of the data is causing inconvenience to make a meaningful analysis.

(4) The R.B.I gives a list of industries that fall within each group. But this list is neither exhaustive nor comparable to the A.S.I. In the case of a few industries, where R.B.I list did not give any guidance, independent choice had to be made.

(5) The structure of industries by ownership could not be done on account of non availability of such data with respect to the time period covered under the study.

(6) Since 1986 the Index of Industrial Production is computed for financial years and for the early years it was calculated for calendar years.

(7) It is not possible to study the structure of modern high-tech industries like software and IT industries as the detailed data is not available.

(8) Very limited variables are available in the ASI report, some variables-technological change, availability of foreign collaboration and demand factors are not available.

CHAPTER 2

CONCEPTS, THEORETICAL ASPECTS AND REVIEW OF LITERATURES

Brief description of the concepts used, theoretical aspects and review of relevant literature may be useful to follow the discussion of the book.

STRUCTURAL CHANGE

The term structure is explained by Ferguson P. R. (1988), as the characteristics and composition of markets and industries in an economy. In aggregate level it speaks about the relative importance of major sectors of the economy. Mukerjee, K. L. (1984), Rao V. (1987), Nagaraj (199), identified the structural changes in the following way- the share of primary sector in Net State Domestic Product comes down at the same time the share of secondary and tertiary sectors increases significantly.

Structural change is defined by Sundrum R. M. (1984), as the transformation between the different sectors with regard to labour force and output. Structural change is explained by Purushothaman Jayasri (1996), as the relation existing among the different segments of an economy.

Sivasubramanian S. (2004), portrays the structural change is the mobilization of resources. He reveals "as economic growth takes place, resources move from sectors with low productivity to sectors with higher productivity, leading to structural changes". Relative change in the sectoral share with regard to GDP and in labour force is defined as structural change (Shandilya, T. K. 2004).

Structural transformation is defined by Todaro & Smith (2004) thus, "it is a mechanism in which underdeveloped countries transform their domestic economic structure from a heavy emphasis on traditional subsistence agriculture to a more modern, more urbanized and more industrially diverse manufacturing and service economy".

The term industrial structure is defined by Devine.P.J and *et. al.*, (1985) as "the relative importance of individual industries or groups of relative industries within an economy".

The structure of industrial sector has been defined by Chenery, H.B & Ckark, Paul (1967), in their study entitled "inter-industry economics" that the inter-dependence and the inter-relations between the different firms under the same industry is termed as the "industrial structure" and the inter-industrial economics is termed as the structure of the industrial sector.

Different authors explain the structural changes in their own style. But in this study, the term structural change means the relative size and weight of different types of industry with regard to principal characteristics.

PRODUCTIVITY

It has been defined by economists, as the ratio of output to input in a given period of time. In other words, it is the amount of output produced by each unit of input.

PARTIAL FACTOR PRODUCTIVITY

This estimates the ratio of total output to a single input, usually labour or capital.

TOTAL FACTOR PRODUCTIVITY

This is the ratio of output of the aggregate measure of the inputs of all the factors of production. Theoretically, this is the true measure of productivity as it incorporates the contribution of all the factor inputs.

GROSS VALUE OF PLANT AND MACHINERIES

It represents the total original value of plants and machineries at the end of the accounting year. It includes the book value of own constructed plants and machineries installed and the approximate rent value of plants and machineries at the time of renting in, but excluding the rented value of plants and machineries rented out. It also includes the total value of plants and machineries acquired by hire-purchase is also included

FIXED CAPITAL

Fixed assets are those, which have normal productive life of more than one year. The fixed capital is the depreciated value of fixed assets owned by the factory, as on closing day of its accounting year. Fixed capital covers all types of assets new or used or own constructed, deployed for production, transportation and living, or recreational facilities of factory personnel. It includes the fixed assets of the head office of the factory and also the full value of assets taken on hire purchase excluding interest element. It excludes intangible assets and assets solely used for post manufacture distribution.

PHYSICAL WORKING CAPITAL

It includes all physical inventories owned/held/or controlled by the factory as on the closing day of its accounting year such as materials, fuel and lubricants, stores etc. that enter into the products manufactured by the factory itself or supplied by the factory to others for processing. It also includes the stock of materials, fuel and stores etc. purchased for resale, semi-finished goods and work in progress on account of other and goods made by the factory which are ready for sale at the end of accounting year.

WORKING CAPITAL

It is the sum total of the physical working capital already defined above and the cash on hand in bank and the net balance of amounts receivable over amounts payable irrespective of duration, advance for acquisition of fixed assets, long term loans including interest there on and investments.

PRODUCTIVE CAPITAL

It is the total of fixed capital and working capital as defined above.

INVESTED CAPITAL

It is the total of fixed capital and physical working capital.

OUTSTANDING LOANS

All loans, outstanding whether short term or long term with interest bearing or not, outstanding according to the books of the factory as on the closing day of its accounting year.

WORKERS

Workers are defined to include all persons employed directly or through any agency whether for wages or not, engaged in any manufacturing process or in clearing any part of the machinery or premises used for manufacturing process or any other kind of work incidental to or connected with the manufacturing process the subject of the manufacturing process, labour engaged in the repairs and maintenance of fixed assets for factory's own use or those employed for generating electricity or producing, coal, gas are included. However, persons holding positions of supervision or management or employed in administrative office, store keeping section and welfare section, sales department as also those engaged in the purchase of raw materials, etc, and production of the fixed assets for the factory and watch and ward staff are excluded.

EMPLOYEES

Employees include all workers and persons receiving wages and holding supervisory or managerial positions engaged in administrative, store keeping and welfare activities and sales department as also those engaged in purchase of raw materials etc. or production of fixed assets for the factory and watch and ward staff.

WAGES

Wages include all remunerations capable of being expressed in monetary terms and also payable more or less regularly in each pay period of the workers as compensation for work done during the accounting year. It includes [a] direct wages and salaries [b] remuneration for period not worked [i.e. basic wages, salaries and allowances payable for leave period, paid holiday, lay off payment and compensation for unemployment if not paid from sources other than employees [c] Bonus and excreta payment paid both at regular and less frequent intervals etc.

TOTAL EMOLUMENTS

Total emoluments are defined in the same way as wages defined above but paid to all employees plus imputed value of benefits in kind i.e. the net cost to the employer on those goods and services provided to employees free of charge or at markedly reduced cost which is clearly and primarily of benefit to the employees as consumers.

FUEL CONSUMED

It represents total purchase value of all items of fuel, lubricants, electricity, water etc. consumed by the factory during the accounting year excepting those which directly enter into the products, as materials consumed. It excludes that part of fuel, which is produced and consumed by the factory in manufacture i.e. all intermediate products and also fuels consumed by employees as part of amenities. It includes quantities acquired and consumed from allied concerns, their book value being taken as their purchase value and also the quantities consumed in production of machinery or other capital items for factory's own use.

MATERIALS CONSUMED

It represents that total delivered value of all items or raw materials, components, chemicals, packing, materials and stores which actually entered into the production process of the factory during the accounting year. Also it includes the cost of all materials used in the production of fixed assets, including construction work for factory's own use. It however excludes all intermediate products consumed during the accounting year.

TOTAL INPUT

It comprises gross value of fuel, materials, etc. consumed and also other inputs viz. [a] cost of non-industrial services received from others [b] cost of materials consumed for rapier and maintenance fixed assets of the factory including cost of work done by others to the fixed assets of the factory [c] cost of contract and commission work done by others on materials supplied by the factory [d] cost of office supplies and products reported for sale during last year and used for further manufacture during the accounting year and [e] purchase value of goods sold in some other condition as purchased.

PRODUCTS

They refer to all products and by products excluding intermediate products that have been completed during the accounting year for sale whether actually sold during the accounting year or not. The products include fixed assets produced by the factory for its use. The value of products is defined to include the ex-factory value (i.e) exclusive of taxes, duties etc, on sale and inclusive of subsidies, etc. if any. It also includes the semi-finished goods and or work in progress representing the excess of semi-finished goods and or work in progress representing the excess of semi-finished goods and or work in progress at the end of accounting year over that at the beginning of the year.

SEMI-FINISHED GOODS

This refers to all materials which have been partially processed by the factory but which are not usually sold after further processing. It includes the work in progress at the end of accounting year, but excludes the value of semi-finished fixed assets for own use of the factory. Their values are computed at the close of the accounting year.

GROSS OUTPUT

Gross output includes the ex-factory value of products and by-products manufactured during the accounting year. It also includes the receipts for industrial and non-industrial service rendered to others, value of semi-finished goods of last year sold in current year and sale value of goods sold in the same condition as purchased.

NET VALUE ADDED

Net value added is the increment to the value of goods and services contributed by the factory and it is obtained by deducting the value of total input and depreciation from value of output.

NET INCOME

Net income represents the share of employees and entrepreneur in the value added and is obtained by deducting the rent and interest paid from the value added.

INDUSTRIALIZED COUNTRY

A country with 25 per cent of who's GDP arising from the industrial sector, of which atleast 60 per cent was in manufacturing and which has atleast one-tenth of its total population (more than ten per cent) employed in industry would be counted as industrialized country, (Sutcliffe, 1971).

THEORETICAL ASPECTS OF RELEVANCE

Interaction between economic development and structural change is well observed in many developed and developing countries in the world. The theory of Neo-Classical economists has highlighted the stability of growth equilibrium in terms of an extremely simple adjustment mechanism between warranted and natural growth rate. Marx and his followers' development theories relate the political set up of the country with the economic development of the country. Similarly, Schumpeter, Rostow, Hirchman etc mark the factors, natural and stages of development in an economy. Colin Clark(1957), Bean(1957) underscored that the upliftment in per capita income is an indicator of economic development and the process of economic development is basically related to structural transformation in the economy from agrarian to non-agrarian economy. Mehta(1976) concludes that there is perceptible positive correlation between, economic development and occupational structure. In an economy, development will take place with a downturn trend in the proportion of population engaged in primary sector and an uptrend in those engaged in industrial and service sectors. Similarly, in the theory of economic development Schumpeter (1969), rightly underlined that the process of economic development is not only an increase in the level of output and income but it should consist of structural changes which will widen the production frontiers. The theories of economic development identified various factors such as components of domestic product, per capita income, per capita consumption, investment, rate of savings, infrastructural facilities employment and structural changes in the economy.

In any nation, economic development is perceived in three broad stages. Development of primary sector like agriculture and allied activities, forestry and logging, fishing and mining and quarrying comprised the first stage. In the second stage, secondary sector, which embodied manufacturing, electricity, gas and water supply and construction undergo considerable development. The development of tertiary sector encompassed trade, hotel and restaurants, railways, transport by other means, storage, communication, banking and insurance, real estate, ownership of dwelling and business services, public administration and other services are the final stage.

Similarly, the industrial development has followed an uniform pattern. The logic of industrial development is the development of agro-based industries such as milling, graining, extracting of oil from oilseeds, tanning of leather, preparing of timber etc are the first stage. The consumer goods industry dominated in the first stage, because in the primitive society, in the initial stage of development as a result of increasing population the demand for food and other primary products would expand this is known as demand side. On the supply side, the consumer goods industries require only elementary and simple technology and the least dose of capital.

In the second stage, the industrial products transform the processed materials in to final consumption goods. It is in this stage that bread and confectionery items are manufactured from flour and sugar, footwear from leather, metal goods from iron and steel. As demand for food, increases it necessitates the adoption of improved techniques or food production such as mechanized agricultural implements, inorganic fertilizers and pesticides.

In the third stage, the demand structure gets diversified. In this stage machines, and other capital equipments are manufactured. These are not meant for direct satisfaction of any immediate consumption want but it facilitates the future process of production. In this final stage the production structure of industrial goods has to be diversified considerably. These structural changes are due to increase in income level and diversification of taste and preferences.

In the circle of structural change Simon Kuznets, H.B. Chennery and W.G. Hoffmann are considered as champions. The summary of these theories is presented here.

Hoffmann Hypothesis

Hoffman (1958) portrays the pattern of industrial growth, which is known as Hoffman's hypothesis. In this, he categorically confirms that the industrial growth of any economy generally follows three stages

"Whatever the relative amounts of the factors of production, whatever the relative amounts of the factors, whatever the stage of technology, the structure of manufacturing sector of the economy has always followed a uniform pattern".

Stage: I The food, textiles, leather and furniture industries, which were defined as consumer goods industries always develop first during process of industrialization.

Stage: II In this stage the capital goods industry is dominant.

Stage: III In the third stage there is balance between each other.

Eventually, why consumer goods industries develop first is due to expansion of capital goods industry requires huge dose of capital and advanced techniques of production as well as skilled labour.

Chennery and Taylor (1960)

On the pattern of industrial growth Chennery and Taylor (1960) remarked important changes. Their explanation slightly differs from that of Hoffmen's hypothesis. According to Chennery and Taylor, the process of industrial development in an economy follows three important changes, those are

(i) A rise in the relative importance of manufacturing industry,

(ii) A change takes place in the composition of industrial output and

(iii) Changes in production techniques and source of supply of individual commodities.

Simon Kuznets

Three shifts in the productive structure, which are associated with modern economic growth first are, the movement away from agriculture (in favour of manufacturing activity) usually referred to as industrialization,, the change in structure within industry proper particularly in manufacturing and finally shifts in structure of service sector.

Stylized Facts

The term "stylized facts" was introduced by Nicholas Kaldor, in the 1958 conference paper on capital accumulation and economic growth. Kaldor explains that the basic requirement of any model is that it should be capable of explaining the characteristic features of the economic process as we find them in reality. He introduced six stylized facts to formulate theoretical model of economic growth and capital accumulation. Those are (a) a steady rate of growth of production and productivity of labour (b) a growing capital to labour ratio, (c) a steady rate of profit on capital (d) steady capital-output ratios over long periods, (e) high correlation between the share of profits in income and (f) the share of investment in output. While allowing these there are differences in the rate of growth of labour productivity and of output between societies.

Rostow's Model

The American Economic historian Rostow has developed the theory in 1960 in which he identified five stages of economic development. In every stage, there has been noticeable transformation occurred.

In the first stage of Traditional Society, the agriculture is important sector, capital is limited, production method is traditional and the producers consume most of the output. In the Transitional Stage the specialization increased, which generates surpluses for trading. Owing to generation of trade the transport and infrastructure developed and the entrepreneurs emerge. In the Take Off stage the industrialization increases. The growth is due to one or two manufacturing industries. The work force transforms from traditional agriculture to modern manufacturing sector. The economic transitions are accompanied by the evolution of new political and social institutions these support the industrialization. In the fourth stage of Drive to Maturity, the economy produces goods and services and the import is less. The technological innovation is providing a diverse range of investment opportunities. In the final stage of High Mass Consumption, the economic structure is geared towards mass consumption. In addition in this stage the consumer durable industry develops considerably and service sectors exist in dominant position.

Lewis's Model

Structural changes in the economy were identified by Lewis through transformation of labour from traditional to modern economy. Lewis produced the dual sector development model in 1954. He assumed that most of the less developed countries in the world had dual economies–traditional agricultural sector, which is naturally, characterized by low productivity, low income, low saving and underdevelopment, on the other hand the industrial sector, which is characterized by higher dose for investment, technological advancement and urbanization.

He portrays that the modern industrial sector would attract workers from the rural areas, because the firms (private or public) could provide wages that would guarantee a higher quality of life. The transformation of labours from traditional to modern economy is naturally to earn higher income. He argued that the higher income leads to saving, saving leads to investment and ultimately investment leads to economic development.

Fisher Clark's Theory

In the theory of Fisher Clark the process of structural change had been addressed that in the early phase of economy, when a country has low income, which dominated by primary products through the extraction of raw materials from agriculture, mining, fishing and forestry. While the country drives to the stage of middle income, the economic structure is dominated by industrial sectors (particularly manufacturing and construction). When the country grows to the high income, the economy is occupied by the provision of service sector.

REVIEW OF LITERATURE:

In this chapter, an attempt is made to review some of the earlier works done on the industrial economy of several countries, India and Tamil Nadu in various dimensions. This chapter consists of four sub sections. In the first section, the growth and development spectrum of industrial economy is presented; the changing scenario of industrial economy is given in the second section, the studies on productivity picture in the industrial economy are embodied in the third section and review of a few studies on the impact of government policy on industrial economy are given in the final section.

Growth and Development

Adhikary (1997) has attempted to explain the industrial growth of Bangladesh over the period 1972-73 to 1984-85. He observed that, the share of industrial output in GDP has increased from 7.28 per cent in 1972-73 to 8.43 per cent in 1977-78. Thereafter, a two-year Development plan was introduced. In this period the contribution of industrial sector to GDP was 8.46 per cent and 8.19 per cent for 78-79 and 79-80 respectively. However, during the second five-year plan period (80-85), the share of industrial sector in GDP tended to increase from 8.39 per cent in 1980-81 to 9.50per cent in 84-85. It may be noted that the share of industry in GDP during 1972-1985 was around 8 per cent.

The Bangladesh government followed specific actions, such as export oriented industrialization and private investments to achieve the objectives of maximizing regional growth. Moreover, several special facilities are provided to the export oriented industries, like duty concession on import of machinery and raw materials, protection against commercial and political risks, encouraging foreign investment and other incentive to the economic growth. The Bangladesh government played a vital role in the industrial development. The initiatives of this government are export oriented industrial policy, permission for private investment, duty concession on machinery and raw material imports and protection against commercial and political risks.

Pawar & Shinde (1993) while analyzing the industrial growth of Maharashtra, revealed that in the Indian Scenario, Maharashtra's share is 16.1 per cent of factories, 17.3 per cent employment and 16.6 per cent and 25 per cent of productive capital and value added respectively. These percentage shares are very high when compared with those of other states. Since the Maharashtra government established several organizations like SICOM, MIDC, IDBI to achieve industrial development in backward districts through providing infrastructural facilities concessions and supply of seed money, several underdeveloped districts have come up. It led to overall industrial development of this state.

Kalipada Deb (2001) conducted a study on the industrial development of Andhra Pradesh over the period 1960-97. He revealed that the annual average growth in industrial production was 9.90 per cent in the seventies, decreased to 6.68 per cent in the eighties, and further to 2.98 per cent during 1990-97. The employment provision by the industrial sector was very low. While, the number of registered factories increased by 35 times, the fixed capital, value of gross output increased 488 times and 338 times respectively. The employment record exhibits an increase of seven times. Fixed capital per employee has increased from 0.04 lakhs in 1960 to 2.38 lakhs in 1995. The author attributes poor infrastructure like scarce power supply and meagre bank finance for the poor performance.

Kalipada Deb (2001) elucidated the industrial development of Tamil Nadu from 1960 to 95 through his research study. He observes that since independence the industrial sector of the state has been quite impressive except for the last few years. Between 82 and 92 the annual average growth was 6.8 per cent it decreased to 1.5 per cent during 92-96. Similarly the growth of manufacturing sector was 7.1 per cent and decreased to 0.6 per cent for the above said period. In the case of factory sector, the value of output has grown by 270 times, the net value added and fixed capital has increased by 189 times and 377 times respectively. Whereas, the capital output ratio increased from 0.33 to 0.46, the growth of employment is 5.6 times only. While the output increased by 48 times per employee, fixed capital per employee increased by 67 times during the entire period. The author concludes that the better position of the industrial economy of the state is due to better availability of infrastructure and provision of bank credits.

Industrial growth of Tamil Nadu was underlined by GOT(2003), that during 1980s the average growth of industrial sector was 4.52 per cent, while during the 1990s the growth rate increased to 5.35 per cent.

Jayasree De (1993) captured the growth of industrial economy of Gujarat in the 60's and 70's. She identified Gujarat as one of the leading industrial states of this country. The petroleum refinery at Koyali setup in 1969 is a mainspring in the history of industrialization of Gujarat. After being separated from Bombay the economy of the state was transformed from agrarian to industrial economy. The availability of local raw materials is the main reason for the development of some industries such as Groundnut oil milling, tobacco processing and chemical industry. Further, dairy industry is another major industry due to the availability of fodder crops. The industrialization of Gujarat is directly linked with the development of power generation, which is also favorable for this state. Moreover, the author attributed the entrepreneurial skills, government incentives, lower taxes, lower prices, and the setting up of the Gujarat Industrial Development Corporation in (1962) as the main reasons for the outstanding development of the industrial economy of this state.

Deb (2001) has studied the industrial development of Kerala during 1960–95. He revealed that, eventhough large number of industrial units were started in India during the planning period; he found no considerable industrial development in Kerala. The manufacturing sector contributed 14.7 per cent of SDP in 1960–61 and 9 per cent in 1996–97. The growth of industrial production as a whole was however, not so depressing. However, the SSI sector developed appreciably. The causes cited by the author for the slow growth of industrial sector were that the trade unions causing loss of mandays, wage and welfare expenditure, insufficient power supply, and other factors played a crucial role for the gloomy picture of industrial sector of this state.

Kaur (1982) observed that in Haryana the contribution of manufacturing sector to the state domestic product had been steadily rising from 1966-67. Its relative share at all India level also increased, in respect of employment and output. The expansion of capital stock was much faster than output and employment. Annual compound growth rate of employment, output and capital in the registered factories of Hariyana recorded higher growth than those of Punjab. The annual rate of growth of capital formation in registered factories of Haryana increased considerably, which was higher than that of Punjab. The author didn't identify any reason for the considerable growth of Haryana.

Kalipada Deb (2001) explains the industrial growth of Karnataka for the past few years. He has revealed that Karnataka's performance is not quite impressive in recent years. The annual compound growth rate of manufacturing sector is 5.3 per cent and the manufacturing share in SDP is

17.2. Similarly, the contribution of employment of secondary sector decreased to 10.71 in 1991 from 12.15 in 1981. But the performance of the factory sector was quite impressive. Here, the value of output increased 256 times, the net value added increased by 224 times. But the per capita value added increased by 19.8 times, and growth of employment is insignificant with four times over this period. In addition, output per employee, increased by 65 times and the fixed capital per employee by 54times. The capital output ratio decreased to 0.14 in 1994-95 from 0.48 in 1960. Moreover the author has underlined on the problematic factors of industrial development, such as unsatisfactory infrastructural facilities, electricity deficit and inadequacy of bank credit.

The industrial development of India since independence is explained by Majumdar and Chopre (1996). They revealed that the country is more or less self-sufficient in the production of consumer goods and some basic items like iron and steel. At the time of independence, Tata iron and steel company at Jamshedpur, Iron and steel company at Burnpur (West Bengal), and Mysore Iron works were the only steel industries. Thereafter, some steel plants in the public sector, such as Bhilai steel plant in MP, Durgapur steel plant in West Bengal, Rourkela steel plant in Orissa, Bokaro steel plant in Bihar, Alloys steel plant at Durgapur, Salem Steel plant in Tamil Nadu, Visakapattionam Steel plant in Andhra Pradesh were established. Besides about are 214 mini steel plants were established, the total capacity of steel production is about 22 million of tones. The other existing industries are cotton textiles, sugar mills and cement industries. Among them, the number of cotton textile mills has increased to 1014 in 1984 form 378 in 1947, the number of sugar mills have gone up to 392 while the cement plants in large sector and in mini sector were 90 and 184 respectively. Thus India today produces everything from a pin to highly sophisticated jet planes.

Growth of industrial economy of India was assessed by Rangarajan C. (2004), he underlined that during 1966-70, a dramatic decline observed in the industrial economy of India, and during 1971-75 the same trend is witnessed. The reasons behind this downward trend are set back in capital goods industries in 1970-75 and decline in consumer goods industries during 71-75.

Srivastava (1986) has analysed the industrial economy of Gujarat using ASI and some other data for different periods. He underlines that the gross output is significantly associated with the raw material and capital inputs. In addition, the correlation analysis showed that among the various variables, there is close association between the variables of industrial growth and institutional finance and industrial shed in the medium and large-scale segments of the industrial sector.

The industrial growth of India has been assessed by Chaudhri (2001), using ASI and NAS data for pre and post liberalization periods. He revealed that the annul rate of growth of manufacturing sector has been fluctuating significantly between 1951-52 and 1998-99. The entire period was classified under the head of high and low growth. He observed that before 1991 period of high growth was invariably followed by periods of low growth. The real net fixed capital stock (NFES) increased from 4.10 per cent in 1991-92 to 10.93 per cent in 1995-96, and the rate decreased to 5.24 per cent in 1997-98. The labour-intensity has come down not only in the capital-intensive goods but also in labour intensive goods. The author says that the industrial deceleration in the 1990s was not only the result of exogenous factors, but also the consequence of economic policies being pursued under economic reforms. He explains this disappointing performance to the adverse impact of import liberalisation and decline in the rate of government demand. Finally, the author suggests that if import liberalisation and other policies resulted not in more efficient production but lower demand and hence lower production and employment, then the policy needs to be seriously re-examined rather than being blindly followed.

The growth of industrial economy of India was analysed by Khan (1980). He concluded that the highest annual average growth rate of industrial production of 11.8 per cent was shown during the period 1959 to 1965. This was the time when the country took the path of large-scale industrialization and a number of new industries were setup. On the other hand, the lowest annual average was exhibited during 1973-74. Owing to the recessionary conditions, the industrial output declined by 0.5per cent per annum during 1966-1967. Between 1975 and 77 growth staged a smart recovery.

Mody and Wang (1997) have explained the industrial growth of coastal China for the period 1985-1989, using output data of 23 industrial sectors in seven coastal regions. They revealed that the there is no uniform growth across the regions and industries. The electronics and telecommunication sector grew only by 5.6 per cent in 85-86 it reached 19.3 per cent in 1987-1988. In most of the coastal region, rapid growth was achieved in leather product, pharmaceutical products, chemical fibres, and metallic products in 1985-1986. In 1986-1987 electronics and chemicals replaced leather and mallic products. The paper products, transport equipment, electronics and pharmaceutical products expanded rapidly in 1987-88, only to lose their position to the apparel industry in 1988-89. The author underlined that the degree of specialization and competition influenced growth. The open-door policies and special economic zones have attraccted investments. In addition to the existing high quality of human capital, infrastructure also contributed to growth.

Deepak Nayyar (1994) attempted to review the factors underlying the industrial stagnation in mid 1960's; he says that the industrial sector witnessed dramatic decline in the mid-sixties, vis., during the decade 1955-65. Total industrial production increased at an average annual rate of 7.8; per cent at the same time manufacturing output increased at 7 per cent. But during 1965-75 the growth rate dropped to just 3.6 per cent and 3.1 per cent respectively. The reason for the stagnation is wars of 1962, 1965 and 1971which diverted potential public investment in to unproductive uses. Moreover, infrastructural bottlenecks and the oil crisis of 1973, balance of payment difficulties and the slack investment of public sector after 1965, are also causative factors.

The annual average growth rate of index of industrial production in India accounted for 4.4 per cent in the seventies.

In the eighties, it was 7.2 per cent. During nineties (upto 1998-1999) the annual average growth rate has been lower at 6.6 per cent. The contribution of industry to GDP rose from 18.6 per cent in 1970 to 27 per cent in 1995-1996. However it came down to around 22 per cent in 1996-1997 and it remained stagnant in the subsequent two years (RBI, 1998-1999).

Attri (1991) has analyzed the industrial economy of India, using NAS Economic Survey and World Bank data for different periods. The main objective of his study is to examine the possibility of rapid and efficient industrialization by fully utilizing foreign trade. His mathematical and econometric calculations show strong growth in different industry groups at more disaggregated level. The strong picture of industrial performance was mainly due to changes in our trade policy. The study concluded that foreign trade plays an important role in the industrialization of the country. Export sector happens to be the next important factor, after domestic demand in the determination of industrial growth.

Industrial growth of Andhra Pradesh during 1980-1998 was analysed by Venkataramaiah & Burange (2003), using ASI and NAS data. This period is sub divided into pre-and post liberalization. They observed that upto 1991 the share of industrial sector increased slowly and then decreased. The state domestic product of industry increased from 12 per cent in 1960-61 to 14.8 per cent, 17.6 per cent and 19.4 per cent in 1970-71, 80-81 and 90-91 respectively, but decreased to 18.5 per cent by 1995-1996. The manufacturing sector also exhibited a similar trend.

The share of value added in the factory sector decreased to 14 per cent in 1991-92 from 16 per cent in 1980 and achieved significant increase of 22 per cent in 1997-1998. The value of ouput has grown at 9.7 per cent per annum over the period. The growth rate is slightly stimulated in the post liberalization period when compared to pre liberalization period. The net value added increased by 9.6 per cent, here also the acceleration was increased from 6.5 per cent to 17.2 per cent from 1980s to 1990s. But employment in manufacturing sector grew only at 3.05 per cent per annum. The liberalization process led to high growth in 1990s. "After the initial pentup demand for manufacturing articles was satiated. The industrial sector was facing a recession. Cheap imports consequent upon trade liberalization as per WTO norms also affect the demand for products of the domestic industry. In the stock market the shares of the companies producing manufactured articles were at very low levels. The infrastructure that is being developed in the state is also largely focused on IT sector to the neglect of the industrial sector.

Gorelal Yadava(1982) studied the development of Bihar for the period 1970-76. He identified the causative factors for the poor performance of industrial sector of this state. They are government policy (licensing system), poor power distribution, lack of entrepreneurs, low plan expenditure and low financial resources.

The industrial economy of Kerala was very depressing, which recorded 3.86 per cent of total population. It produced only 2.5 per cent of the national industrial output from factories and registered 12th place among the Indian states in 1994-1995. The investment on industrial sector was a major challenge in this state, especially in the post-liberalization period. The causes for this disappointing performance are labour disputes, non-availability of land at affordable prices and erratic trend in power generation and transmission. The author suggests that (a) the state government should follow an approach more vigorous than in the past by reformulating labour policies, with the co-operation of trade union, a climate of confidence and a conductive environment for private investment is created in Kerala, (b) the government should take steps to invit private participation in power generation (M.M. Thambi, 1999).

The revolution in the industrial sector and natural sequences of industrialization was underlined by Hughes (1968). He revealed that the industrial revolution occurred during 1770 to 1825. During this period the acceleration of mechanization was impressive, which includes steam power of the manufacturing sector, which led to identifiable change in economic structure and growth of Great Britain. "The pattern of industrialization in other countries after 1800 has been broadly similar in many respects to that experienced by Britain, although of course, the permutation was never the same in any two countries. Textiles first (along with food processing) has been almost the rule in industrialization, followed by transportation development, heavy industry and more sophisticated enterprises like metal working chemicals, and electronic. In most cases, substantial advances in agricultural output or increased foreign trade, or both have been concomitants of industrial development" (Hughes, J.R.T, 1968).

Structural Change

Adhikary (1997) identified the industrial transformation of Bangladesh during the period 1971-85. He elucidates that the number of industries had increased by 24 per cent. Gross value of production had increased by 19 times, and total fixed assets had increased by 8 times during the period of analysis. The industries like textiles (Jute & cotton), chemicals and its products, food and beverages, machinery and tobacco contributed a higher value of production. Nevertheless, the percentage share of some agro-based industries to total product had drastically come down, i.e., textiles from 44.9 per cent to 30.7 per cent tobacco 13.1 per cent to 7.0 per cent, Food and Beverages 11.2 per cent to 11.0 per cent during 1972-73 and 84-85. In contrast to the downward swing, an extraordinary progress was achieved by chemicals and chemical products from 10.6 per cent to 15.4 per cent in the same period. The percentage share of total fixed assets of traditional industries has also come down.

In terms of value added and employment, the Bangladesh industries have scored 16 times of value added and tripled the average of daily employment during this period. In the industrial group the higher value added products are contributed by textile, chemical, tobacco, machinery and food and beverages industries. In terms of percentage share of decreasing trend appeared in textiles and tobacco industries and the daily employment also decreased. The employment opportunities increased steadily in chemical and chemical products, machinery and basic metals. The author argued that the low levels of technology and managerial efficiency are contributory factors for the non-achievement of the planning strategy in the industrial economy of Bangladesh.

Allen & Stevenson (1974) have observed the structural changes of Italy's economy through export, during the period 1950-72. They revealed that, the rapid export growth of Italy was associated with two important structural changes; one is related to commodity composition and another geographical distribution. In terms of export, the manufacturing goods increased, while primary industries came down. In addition the composition of manufacturing export also changed, i.e., the importance of textiles and food products in exports had come down gradually. Contrarily, the export of vehicles, machinery, metallurgy and clothing had increased. More interestingly, the engineering, chemicals and clothing industries alone contributed to the total export of 63 per cent during 1952-71.

Chenery (1980) distinguished the industrialization of the nine semi-industrial countries of the world during 1955-73, using input output data for finding the relation between industrialization and exports. He revealed that countries like Korea, Taiwan, Israel and Norway increased their manufacturing growth mainly due to expansion of exports over the study period. Some other countries like India, Brazil, Chile, Uruguay and Argentina have development based on import substitution. The author concludes "the effect of trade policy on industrial structure is quite striking. Although import substitution is an important feature of early stages of industrialization in all developing countries it can be accelerated to retarded by trade policy. The later stage of expansion of manufactured exports is more susceptible to policy influence and it shown to have to large extent on the subsequent course of industrial development".

Devine and *et. al* (1985) have distinguished the structural transformation of British economy during 1968-81. This study is based on the net output and employment data for this period. They revealed that the economy of Britain had undergone radical structural change that is, the importance of agriculture came down, by contrast the service activities had expanded, at the same time the manufacturing sector experienced a fluctuating trend. In the British economy, the relative importance of manufacturing sector has come down, in terms of both net output and employment. Contrarily, the importance of service industries (transport, distribution and wide range of governmental, commercial and leisure activity) share has correspondingly expanded in terms of net output and employment.

The structural changes in Kenya's industrial economy was analysed, over the period from 1980's to 1990's. The authors Dorathy Mc Cormick and Paul Ove Pedersen (1999) have expressed that, during 1980's the export of Kenya comprised of 60 per cent of processed and unprocessed food and beverages, followed by 20, 13 and 1per cent respectively of non-food industrial products, fuel and lubricants and machinery and transport equipments respectively. This scenario was changed during 1990's, the export of consumer goods, doubled and non-food products increased to 30 per cent. In contrast, the export of food and beverages decreased to 52 per cent in mid 1990's. The author underlined that the export of this country has increased by taking advantage of the creation of Preferential Trade Agreement (PTA) in 1984 and the gradual liberalization of trade with its neighbors.

Sharma (2000) explains the structural transformation of the industrial sector of Nepal. He observed that, the share of manufacturing sector in GDP rose from 4 per cent in the pre-liberalization period to above 7 per cent in the post liberalization period. Similarly, the share of manufacturing sector in the total exports rose from about 36 per cent to above 75 per cent. Due to the restrictive trade regime, the output was dominated by import substitution until the mid 1980s, while the output of export oriented industries was nominal. But the share of export oriented industries has increased from 13 per cent in 1980 to 28 per cent in 1993–94. The industries paper & printing, chemicals, rubber and plastic iron and steel, ship building, motor vehicles and other transport equipments experienced impressive growth in output upto 1980, but fell in recent years.

The Portugal economy has undergone structural transformation during 1961-1990. The industrial sector has increased its share by three times of the total output within the secondary sector. Manufacturing sector contributed a major share and the expansion was concentrated in the large-scale enterprises with modern technology. Similarly, the service sector has doubled its share, but the contribution of primary sector came down.

In the export of Portugal, a few products like canned fish, raw and manufactured cork, cotton textiles, and wine dominated in the earlier period of 1960s. This scenario was changed for the following phases- both consumer and export goods registered significant growth in export.

Singapore economy experienced noticeable changes over the period 19601-1995. The rapid growth of this economy was accompanied by changing economic structure. In the GDP of Singapore, the share of primary industries (agriculture, quarrying) came down and the share of industrial sector's was maintained at a certain level. But the share of financial and business service sector increased noticeably. Similarly, the dramatic expansion occurred in financial and business sector over the past three decades. Moreover the industrial composition of the manufacturing sector changed with the favour of more capital-intensive industries like electronics, from the labour intensive industries such as concrete products, cement and rubber.

The Structural change in the economy of Republic of Korea was assessed by Asian Development Bank (1997 & 98). It highlighted that all the sectors in the economy of Korea (expect-service) exhibited lower growth between 1994 and 1996. The growth of manufacturing sector decreased from 10.7 per cent to 6.9 per cent and its employment also decreased during this period. The growth of construction also revealed the same trend. Sluggish investment on equipment and heavy and chemical industries were the cause for this deceleration.

Carbaugh (2000) has underlined the structural changes in the industrial economy of Japan by export of this country, over the period 1950-1990. Japan has become a technological leader in the post-world war II era. In 1950's, the export of Japan consisted primarily of textiles and other low-tech products. In the decades following 1960's its exports included capital-intensive products, such as autos, steel and ships. Further this scenario experienced considerable changes during 1980's and 1990's. In addition, It was a period were Japan became a major world competitor in high tech goods, such as optical fibers and semiconductors.

Kulkarni and Sun (2004), analysed the economy of Taiwan. They elucidated that Taiwan economy recorded considerable growth. Its per capita GDP was $196 in 1952 and jumped to $2344 in 1980 and climbedup to $13233 in 1997. Its share of global exports rose from 0.16 per cent in 1950 to 2.23 per cent in 1997. The industrial product was shifted from agro-based industries to metal, chemical and hi-tech industries. The export-oriented industries have grown noticeably and the industrial structure was diversified considerably. These impressive growths were mainly due to comparative advantages in international trade, in addition to government policies, such as, strategy of promoting growth of labour-intensive export industries; export promotion policies. Cheap credit and raw materials are made available to exporters. In addition, competitiveness of Taiwanese labour, and education have played a crucial role in the faster growth of Taiwan's economy.

The structural transformation in the industrial economy of Taiwan was analysed by Clark(1989), He revealed that in export of food, textiles and wood manufactures contributed more than 50 per cent of Taiwan's economy in 1970. This picture has changed considerably i.e. their contribution came down to 33 per cent in 1980. The share of electronics, (combining both high technology and skilled labour-intensive assembly) rose from 12 per cent to 18 per cent. Heavy industries such as, rubber and plastic, metal manufactures and machinery also became more important as their combined share in

Taiwan's export mix tripled from 6 per cent in 1970 to17 per cent in 1980.

The changing pattern of industrial structure of Sub-Saharan Africa for the period of 1980-87 was assessed by Saha (1991), he revealed that most of the manufacturing industries are involved in the processing of primary products, from its agriculture, forestry and mining sector. Between 1980 and 87 the share of Africa's manufacturing value added (MVA) directly relatable to the processing of primary products has in fact increased from 61.6per cent to 65.3 per cent. During 1987, industries such as food products, beverages, tobacco, textiles, apparel, leather, footwear, wood products, furniture non-metallic mineral products and non-ferrous metals contributed two-third of the country's MVA.

Nishimizu & Robinson(1986) have analyzed the structural change and total factor productivity of Korea, Turkey, and Yugoslavia. They compared it with Japan using World Bank time series data, for the period 1950s to 1970's. They concluded that more than two thirds of all industries (apparel, leather, furniture, paper, chemicals, petroleum and coal stone, clay and glass, basic metal, fabricated metals, machinery, electrical machinery and transport equipment) have recorded a growth rate of 9 to 15 per cent in Japan. Korea recorded 17 to 27 per cent growth 9 to 18 per cent by Turkey and 6 to 13 per cent by Yugoslavia. No industry has revealed slow growth in the countries. The faster growth in heavy industries and slower growth in light industries were observed.

The structural shift in the economy of Latin America was assessed by UNIDO (1997) for a period of 25 years from 1970 to 1995. During this period manufacturing sector's value added grew at a lower rate than the service sector. The share of manufacturing sector in GDP fell from 25 per cent to 22.7 per cent over this period. In contrast, the share of service sector in GDP rose from 6.1 per cent to 58.4 per cent by 1995. This shows the inter sectoral transformation of this country during the above-mentioned period (UNIDO, 1997), this obvious structural transformation must be influenced by a number of service industries.

UNIDO (1997) revealed the industrial transformation of third world countries over the period 1970-1994; it observes that "the developing countries as a whole have gradually been moving towards industrial structures based on high-technology industries rather than those dominated by labour-intensive, resource-based low-technology industries. Manufacturing industries in developing countries have also diversified over the years. In 1970, low technology industries like textiles and petroleum were among the top three manufacturing industries. They were replaced by high-technology industries, such as electrical machinery and transport equipment, as a result of strong growth rate in those industries. High technology industries have registered a strong growth of 6.9 per annum, raising their share of MVA from 11.4 per cent in 1970 to 17.1 per cent in 1994".

Surendra (1970), explains the structural changes in the industrial economy of major industrialized countries, such as Great Britain, France, Germany, United States, Belgium, Switzerland, Italy, Japan and USSR, for different periods. In the course of industrialization of these countries, there was noticeable decline observed in consumer goods in total industrial output. In the beginning of industrialization, consumer goods accounted for two thirds or more of total industrial output in these countries and remainder were producer goods. In the process of industrial development, the stage of these two sectors was almost reversed i.e., the share of consumer goods came down to around one-third of total industrial output and producer goods increased their share correspondingly.

Bhagwati and Desai (1970), concluded that a substantial change underwent in Indian industries during the plan periods. It is observed that the relative shares of gross value added, gross output at market prices and factor prices of consumer goods declined, at the same time the investment goods rose sharply. This transformation was obvious in metals, machinery and chemical industry.

Economic Survey (2001-02) revealed that in terms of use-based classification the overall growth rate of consumer goods was 8.2 per cent in 2000-01 and decreased to 5.0 per cent in 2001-02. The performance of consumer durable and non-durable goods was 17.8 per cent and 5.3 per cent but decreased to 12.5 per cent and 2.3 per cent in the successive periods. Similarly, the growth of basic and intermediate goods decreased form 5.1 per cent and 4.8 per cent to 2.2 per cent and 2 per cent respectively during the same period.

Within the industrial sector the negative growth recorded by six 2-digit industry groups such as food products, cotton textiles, jute and other vegetable, fiber textiles, textile products, wood and wood products and metal products. However, four industry groups registered growth rate of over 10 per cent, they are beverage, tobacco and related products, leather and its product and fur products, rubber, plastic, petroleum and coal products and other manufacturing industries.

Changes in the industrial economy of Andhra Pradesh for the period 1981-91 was analysed by Sudhakar Reddy(1994). In the industrial mix of this state, beverages, and tobacco, food products, and cotton textiles accounted for 76 per cent of total industrial employment in 1961. During the course of economic development, their contribution decreased to 59 per cent in 1981, at the same time the industries producing machinery, and machine tools, metal products, paper and paper products and transport equipment and parts increased their share. The author underlined that the agricultural development, improvement in forest output, income distribution and availability of labour force are causative factors for the industrial development of this state.

Pawar & Shinde(1993) have analysed structural changes of Maharashtra State, from 1961 to 87 using secondary data. They revealed that Maharashtra is one of the industrially advanced states in this country. She is endowed with large amount of fertile lands, forest wealth and mineral resources; they are responsible for the industrial development of the state. The industrial sector of this state has undergone massive diversification. The well developed industries are textiles and chemicals and chemical products, machinery and machine tools, food processing transport equipment and other manufacturing industries. These have important place in the industrial economy of the state. The role of traditional industries in respect of value added and employment have come down. Ironically, the modern industries experienced a dramatic increase.

Deb (2001) studied the industrial development of several states in India such as Andhra Pradesh, Tamil Nadu, Karnataka and Kerala. He revealed that these states experienced different levels of growth for different periods, but they have been undergone a uniform pattern of change in the industrial structure. Naturally, the agro-based industries like food products, textiles, leather and paper products developed in the earlier phase. Their contribution in investment, output, value added and employment is very high. During the course of development, of the economy the modern industries such as chemical and chemical products, engineering and computer oriented industries have replaced the traditional industries.

Jayasree (1993) has studied the structural transformation of industrial economy of Gujarat during 60's to 70's. She revealed that the major industrial units in this state are textiles, fertilizer, chemicals and petrochemical, drugs and pharmaceuticals, dyestuff, cement, paper, vegetable oil, engineering and some other agro-based industries. The growth of factory employment steadily increased up to 1982, thereafter it decreased. The main cause of this is the closure of a number of textile factories and other related industries. Conversely, tremendous increase was achieved by various branches of chemical and chemical producing industries. This deceleration in the employment generation of textiles is mainly due to poor market, lack of modernization and low output. It may be noted that the engineering industry is showing a steady growth in this state. The author concluded that in the beginning stage the industrial structure was concentrated with textile industry; but later it was diversified, it was replaced by chemicals, food processing, non-metallic mineral products, paper & paper products. Also "the increase of factory employment in Gujarat is highly correlated with the growth in the employment in chemical industries, non-metallic mineral products, food beverage and tobacco processing, various miscellaneous and service industries.

Vinod Vyasulu & Arun Kumar (1997) have attempted to examine the structural change in the industrial sector of Orissa for the period 1966-67 to 88-89. The main source of information for this study is ASI. He revealed that in the industrial structure the performance of metal alloys industries are appreciable. Similarly, the other important factories are wood and wood products, food and food products, cotton textiles, paper and paper products, chemical and chemical products, non-metallic products and other manufacturing industries. These indicate that the industrial pattern is not well diversified in this state as the traditional industries are playing the main role. In terms of annual average growth rate these industries, showed a positive growth in all the industry groups. Particularly the chemical products and non-metallic products grew at a much higher rate in terms of number of factories and number of employees. The overall extraordinary growth was due to the high growth of chemicals and its sub-products in 1960's and other manufacturing in 1970's.

Bhuvaneshwari (1991) made a study of the industrial sector of Tamil Nadu covering the period 1960's to 80's. The main data source was the Annual Survey of Industries and Tamil Nadu Economic Appraisal. Her analysis revealed that in terms of industrial mix the traditional industries like cotton textiles, sugar factories, cement and leather industries dominated during the earlier period. But the industrial groups like chemicals; fertilizers, machine and machine tools and transport equipments dominated during later period (70's and 80's) in terms of value added. The agro-based industries lost their importance to the chemical, mineral and metal-based industries. In other words, the importance of consumer goods industries came down during the study period. Contrarily, the basic goods, capital goods and intermediary goods have gained their share during the same period.

Ahluwalia (1998) has explained the structural change and diversification of Indian industries since independence. Her study revealed that at the time of independence the agro-based industries such as textiles and sugar dominated the industrial scenario, thereafter, this structure was changed. The process of structural diversification in the industrial sector began in second five-year plan. After independence, particularly in 1956 consumer goods accounted for nearly 50 per cent in the weight of index of industrial production. Contrarily this picture was changed in 1980-81, i.e. the importance of consumer goods had decreased. Numerically, the share of consumer goods has come down to 30 per cent in 1980-81, in contrast, a steady increase was achieved by the capital goods in the same period.

In the industrial composition of India the industries producing textiles, wool, chemicals, rubber, petroleum, and electric machinery have increased at the rate of more than 8 per cent during 1970s. But during 1980s the other manufacturing increased up to 15 per cent. At the same time rubber, petroleum, non-metallic products, textiles, leather and electrician machinery increased more than 10 per cent. In the industrial economy of India textile and electrical machinery industries increased 10 and 9 per cent respectively during 1990s. (Ramanjaneyuly, M, 2005).

Rajeswari V. (1989) has examined the structural changes in Andhra Pradesh economy from 1966-80. For this purpose the author has taken the variables such as employment, gross fixed capital, gross value added, the main source of data is ASI. She focused that in the early stage of industrialization, agro-based (or) resource based industries (sugar mills, rice mills, oil crushing, tobacco products, paper) products dominated. Later on, a few high capital-intensive industries were developed. This is due to the introduction of industrial estate sales tax concession and power tariff concession. These structural changes started particularly after 1973. The importance of agro-based industries decreased while foot loose industries increased. Similarly, in terms of use-based classification, higher rate of growth was recorded by the capital goods followed by basic goods. By contrast, the consumer goods recorded scanty growth. The author reported that the resources are not properly utilized for the process of industrialization in this state.

Industrial development of Rajasthan was assessed by Somar. S.S(1999). He revealed that during the period of 1980-91, in the industrial mix of this state, there is a considerable increase in the consumer goods and forest based industries, engineering and water works. At the same time there is a deceleration observed in the production of agro-based, and animal based, mineral based industries.

Thangamuthu (1973) has given a clear picture in his M. Lit. thesis about the structural changes of Tamil Nadu industries during 1951-1965. He analysed the pattern dimension of structural changes and also identified the factors responsible for structural changes. His study revealed that the relative share of agro-based industries such as textiles, food processing furniture and other agro-based industries has come down. Industries such as chemicals, metal products, engineering and transport equipment, paper and printing, and the construction materials, have gained noticeable progress, in terms of total investment, labour employment and value added. However, the transport equipment, chemical industries, metal products and engineering industries have overtaken all the other industries. In addition the author has concluded that the change in the industrial structure is determined by the changes in the pattern of capital structure in different industries.

The structural change in the industrial economy of Hariyana was assessed by Kulwinder Karu (1982) over the period 1966 - 1998. He observes that in 1966 about 67per cent of the total employment came from cotton textiles, manufacturing machinery and electrical apparatuses, food processing, transport equipment and metal products. In 1978, these industries provided 60 per cent of the total employment. In the industrial composition, the share of food processing industry declined and the cotton textiles fell from 18 per cent to 15.98 per cent but the basic metals increased its share, at the same time machinery and machine tools maintained their relative share. The basic metals, chemical and chemical product industries made significant improvement with 52.63 per cent increase of employment. The share of electricity machinery and transport equipment remained stable, but the other industries such as woolen textiles, wearing apparel and rubber products gained considerably. To sum up, the agro-based industries lost their share but metal and chemical based industries gained.

Bhagavan Reddy (1988) has made a study on industrialization in India and its impact on employment. He revealed that the basic industries achieved annual compound growth rate of 4.7 per cent to 12 per cent during 1951-60, it slipped down to 10.4 per cent during 60-65, and further down to 6.2 per cent by 65-70 and 76-83. The growth of capital good ranged from 19.6 per cent to negative growth of 1.4 per cent. The performance of consumer goods came down gradually. Similarly, the trend of intermediate goods also came down during the period.

As a whole the author concludes that the contribution of industrial sector to employment was disappointing over the analyzed periods. This is mainly due to adoption of more capital-intensive techniques in production and distortion in factor and product price. In addition, the author suggested encouragement of rural industry & services for maximizing employment.

The structural changes in the industrial economy of India explained by Gobal Ial Jain (1999) The study concludes that the value added share of consumer durable goods accounted for 2.5 per cent in 1960-61, which experienced the highest growth rate of 10.7 per cent per annum. Nevertheless, the intermediate and consumer non-durable groups dwindled. In the input based, the chemical based and metal-based industries recorded impressive growth rate. While the traditional agro-based industries grew at a low rate.

Devadason (2004) has analysed the trade pattern of Malaysian economy using panel data for the period of 18 years from 1983-2000. He concluded that the high intra industries trade increased their employment and wage shares over the period of analysis.

The structural changes in the industrial economy of India for the period 1951 to 64 using CMI and ASI data were studied by Sinha (1988), who revealed that the traditional industries including cotton textiles, jute textiles and sugar had lost their importance in terms of value added. Specifically, the dominant position of cotton textiles had declined considerably. But the importance of modern industries like general engineering and chemicals had increased noticeably.

The industrial development of Punjab was explained by Mahajan V. (1986). He underlined that as a result of the efforts in the first three plans the industrial economy achieved considerable progress. The number of registered working factories and workers engaged in factory sector had increased. In the industrialization, the agro-based industries revealed a strong growth. In the recent periods, the prospect for light engineering industries with high value added output is also good. "Notwithstanding the fact that there are flourishing rural and urban markets for industrial products including consumer goods, large-scale consumer industries have been slow to develop. Thus, there is a need for massive forward push to the process of industrialization, more particularly in sectors which will create large employment potential".

Changes in the industrial structure of India are explained by Venkatasubramanian (1993). He revealed that at the time of independence the industrial products of India comprised cotton textiles, jute manufacturing and a limited quantity of ores. This structure was changed after a certain period. India was able to produce a wide variety of products covering a wide range of consumer, intermediate and capital goods. In terms of export, the industrial products; particularly engineering groups have become a growing component. In toto, the relative share of some traditional industries including food and textiles has declined. In contrast, the relative share of new industries such as chemicals and engineering goods has increased considerably.

Krishna (2002-04) has analysed the growth and diversification of Indian economy for the period of 40 years (1951-90). The capital goods share in terms of value added of industrial sector increased steadily at a higher pace from 4.7 per cent in 1956 to 23.7 per cent in 1990. The share of basic goods also increased, to 38.4 per cent from 22.3 per cent. But the consumer goods group declined considerably from 48.4 per cent in 1956 to 20.5 per cent n 1990.

In 1980s electrical machinery had a growth rate of 20.1 per cent, rubber, petroleum etc. (11.6 per cent), chemicals etc (10.81 per cent) non-metallic mineral products (9.9 per cent), non-electrical machinery (9.3 per cent), food products (9.2 per cent), paper and printing(9.2 per cent) and transport equipment (8.6 per cent). Among the industries, textiles (4.9 per cent) and basic metals (3.9 per cent) grew slowly. Higher growth was registered in several industries belonging to either metal-based or chemical based industries groups. During 1970-89, heavy industry such as machinery, transport equipment and chemicals improved their share from 34 to 43 per cent of manufacturing value added, but there was a considerable reduction in light industry from 34 to 23 per cent.

The structural changes in the industrial economy of India was explained by Sidip Chaudhri (2002), He revealed that between 1960-65, the manufacturing sector achieved 29.9 per cent growth with regard to net value added, this growth is mainly by the influence of sub-sectors growth such as basic, intermediate and capital goods. This was in consonance with the initial aligning strategy, when an attempt was made to develop the basic and intermediate goods. But during 1990-91 to 1997-98, the growth performance of consumer goods was appreciable (16.9 per cent) at the same time 16per cent and 12 per cent growth was achieved by basic and capital goods respectively. Similar trend is observed during 1980s, though the contribution of capital goods is somewhat higher and that of consumer durable is marginally lower. With regard to employment significant growth was achieved by the textile garments (15.37 per cent compound annual growth), industrial organic and inorganic chemicals (9.18 per cent) and plastic product (7.35 per cent).

Burange (1999), analysed the industrial structure and growth of manufacturing sector in Maharastra for the period from 1979-80 to 1994-1995. For this purpose he used ASI data and this study yielded that in 1960, the consumer goods industry contributed 52 per cent of value added, and 48 per cent was accounted for by capital and intermediate goods. This scenario was changed in 1980-1981 as consumer goods industries accounted for 35 per cent, similarly the capital and intermediate goods industries accounted for 65 per cent. In 1994–1995, the consumer goods industries decreased further to 17 per cent and the capital and intermediate goods recorded 83per cent of value added. The contribution of agriculture related industries (20-21 to 29) decreased in terms of fixed capital, employment, value added and value of output; by contrast the share of the non-agricultural related industries increased. In the industrial composition, food products, rubber, plastic, petroleum and coal products, manufacture of chemical and chemical products, basic metal and alloys industries and the manufacture of electrical and non-electrical machinery accounted for 67 per cent of fixed capital. In terms of value of output of food products, rubber, plastic, petroleum and coal product, chemical and chemical products, electrical and non-electrical machinery and transport equipment are amounted 69.66 per cent in 1994-1995. As for net value added only four industries (rubber, plastic, petroleum and coal products manufacture of chemical and chemical products, electrical and non-electrical machinery and transport equipment.) contributed 56.77 per cent. As regard employment, 49 per cent was provided by food products, cotton textiles, rubber, plastic, petroleum and coal product and electrical and non-electrical machinery.

The performance of employment generation was very poor in this state, due to the decline in agricultural related industries. The capital-intensive industries are becoming more dominant in this state, the structural ratios explain the increasing capital intensity, falling employment and consequently rising labour productivity and falling labour cost in this state.

The structural changes in the industrialisation of Andra Pradesh has been assessed by Munirathna Naidu(1995) for the period 1970's-80's. In 1950 the output of basic and capital goods was only 20 per cent but in 1980 it increased to 50 per cent. The production of engineering goods improved to 11per cent in 1980. The other industries such as food and agro processing, pulp, paper and other forest based industries, textiles and jute industries, accounted for 54.62 per cent in 1971 but declined to 47.37 per cent in 1982. In contrast, the capital goods, chemicals, drugs, pharmaceutical and leather goods industries made progress. Between 1960-61 and 1980-81, the number of non-agricultural labourers rose by 86.4 per cent and agricultural labourers increased by 56.6 per cent. The export of engineering goods has boosted the settingup of engineering companies by both central and state governments. In addition the author identified the infrastructural setback and low allocation during the planning period for industrial sector as the obstacles for industrial development.

Unni and *et al.* (2001) have analysed the growth and structural changes in the industrial economy of Gujarat and compared it with all India level for the period 1978-95 using NSSO data. They revealed that due to collapse of textile industries low growth was recorded during 1978–85. The employment generation of organized sector came down due to decline of cotton textiles. In contrast, there was a massive growth achieved by capital-intensive industries that is chemical and related industries. The other important industries are basic metals, machinery and equipment, transport, equipment and food products in terms of output. Their contribution to total output is considerable. There has been perceptible structural transformation in terms of employment and output. There was observed during the mid 1980 particularly during the reform period. The expansion in output was higher than the employment. This was because during the reform period the capital - intensive industries such as chemical and chemical product grew and labour-intensive industries like cotton textiles declined and the restructing of the state public enterprises also contributed to the decline in employment. It is to be mentioned that in Gujarat there was a huge increase in investments in the organized manufacturing sector in the post reform period as a result of liberalization. Finally the author highlights that the strategy adopted by the state during the 1980's for the physical infrastructural development, (which has contributed in 1990's) is the main reason for the growth of manufacturing sector in Gujarat.

The structural changes in the industrial economy of India in terms of output were assessed by Khan (1980), for a period of 25 years starting form 1951, using CSO & RBI data. His analysis explains that the weight of capital goods industries in total industrial production was only 4.71 per cent at the end of the first five-year plan. While intermediate and consumer goods industries recorded 24.59 per cent and 48.37 per cent respectively. Due to the adoption of the industrial policy resolution of 1956 (The absence or inadequacy of machine producing capacity was sought to be set right by the industrial policy resolution of 1956) Considerable expansion and diversification was achieved by basic and capital goods industries. The basic and capital goods have increased their respective weights in the industrial production while the weight of consumer and inter mediate goods industries sloped downwards over the study period.

In the industrial composition, the share of food, textiles, rubber products, petroleum and coal and basic metal has shown a declining trend in terms of output. In contrast, the share of chemical and chemical products, metal products, except machinery and transport equipment, electrical machinery, apparatus, appliance and transport equipments increased over the period of analysis.

The performance of industrial economy of India was discussed by Manmohan Singh (1985) at the time of independence. The industries were confined to cotton textiles, jute manufacturers and limited quantities of ores. The other industries like power plants, steel units, heavy engineering projects, chemicals, drugs and fertilizers were generally beyond the horizon of the entrepreneurs. During 1980-1985, the industrial production increased by about five times and the industrial structure had been widely diversified. Covering broadly the entire range of consumer, intermediate and capital goods. Owing to rapid industrialization the role of traditional sector, like food and textiles had declined, contrarily chemicals and engineering goods increased very substantially. Rapid industrialization was accompanied by a corresponding growth in technological and managerial skills.

The growth of industrial sector in India, during eighties was explained by RBI (1998-1999), during this period the basic and capital goods sectors grew at a faster rate. In the nineties, the intermediate goods sector showed faster growth. Ironically, the basic, capital and consumer goods sectors recorded deceleration in the rate of growth. This was mainly due to the restructuring in the industrial sector, in general and in the basic and capital goods sectors, in particular.

Growth and structural change of the industrial economy of Kerala was assessed by Alice Albin (1990) for the period 1960-1980, National Account Statistics, Annual Survey of Industries, Directory of Manufacturing Establishment and National Sample Survey are the sources of data for her study. To analyze the industrial structure she divided the entire period into two sub periods viz., 1961-1971 and 1972-1981. She observed that in terms of value added only 3 industries have recorded negative growth in the first phase. Except the non-metallic mineral product and transport equipment, all the industries registered decline in growth in terms of value added in the second period. Only four industries, recorded negative growth (canning and preserving of fish, miscellaneous food products, coir and coir products and printing and publishing) for the whole period.

Regarding employment, several industries such as miscellaneous food products, coir, printing and publishing, non-metallic mineral products and basic metals and alloys showed negative growth in the first period. Among them, coir, printing and publishing revealed negative growth in the second period also. Only a few industries such as textiles and wood products, non-metallic mineral products and basic metals and alloys accounted for higher growth in the second period. From the above, it may be concluded that Kerala experienced a slower growth in value added and employment in the study period and this slower growth was seen in almost all the industry groups.

Subrahmanian (1990), studied the industrial development of Kerala using ASI data for different periods. In terms of industrial structure, the author says that "the region tends to specialize in resource based industries like food processing, wood and wood products, paper and paper products, rubber and rubber products and non-metallic mineral. The analysis did not show any significant change in the industrial base of Kerala. The industrial structure is too lopsided to ensure inter-sectoral linkages and agglomeration economies for the overall industrial progress".

Todaro (1997) has explained the industrial composition of Indian industries. He reveals that India is the seventh largest country in the world and the largest country in South Asia. In the industrial sector cotton and jute textile production is still the most important industrial activity. Whereas, publicly owned and operated large manufacturing companies producing steel, machine tools, electricals and transport machinery, and chemicals have played significant role since 1960. Yet in early 1990's, many of these state owned enterprises were being transferred to private hands through the process of privatization.

Thomas (2002) has analysed the manufacturing sector of the Indian economy over the period 1979-1980 to 1997-1998; he used the ASI data for his multi dimensional aspects of analysis regarding structural change. He revealed that the chemical and related industries increased their importance in the value added during the two decades. On the other hand textiles and its related industries lost their share. In terms of employment the food industries provide considerable employment. The manufacturing of chemical and food products created large number of new jobs and investment in 1990's. In contrast to this, the agro based industries such as cotton and jute textiles suffered considerable loss of jobs in the 1980 and it continued in 90's also. Increase in the manufacture of transport equipments in the 1990's is probably the reflection of the recent boom in demand for passenger vehicles. Large share of investment has moved into the production of basic metal and alloys such as iron, steel, aluminum, etc. These two industries were the fastest growing segments of Indian manufacturing in the 1990s. Significant variation in the growth across industries and regions is the notable point, the author mentioned.

Dhal (1996), has exemplified the impact of technical change on the economic growth of India during 1980's and 1990's, using data form planning commission technical notes data. In this study, he explains the structural changes in the industrial economy of India. Within the manufacturing sector textiles, petroleum products, chemicals, electric machinery, electronic equipments and transport equipment increased their share in 1979-80, 1984-85 and 1989-90 to the gross output of the economy. Owing to import substitution the contribution of minerals, basic metals and machinery sector was appreciable. At the same time the contributions of technological change were made in the case of crude petroleum and natural gas, and miscellaneous minerals.

Even though, Andhra Pradesh is agriculturally advanced state, contribution of non-agro based industries was very high. The major productions of this state are basic metals, non-metallic mineral products, beverages and tobacco, food, and textile products. The entire period (1980-81 to 1997-1998) witnessed stagnation in agro-based industries in contrast to the significant growth of non-agricultural. The industrial growth accelerated in the post liberalization period as compared to the pre liberalization period. During the post-liberalization period the annual growth rate of chemical and chemical products of which drugs and pharmaceuticals is an important component, has more than doubled. Ironically, the agro-based industries have come down with regard to growth. Considering the growth of employment also the non-agro based industries are higher when compared with agro-based industries, while the employment in electricity increased in the post-liberalization period. The registered manufacturing of the factory sector during the decade of 1980s and 1990s grew steadily aided mainly by the public sector undertakings. The author identified that; the state may have to focus on selected localities by providing the necessary infrastructural facilities to promote industrial development (Venkataramaiah & Burenge, 2003).

Hashim (1991), has analysed the forty years of Indian Economy (1950-1990) using CSO data, he has analysed the consumption expenditure, GDP and sectoral contribution to growth. Regarding the industrial economy he explains that, the mining sector recorded 6.79 per cent growth in the eighties from 4.58 per cent during the fifties, at the same time the manufacturing sector recorded significant growth, within the manufacturing sector, the growth rates of electricity, gas and water supply was high, however, there was deceleration in the construction sector over the decades. There was no considerable increase in growth of trade, hotels and restaurants, but transport and storage grew faster during the study periods.

Considering the consumption, the proportion of food in the total private consumption declined from the fifties to the eighties. Within the food group the shift was recorded from cereals and pulses in favour of sugar, gas and oil to some extent, but more in favour of fruits, vegetables, milk and animal products. A significant increase occurred in the share of clothing and footwear, durable consumer goods, transport and communication, recreation and education. The structural transformation from the consumption pattern is very clear.

Prakash (1999) documented the changes in employment in Kerala's economy. The tertiary sector recorded higher employment when compared to other sectors. Fairly, higher growth of employment was recorded by construction, transport, storage and communication, trade and commerce and other services. There was a decline in the share of primary employment and stagnation in the contribution share of secondary employment and an increase in the share of tertiary employment in 1980's.

Productivity Picture

Bhatia (1990) has compared the manufacturing productivity of Indian industries with those two countries such as U.K. and U.S. over the period 1965-85. His mathematical analysis explains that the total factor productivity of Indian Industries tend to comedown during 1965–75. Thereafter it increased, particularly the upgradation of this productivity increased substantially during 80-85. In UK, productivity index rose during 65-73, and was maintained during 73 to 82, than increased in the period of 83 to 85. However, the US productivity index had been steadily increasing during the period of analysis. It is noted that the upward trend of productivity index of Indian industries after 1975 was greater than that of UK and US. Moreover, the author concluded that the lower capital, labour ratio, low level of technology, relative higher share of housing in the fixed capital stocks and socio-demographical conditions are responsible for very low level of productivity in Indian industries for certain period.

Chen (1997) studied TFP for five Asian Countries such as Hong Kong, Singapore, Korea, Japan and Taiwan for the period of 1955 to 1970. Chen extended his analysis to estimate TFP for all sectors such as agriculture, manufacturing and service. According to him, the developing countries tended to have higher capital share in income (in the range of 0.4 to 0.5) compared with developed countries (in the range of 0.25 to 0.3). The source of growth pattern showed that factor inputs play an important role on growth at aggregate level. It is to be mentioned that in manufacturing sector the growth of inputs played an important role in explaining the growth of output.

Mullen & Williams (1990) scanned the Total factor productivity differential in manufacturing sector for 29 standard metropolitan areas in US from the period of 1958 to 1978. They found that high growth of output was related to the high growth in productivity. There was also a positive correlation between manufacturing output growth and the newness of capital. Fast growing metropolitan had relatively high proportion of new factories with the latest technology.

Dawling & Summers (1998) examined TFP for seven Asian countries for the period 1970-1992 using gross domestic product (GDP) data. They concluded that the estimates of TFP were sensitive to a number of external factors and also to the stage of economic growth and development in a given country. The external factors include the process of technological transfer, the external trading environment, the level of economic growth, and the distortions and biases inherent in the measurement of capital and labour in developing economies. There were evidences to prove that TFP was higher in the periods of rapid economic growth and when the international trade environment was more conductive to international exchange of technology.

Jantan & Sahlan (2002) have reviewed the Total Factor Productivity of selected 22 districts in Malaysia over the period 1991-1996. They have observed: "The growth of inputs i.e., capital and labour, accounted to 78 per cent of the growth of manufacturing output, while the contribution of technical progress was 22 per cent. These findings suggest that developing economies rely heavily the newer machinery to promote growth. This is true because the early stage of economic development depends on new investment in capital.

Wulong Gu and Muns Ho (2000) have compared the productivity growth of two countries viz. Canada, and United States for the period from 1961 to 1995. Their work revealed that there has been a steady slow down in the growth of output, input and productivity in both countries during the sub-periods of 1961-73, 73-88 and 1988-95.

Sharma (2000) elucidates the Total factor productivity growth of manufacturing sector in Nepal's economy during the pre and post liberalization period. His Tornquist index number formula yielded the result of reduced overall productivity growth during the period. The fall of productivity growth is more in pre-liberalization period than in the post-liberalization period.

It is noteworthy to mention that the productivity growth of export-oriented industries is very high in the pre-liberalization period but not in the post-liberalization period. Owing to external competition, better technologies and imported inputs the productivity of import substitution industries increased considerably in the post-liberalization period. The author concludes that there is not much impact on productivity growth through liberalization.

The performance of manufacturing sector for twelve industrially advanced countries was analysed by Kaldor (1963) for the period from 1953-54 to 1963-64. This study reveals that the countries, which had highest growth in output, had the largest increase in productivity and also labour input.

A study was conducted by Nicholoson and Gupta (1960) on 138 industries in British during 1954. This study reached the conclusion that there is a marked association between output changes and productivity changes. In addition they concluded that the industries, which reveal higher rate of increase in output also had high rate of increase in productivity.

Lomas (1959) has analysed the productivity trend of 14 industries group of United Kingdom. The period of this study was 1907 to 1960. This study yielded the result that there is highly positive association between the growth of volume of output and labour productivity.

The relationship between productivity and output analysed by Maddison (1955), for British manufacturing, revealed that the growth of productivity seems to be highly correlated with output.

The productivity picture of manufacturing industries of the United States was ascertained by Kendrick (1961). His analysis covered the period from 1899 to 1953 and various sub-periods. This rank correlation co-efficient analysis concluded that between rate of growth of output and output per unit of labour input for the 33 industry groups was 0.68 for the whole period, and recorded 0.69 for 20 manufacturing industries. The negative association (-0.10) between the rate of growth of output and output per man-hour was only 12 for industry groups for the entire analysed periods.

Industrial productivity of Nigeria has been assessed by Anyanwu (2000), for the period 1966 –1998. It concluded that there was a little productivity growth during the analysed period. This is mainly due to numerous problems like low level of technology, low level of capital utilization rate, high cost of production, inflation and poor performing infrastructure. This study suggests the following steps to achieve higher productivity upgrading the technological capacity, reducing cost of production, increasing investment, reducing dependence on imports, stimulating demand for manufacturers and rehabilitation and development of infrastructural facilities.

Mieko Nishimizu & Robinson S. (1986) assessed total factor productivity of Korea, Turkey and Yugoslavia; they compared it with Japan for the period of 1950's to 1970' using World Bank time series data. They revealed that the total factor productivity growth rate in Korea was 1.77 per cent, which is above that of Japan. In the case of Turkey it is 1.05 per cent and Yugoslavia it is 1.95 per cent, both values are below that of Japan. This total factor productivity growth indicates that the there is significant difference among the countries. The authors suggest that the productivity difference among the countries might be atleast partly caused by the nature of the economic policies followed by each country.

Ahluwalia (1985) has calculated the total factors productivity of Indian industries over 1959 to 80 using ASI data. She computed the so-low and Translor methods of total productivity, which covered twenty (two digit) industries. She revealed that the efficiency in factor use in manufacturing has decreased over this period. In terms of inter-industrial scenario the rubber products, miscellaneous industries, food manufacturing, wood and cork, metal products, leather and fur products exhibited a declining trend in total factor productivity growth. Similarly the other important industries like chemical and non-metallic mineral products declined. Contrarily, the two industries such as footwear, furniture & fixtures, achieved a growth of 2 per cent to 3 per cent of total factor productivity for this period. In the case of use-based and input-based categories, there was a declining tendency in the total factor productivity growth over this period (this excluded capital goods and consumer durable goods). Moreover, the author worked out the capital output ratios and labour productivity for twenty (two digit) industries of the same period, which shows that there is a statistically significant trend in all the industry groups. It was observed that the growth of capital productivity was overwhelming due to capital deepening. But in most of the industry groups, the efficiency in use factor decreased.

Vinod vyasulu, & Arunkumar (1997) has analysed the productivity trend of Orissa's industries for the years 1966-67 to 88-89. It revealed that, except the industry group, chemical and its products all other groups witnessed a positive growth in labour as well as capital productivities over this period. But in the case of capital productivity and capital intensity of cotton textiles exhibited higher growth. The industries like non-metallic product, metal alloys and other manufacturing industries scored higher value added per employee.

In addition, the author underlined that "From the policy point, the main issue will be to work out strategies that help in the substantial decentralized growth of industries in a highly backward state like Orissa. Attention especially in areas like a decentralized rural industry is called for. The present pattern of industrialization is largely inadequate and the state has to actively intervene in the promotion of these industries suitable to the resource endowment of the states".

Shanthi(1981) has analysed the productivity trend of Tamil Nadu industries for the period 1959-1971. She has taken data from various ASI reports for 23 major industries. In this study the author highlights that the capital output ratio and capital value added ratio have shown increasing trend during the period of analysis. In terms of technical co-efficient, the value added per employee has increased only 4 points and the real wages per employee has gone up by 6 points.

The productivity trend in India for the period 1951-1964 was analyzed by Sinha (1988), using CMI and ASI data for selected 10 industries. It revealed that there has been an improvement in labour productivity. There has been more than 3per cent improvement in labour productivity per annum in sugar, cement, chemicals and general engineering industries. The productivity increase in traditional industries like cotton textiles, woolen textiles and jute textile has not been so impressive. Moreover, the author identified the man-power problem, problem of production techniques, management problem, and some other problems as contributory reasons for low productivity.

The labour productivity of Indian industries was assessed by Chenchankar (1969) for the period 1946-58. His study concluded that during the analysed period the rise in labour productivity and real earnings was not even and labour productivity increased by 57 per cent, the money earning by 204 per cent and the real earnings by 54 per cent. In the case of traditional industries, the real earnings remained at a higher level than the labour productivity. In contrast, the opposite occurred in modern industries.

Chaudhuri (2002), calculated the productivity of Indian industries for the period 1990-1991 to 1992-1998, using ASI and NAS data. He revealed that in the registered manufacturing sector, labour productivity has increased steadily from 0.45 in 1990-1991 to 0.65 in 1995–1996, since than it stagnated at this level. The compound average rate of growth of labour productivity has been 5.6 per cent for the entire. There is a marginal increase revealed by the capital productivity. The compound average rate of growth of capital productivity is recorded as 0.76 per cent for the entire period.

Unni, Lalitha and Uma Rani (2001) have assessed the productivity trend for Gujarat and compared it with all India for the period 1978-95 using NSSO data. They concluded that in Gujarat, the organized sector reforms period saw a sharp increase in labour and capital resulting in high growth of value added. The growth of capital intensity was relatively higher resulting in a negative growth of capital productivity over the analyzed period. In this state, the increase in capital intensity and decline in capital productivity in the reforms period appeared in all the user groups, except intermediate goods. This study concludes that the growth of manufacturing sector in Gujarat was better compared to the national level and this growth was accomplished by the physical infrastructure development.

Goel (2003), attempts to test the impact of infrastructure on productivity for the period 1965-99 in India using twenty-three types of infrastructural variables. They grouped all the variables under two broad categories, such as economic infrastructure and social infrastructure; the economic infrastructure includes five sectors namely electricity, banking, irrigation, transport and communications. Similarly social infrastructure includes two sectors viz., education and health. Her principal component analysis yielded the result that both economic and social infrastructures significantly affect the cost and productivity of registered manufacturing sectors in India. She concluded that the infrastructure plays a positive and significant role in the productivity.

Siddharthan (2004), reviewed six studies on industrial productivity of Indian industries Das, (2003), Ray (2003), Goldar Ranganathan and Banga, (2003), Siddharthan and Lal, (2003), Banga, (2003) and Narayanan, (2003). After reviewing all these studies the author concludes that these studies do not support the hypothesis that an increase in productivity efficiency in Indian industries is the result of economic liberalization.

Deb Kusum Das (2004), analysed the total factor productivity for 75 three-digit industries of India using ASI data for the period of 1980-2000. His study identifies four distinct phases of India's trade liberalization (1980-85, 86-90, 91-95 and 96-2000). This study shows that for the entire period total factor productivity growth recorded 0.08 per cent over 75 three-digit industries. Among these only two industries viz., weaving and finishing of cotton khadi and tanning, curing and finishing of leather contributed 50 per cent of the total factor productivity for the period 1980-2000. The author concludes that the total factor productivity growth in the 1990's was lower than in the 1980's. Moreover, the total factor productivity growth for the three use based sectors for the second half of the 1990's was lower, when compared to the first half (1991-1995).

"Two possible explanations for the slowdown in TFP growth may be offered. First industrial production in 1990-1991 and 1991-1992 was constrained by factors such as import compression, tight money policy, inflationary pressures and fiscal contraction initiated by the government as part of the macro economic stabilization programmers. These led to a recessionary trend in the manufacturing sector. Secondly mergers began to pick up only towards the end of the 1995 and constraints operate in the functioning of the labour markets, particularly the exit policies that ought to supplement the trade liberalization attempts".

The small scale organized industrial sector of Kerala was analyzed by Thampy(1990), for the period 1970-1971 to 1982-1983, based on the ASI and Indian Labour year book data. This study revealed that the wage per worker increased more than three times, while the productivity increased less than two times. In terms of value added per worker Kerala had been lagging behind the national figure. Among the major Indian states, Kerala accounted for considerable rank in case of wage per employee but very low in both labour and capital productivity.

A study was conducted by Aggarwal, A.K. and Ganesh Kumar N. (1991), for the purpose of analysis of productivity performance of Indian industries using cross section and time series data for different period. The cross-section data analysis support the verdoorn's law, and the time series analysis of the causality test suggests that this slow/declining rate of growth of productivity could be partly explained by the small size of the market and the slow growth of demand for industrial goods. The authors suggest that to improve growth of productivity in industry, efforts should be focussed on developing new market for industrial goods.

Subramaniam (1992) has calculated the productivity growth of cotton textile industries in Tamil Nadu, for the period 1975-1976 to 1985-1986. The Annual Survey of Industries and Tamil Nadu-An economic appraisal are the data sources for his study, and value added, labour and capital are the variables. This study concludes that the partial labour productivity has increased at an annual average growth of 2.42 per cent, at the same time the capital productivity declined around 24.5 per cent. The predominant influence behind marginal increase in labour productivity seems to be capital intensity. The total factor productivity shows that the declining trend (the Kendrick indices explains that the total factor productivity has declined at an average rate of 10.25 per cent while Solow's indices show a constant annual average decline of 14.89 per cent). This downward trend may be caused by decline in capacity utilization (due to workers strikes) severe power cut, increasing cost of raw cotton, labour and electricity.

The capital output ratios for the Indian industrial economy during the period covering 1950-1951 to 1989-1990 were calculated by Rangarajan, C. and Kannan, K. (1994). They used the relevant data from different published papers. This study explains that during 1960's agricultural sector recorded 122 per cent of increase followed by 104, 82, 68 and 61 per cent by banking and insurance, manufacturing, transport and electricity respectively. In 1970's the construction sector accounted for 111per cent increase and 104, 87 and 34 per cent of growth was contributed by trade mining and quarrying and electricity. During 1980-88, agriculture, fisheries, manufacturing, electricity, transport, real estate, public administration and others recorded lower growth of incremental capital-output ratio. By contrast, construction, trade banking recorded increase in incremental capital-output ratio for the same period.

Impact of Policy

Uma Kapila (2002), has analysed the impact of the industrial policy on the industrial sector of India. She observed that "the major policy changes initiated in the industrial sector since July 1991 viz removal of entire barriers, reduction of areas reserved exclusively for public sector, rationalization of the approach towards MRTP, liberalisation of foreign investment policy, far reaching liberalisation of import policy with respect to intermediates and capital goods may have all contributed to the upward surge in industrial growth".

The impact of liberalization on industrial sector of Maharastra was assessed by Burange L.G. (1999). He classified the analysed period in to pre-liberalisation and post-liberalisation periods (1980-81 to 91-92 and 91-92 to 94-95). This study revealed that the successive reduction in taxes and import liberalization with export promotion had boosted Indian industry. In addition, the liberalization policy facilitated private investment, technical and financial collaboration with foreign entrepreneurs. All these helped the manufacturing sector of India in general and Maharashtra in particular. In conclusion manufacturing sector of Maharashtra recorded high growth of output, employment, fixed capital, and value added during the post liberalization period. However, the overall performance of some agro based-industries such as cotton textiles, non-metallic mineral products and leather and leather products decreased further in the period under review.

Yumkella and *et.al* (1991) have assessed the impact of globalisation on industrial structure. They observe that the globalisation has facilitated structural shifts in most economies in favor of the service sector. In the OECD countries, the share of manufacturing sector to GDP and its share of total employment peaked at the end of the 1960s. But the share of manufacturing in total employment fell from 28 per cent in 1970 to 18 per cent in the mid-1990s. The most visible feature of globalisation has been the massive increase in international trade that had flowed and investments particularly since the late 1980s. In the 1990s foreign trade and foreign direct investment have been the principal propellants of rapid economic growth and structural transformation in the emerging economies.

The impact of new economic policy on output and employment in manufacturing sector of Punjab was assessed by G. K. Bhatia (1999). He shows that the annual average growth rate of output has increased by 16per cent during the pre-liberalisation period decreased slightly (15.69 per cent) during the first phase of liberalization then increased to 18per cent during the second phase of liberalization (1985-1986 to 1991-92). Employment registered twelve per cent increase during the pre-liberalisation period but fell to 10 per cent and 7 per cent during the first and second phase of liberalization in this state.

Considering the structural ratio, fixed capital per factory increased nearly four-fold during the pre-liberalisation period and extraordinary growth appeared in the post liberalization period. Similarly the fixed capital per employee has increased sharply. But the level of employment per lakh of capital, emoluments in output and value added registered a down ward trend.

Howard Pack (2000) has examined the impact of industrial policy on the industrial sector of two countries viz. Japan and Korea. He assumed that if infact the industrial policy played an important role for development. It may be a lesson for other countries. Ironically, if the role of policy was limited, more conventional policies should be pursued.

Howard pack (2000) has analyzed the impact of government policy on the industrial structure. He compared Japan with Italy, Finland, Austria, Australia, France and the Federal Republic of Germany. Similarly, Korea is compared with Uruguay, Portugal, Malaysia, Mexico and Panama. He underlined that there are a few substantial sectoral differences in the production structure between Japan and its bench mark countries and Korea and its bench mark countries. Particularly in both countries, the combined metal products, machinery and electrical equipment sectors have achieved high growth. The author underlined that this trend suggests that the government policies may have had their intended impact on sectoral structure.

Since independence the industrial policy of India, concentrated on rapid industrialization with diversification of the industrial structure (which is one of the important objectives of industrialization). At the time of implementation of Mahalanobis model, various steps were taken for the establishment of machine tools industries, heavy electrical, machine building and other branches of heavy engineering industries. In terms of structural transformation of Indian industries, the share of capital goods in industrial value added had increased from 4.7 per cent in 1956 to 23.7 per cent in 1990. Similarly the share of basic goods increased from 22.3 per cent to 38.4 per cent during the same period. Contrarily the share of consumer goods declined sharply from 48 per cent in 1956 to 20.5 per cent in 1990.

The author cited Ahluwalia's conclusion for industrial declaration to slow down in public investment, poor management of the infrastructural sector, slow growth of agricultural income and restrictive industrial and trade policy.

Chaudhari (1989), underlined that the policy reforms, which promoted efficient competition and to long-term changes in industrial structure.

CRITICAL REMARKS

From the foregoing review of studies, it is understood that the industrial development is an unambiguous process for not only economic development but also overall sustainable development of the country.

One of the distinguishing characteristics in the process of industrial development is structural changes. The study on growth and structural changes in the industrial economy of India has been made by several authors. Among them Ahluwalia (1999), Chaudhri (2001), Khan (1980), Nayyar (1994), Chandrasekar (2000), Attri (1991), Reddy (1988), Jain (1999), Venkatasubramaniam (1993), and Hashim (1991), Balakrishnan & Sureshbabu (2002), they concentrate on various aspects. A few studies were made on different aspects in Tamil Nadu by Kurian (1995), Thangamuthu (1973), Dhanajayan (1985), Bharathan (1980), Shanthi (1981) and Vijayalakshmi (1994). However, analysis on growth structural change, and productivity trend in the industrial economy of Tamil Nadu were very meagre, particularly in regard to the concentration on each and every segment.

But from the available studies, the pattern and dimension of industrial development is identified. They have concentrated on growth in index of industrial production, industry wise and classification (use and input- based classification) wise growth performance.

The above mentioned authors have used the factors to assess the growth and structural changes in the industrial economy. Those are, national income, labour force, imports, exports, and aggregate level. Similarly, in a few studies, to assess the structural transformation in the industrial economy they have used the criteria such as number of factories, productive capital, number of persons employed, value of output and value added and they have underlined the factors governing for dramatic and poor growths.

On the whole, the earlier studies examined the industrial economy on an aggregate level. The aggregate level study may hardly reflect the full spectrum of industrial economy of a region. In the backdrop, the authors of the book made an attempt to estimate the performance of each and every segment of industrial economy of Tamil Nadu in general and structural changes in particular. The focus of the work was on growth of sub-sectors (mining, quarrying, electricity, gas and water supply), exports, imports, generation and consumption of electricity, analysis on two digit, analysis on three digit (use and input based, agro and non-agro based comparison) and partial and total factor productivity.

The real contribution lies in the comparison between pre and post reform periods and in understanding the implications of new industrial policy on the industrial economy of Tamil Nadu. The comparison has been made on growth, structural change, and productivity. Hence, this is a necessary study in the contemporary economy as the structural changes are distinguishing characteristics and merits of industrial development.

CHAPTER 3

INDUSTRIAL PROFILE

In this chapter, a brief note on the industrial economy of Tamil Nadu is presented. It coveres the sub-segments such as infrastructural development, major financial institutions, structural change in the aggregate economy, per capita income, trend of financial allocation during the five year plans, and foreign trade.

Tamil Nadu is a State situated in the south eastern extremity of the Indian subcontinent. Map of this state is enclosed at the end of this chapter. It is bounded on the north by Karnataka and Andhra Pradesh on the east by Bay of Bengal, on the south by the Indian Ocean and on the west by Kerala State. Tamil Nadu covers a little over 130,000 sq km, representing about 4 pre cent in India's total geographical area (MIDS, 1988).

ENDOWMENT OF MINERALS:

Generally, in any nation the endowment of mineral resources is of vital importance for a strong industrial base. The State of Tamil Nadu is poor in the mineral resources. The available minerals in the State include limestone, lignite, granite, clay, gypsum, feldspar, graphite, magnesite, crude mica, bauxite, bilmenite and iron ore (www.tidco.com). A few of these were exploited economically, the rest remained as small deposits. Among them, lignite, mangnesite, gypsum, limestone and clay are exploited on a commercial basis. The Techno Economic Survey of the State (1958) had given the following note about the mineral and natural resources of Tamil Nadu, that "the Physical resources basis of the State is ostensibly weak. It is deficient in key minerals essential for rapid economic development on modern lines. Of coal, there is none, iron available is not of high grade; other metallic minerals are not plentiful, forest resources too are meager. Power development is reaching or will soon reach the point of saturation. The centers of industry in the region are far from the main fields of raw materials supplies". (Cf. James and Kurien, 1979).

Table 1
Production and Value of Major Minerals in Tamil Nadu in 1999-2000

Name of the Mineral	*Quantity (tonne)*	*Value (Rs in thousands)*
Bauxite	137712	11315
Dunite	12164	1876
Felspar	10714	2119
Fireclay	35293	37583
Garnet (Abrasive)	208382	55919
Graphite	2170	807
Lime Kankar	206038	24314
Limestone	5447748	1215841
Lignite (in '000')	17551	8384639*
Magnesite	245980	299286
Petroleum Crude (in '000')	521	1807349*
Quartz	16065	5458
Silica Sand	1354	1036
Steatite	238	16
Vermiculite	1281	3001
Total		11850559

Included in Andhra Pradesh.
Source: Statistical Handbook of Tamil Nadu, 1999-2000, p-188

Spatial Distribution of Mineral Resources:

In Tamil Nadu, the distribution of mineral resources, as elsewhere in the country is directly related to geological formations, particularly, the crystalline rocks of Archean age. The mineral deposit occurring in the Archaean rocks include iron ore, magnesite, mica, chromite, barytes, berly, limestone, copper and pyrites (Ramesh & Tiwari, 1983).

In Tamil Nadu most of the minerals are available in a few districts like Salem, Coimbatore, South Arcot, Tiruchirappalli and Tirunelveli. Among these, Salem district contains rich deposits of bauxite, magneite, iron ore, limestone, chromite, corundum and bauxite is available at Shevaroy Hill. Gypsum and small quantity of phosphatic nodules are colleted from Tircuhirappalli district. The coastal areas such as Kanniyakumari, Tirunelveli and Chinglepet district produced salt; lignite is available at Neyveli (South Arcat district). Crude oil and natural gas have been discovered at Karaikal and Narimanam (Gopal Singh, 1995).

Forest Resources

In the total geographical area 17 per cent was under forest, timber and sandalwood are the main products from the forest source. In addition, tea, wattle bark and cashew are some of the minor products.

MAJOR INDUSTRIES

Historical Phases of Industrial Development of Tamil Nadu

From the historical phase, Tamil Nadu has been a frontline industrial State in India. Under British rule, Madras (Tamil Nadu was called before 1956) being one of the leading industrial regions. At the time of independence, Madras and Coimbatore were two main industrial and trading centers. In these, Madras had strong administration power and possessed various trading communities. This State, Madras had well-developed infrastructure some of the people had entrepreneurial and managerial capacity. Most of the textile industries are concentrated in Coimbatore (Rosen, 1988).

The establishment and growth of modern industries in Tamil Nadu (up to independence) have been classified under three phases. During first half of the 19th century the factory sector of the State was dominated by sugar, textile and leather industries. Three, sugar producing industries were established in South Arcot district and another at Pugalur. Similarly, the textile industries were established at Madras, Coimbatore,

Madurai and Tuticorin (The first textile mill, Harvey's at Ambasamudram). Where as, Leather tanning industries (the process of converting hides into leather) were established at North Arcot district.

The second phase covers the period from 1870s till about the First World War. During this period the factory sector was dominated by cement industries. There were three cement plants setup at Madukkarai, Thazhayuth and Dalmiapuram. During the period of 1930s at Mettur a large-scale chemical industry was established to produce caustic soda, liquid chlorine, hydrogenated oils and bleaching power. In addition to the already existing industries, cotton textiles were expanded with the help of the Pykara Hydro Electric Power Project during this period.

The third phase was the period between the two world wars. During this period, engineering and transport equipments industries emerged. From this period the capital goods sector was strengthened with Integral Coach Factory (ICF) and TI cycle factory started at Madras. They were established by public and private sectors respectively.

Since mid-fifties to late seventies, the industrial structure of Tamil Nadu was characterized by substantial diversification, dominated by the capital and intermediate goods sectors. During the end of the seventies, the role of traditional industries such as cotton, sugar and cement slipped down. In contrast, industries such as nylon tyres yarn, phospetic fertilizers, railway coaches, commercial vehicles and automobile components dominated in terms of total industrial output.

Current Scenario of Important Industries in Tamil Nadu

Tamil Nadu has emerged as one of the front-runners in the Post-liberalization era by attracting a large number of investment proposals. The salient features of the industrial economy of Tamil Nadu are as follows:

In terms of industrial output, Tamil Naud recorded third place, and second place in the case of value addition. Similarly, it recorded second place in terms of number of factories, total workers employed in factories and foreign direct investment flow.

In the case of production of different industries the role of Tamil Nadu is very appreciable in total Indian output of heavy commercial vehicles it contributes 27 per cent, 35 per cent of Auto components, 49 per cent of Railway coach, 26 per cent of Motor cycles and mopeds and 17 per cent of News print where contributed by Tamil Nadu. Whereas, in the case of Cotton yarn Tamil Nadu contributed 32 per cent, and 50 per cent, 70 per cent and 32 per cent of power driven pumps, leather products, and safety matches and software products respectively.

During 2001, India's industrial output Tamil Nadu's share was 11 per cent. The strength of Tamil Nadu is not only in traditional industries, but also in several newly emerging industries. In order to develop and promote the industrial economy of Tamil Nadu the government has been taken several efforts.

Mineral Based Industries

The important mineral wealth of the State is granite, limestone and lignite. Over the years, the granite industry has grown from strength of strength contributing more than 35 per cent of the country's exports. The export of Tamil Nadu in the case of granite products and other minerals is Rs. 4 billion and 5.1 billion respectively during 1996-97, and they increased the subsequent years.

Engineering Industries

The engineering industries include automobiles, bicycles, castings and forgings textile machines, electrical and non-electrical machinery, pumps and transport equipments. The engineering exports from Tamil Nadu is around Rs 11.5 billion (US dollars 320 million) of which automobile ancillaries alone contributed around 150 million US dollars. In the all India export of automobile industry the State contributes nearly 50 per cent. The strong engineering base consists of a network of nearly 3000 units, employing a skilled workforce of more than 2.5 lakhs, making high quality inputs such as castings and forgings and a wide variety of ancillary products.

Textile and Ready-made Garments

Textile is an important industry in Tamil Nadu, in the entire exports of cotton yarn and fabrics of India, Tamil Nadu contributes more than 22 per cent. In 1996-97 the export of cotton textiles was $ 2.1 billion and it is estimated that it would reach more than 5 billion by the end of 2005 AD. In the textile products several countries such as USA, UK, France and Germany are principal buyers from Tamil Nadu. However, the textile industries are facing several problems viz stiff competition in international market, lack of demand in local market, financial difficulties for modernization and expansion, shortage of raw materials and high cost of power tariff and so on (DEAR, 1999-2000).

Leather-Based Industries

Historically, Tamil Nadu dominates in leather-based industries; due to the availability of raw materials. In the country's total export of leather and leather related products, the share of Tamil Nadu more than 50 per cent. By the end of 1996-97, the leather exports were $ 900 million and the ambitious target of 4 billion US dollar was fixed for 2004.

Agro-Based Industries

In the agro-based industries, the industry producing food industries are fast developing in the State due to the existence of appropriate climatic conditions. In Tamil Nadu, the Madurai-Dindugal belt is having favorable climatic conditions for the cultivation of a variety of fruits and vegetables. The floriculture industry is also poised for a quantum leap in the next few years in and around Coimbatore, Dharmaprui and the Nilgiris as they have been identified as places ideally suited as places ideally suited for the cultivation of flowers like Rose and Chrysanthemum. Of these, Coimbatore has been identified as an intensive floriculture zone.

Chemical and Petro-Chemical Based Industries

Traditionally, the State of Tamil Nadu has a strong base in the case of chemical industries. Manali (Chennai) has emerged as a major petro chemical complex. Major chemical and fertilizer plants have also been established at Cuddalore and Tuticorin. Dupont, USA has recently commissioned a large plant for the manufacture of nylon at Gummidipoondi near Chennai. Other major projects in Pipeline are Norsk Hydro (PVC), SPIC (PTA/PFY), etc. In addition, 3 new refineries are proposed to be setup at Cuddalore, Tuticorin and Ennore. The petro chemical industry is in the doorstep of rapid expansion in Tamil Nadu.

Electronics Industries

The electronic industries are comingup and getting priority attention in recent years with a turnover of 270 million US dollar. There has been a boom in consumer electronics giving rise to a wide range of consumer products (apart from computers and associated hardware).

Supportive Agencies

In 1949, the first major financial institution was setup in Tamil Nadu, and it was called Madras Industrial Investment Corporation (MIIC). Thereafter it was named Tamil Nadu Industrial Investment Corporation (TIIC). There are 57 financial institutions sponsoring long term and short term financial requirements of industries in the country. These include, 11 all India institutions and 46 State level financial institutions. Among the eleven all India financial institutions, five are development banks. The Industrial Development Bank of India (IDBI), Industrial Finance Corporation of India (IFCI), Industrial Credit and Investment Corporation of India (ICICI) and Industrial Investment Bank of India (IIBI) are providing financial support and undertake promotional and developmental activities of medium and large industries. Small Industries Development Bank of India (SIDBI) is giving financial assistance for small scale industries.

The other important promotional agencies are Tamil Nadu Industrial Development Corporation (TIDCO), State Industries

Promotion Corporation of Tamil Nadu (SIPCOT), Tamil Nadu Small Industries Development Corporation (SIDCO), and Electronics Corporation of Tamil Nadu (ELCOT). These agencies are undertaking project financing, and they provide infrastructural facilitates and worksheds, and they are helping to the establishment of growth centers implementation of investment subsidy and Sale Tax Deferral Schemes (DEAR, 1999-2000, & MIDS, 1988).

INFRASTRUCTURE SCENARIO

Infrastructure is a prerequisite for the industrial development of an economy. Srivastave (1986) rightly remarked that in most of the developing countries including India the strategy of infrastructure development has been used as a tool for developing industries in backward areas.

Power Resources

Power plays an important role in the industrial development and diversification in any country. The health of the industrial economy largely depends upon energy security and availability. Abundant and cheap (in terms of price) power is indispensable for running industries successfully. The energy sources are classified as conventional and non-conventional sources. The conventional source comprises oil, coal, natural gas and the non-conventional (renewable) source consist of bio-mass, wind solar and hydel power.

In Tamil Nadu, among the available sources of power, Thermal-Electric power occupies pre-eminent place with the contribution of 80 per cent of total power generation in 1999-2000 and it increased further to 84 per cent in 2002-03. The significant role played by the power source is due to good performance of Neyveli Thermal station, Madras Automic power. The other sources of power generation are Hydro, Wind and Gas. As the performance of the hydel stations depends on the vagaries of monsoon, the inflow and storage in the resources play an important role. The remaining two sources viz Wind and Gas contribute (independently) less than 5 per cent. The performance of power generation of Gas is very appreciable as it has gone up from 0.9 per cent in 1999-2000 to 3.4 per cent in 2001-02.

The investment for power generation in Tamil Nadu has been very high. Cumulatively, up to the IXth Five-year plan over 22 per cent of the expenditure had been devoted for power infrastructure development. During the First three plan periods, the power sector received the highest allocation of 34 per cent 42 per cent and 34 per cent respectively. But only 20 per cent of the plan outlay has been earmarked for energy development in the Tenth plan (DEAR, 2001-02).

Power Development

The trend of development of power sector in the past 20 years can be analyzed with reference to capacity, generation, and purchases, gross and net power availability. Table 2 revealed that the total installed capacity had increased more than 100 per cent, as it increased from 3109 MW in 1982-83 to 7924 MW by 2001-02. During the same period, the generation and purchases of power have increased from 7382 to 25562 and 3081 to 18358 million units respectively. Similarly, the gross availability of power and total sales within the State have increased from 10463 million units to 43920 million units and from 8223 to 35064 million units respectively in the above said period.

Source wise Power Generation

Table 3 shows that the hydor electric power is in predominant place in 1980-81 with the share of nearly 67 per cent. But its contribution has been decreased over the study period and it came down to 11 per cent in 2002-03, this deterioration trend could be attributed by failure of monsoon. The other important source of power generation is Thermal. Its contribution was 33 per cent in 1980-81 and it improved to nearly 85 per cent in 2002-03, this is due to the improvement of the installed capacity of Ennore, Mettur and Tuticorin stations. After 1986, one million units of Wind mills were made available in this state. At the same time Gas source provided nearly 5 per cent of the total power generation.

Table 2
Power Developments in Tamil Nadu-A Trend Analysis

Year	*Installed Capacity (MW)*	*Generation*	*Purchases*	*Gross Power availability*	*Total Saleswithin State*
1982-83	3109	7382	3081	10463	8223
83-84	3344	6929	3401	10330	7861
84-85	3344	9382	4130	13512	10496
85-86	3668	8632	4725	13357	10090
86-87	3987	9450	5460	14910	11401
87-88	4558	9346	6273	15619	11760
88-89	5123	11224	6394	17618	13639
89-90	5473	11845	6428	18273	14124
90-91	5744	13219	7574	20793	16117
91-92	6019	13833	8087	21920	17040
92-93	6090	16958	7257	24215	18988
93-94	6158	17628	8087	25715	20157
94-95	6578	19917	9158	29075	22936
95-96	6908	21975	9146	31121	24413
96-97	6908	22953	9747	32700	25598
97-98	6916	23066	10999	34065	26740
98-99	7120	22141	13031	35172	27657
99-2000	7204	23549	14764	38313	30238
2000-01	7513	25147	16617	41764	33216
2001-02	7924	25562	18358	43920	35064
TGR (% P.A)					
1982-2000	4.99	7.63	8.56	7.97	8.19
1982-97	6.39	9.02	8.04	8.69	8.9
1997-02	3.33	2.48	13.81	6.4	7.82

Source: Data computed from Tamil Nadu-An Economic Appraisal, Various Issues.

The following bar diagrams clearly explains the power generation of Tamil Nadu over the period 1980-2000.

Consumption Pattern: [Electric power]

It is necessary to discuss the consumption pattern of electricity for different categories. The consumption of industrial sector accounted for nearly 48 per cent in 1980-81, decreased gradually to 33 per cent in 2002-03 this may be due to higher cost and sever power cuts. Though, the domestic consumption has increased considerably from 9 per cent to 24 per cent during same period, the commercial purpose and lighting and

Table 3
Source-wise Power Generations in Tamil Nadu

Source	*1980-81*	%	*86-87*	%	*90-91*	%	*95-96*	%	*99-2000*	%	*2002-03*	%
Hydro	4925	66.8	3319	35.1	3982	30.1	4714	21.5	4444	18.9	2724	10.9
Thermal	2446	33.2	6131	64.9	9207	69.6	17220	78.4	18861	80.1	21080	84.6
Wind	0	0.0	0	0.0	30	0.2	23	0.1	27	0.1	18	0.1
Gas	0	0.0	0	0.0	0	0.0	18	0.1	217	0.9	1107	4.4
Total	7371	100	9450	100	13219	100	21975	100	23549	100	24929	100

Source: Data computed from Tamil Nadu-An Economic Appraisal, Various Issues.

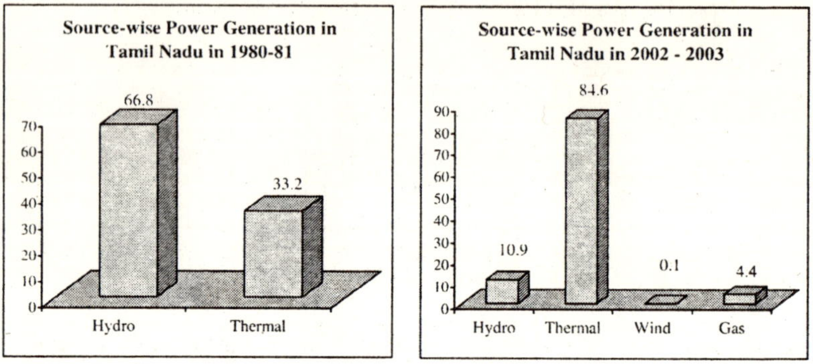

Figure 1: Per centage Share of different Types of Power Generation

water works has increased a little bit during this period. Agricultural consumption has increased with wide fluctuations. Only the consumption for 'other uses' has decreased from 7.4 per cent to 5.1 per cent in the above said period.

Table 4
Category-Wise Consumption of Power in Tamil Nadu [in MU]

Category	*Domestic*	*Commercial*	*Industrial*	*Agri-culture*	*Public light and Water Works*	*Others*	*Total*
1980-81	793	573	4036	2346	80	626	8454
%	9.4	6.8	47.7	27.8	0.9	7.4	100
1986-87	1569	587	5058	3114	178	895	11401
%	13.8	5.1	44.4	27.3	1.6	7.9	100
1990-91	2632	1093	7026	3947	134	1285	16117
%	16.3	6.8	43.6	24.5	0.8	8.0	100
1995-96	4150	1630	10140	6626	524	1343	24413
%	17.0	6.7	41.5	27.1	2.1	5.5	100
1999-2000	5678	2731	11152	8983	740	956	30238
%	18.8	9.0	36.9	29.7	2.4	3.2	100
2002-03	8837	3632	11974	9030	1038	1836	36347
%	24.3	10.0	32.9	24.8	2.9	5.1	100

Source: Data computed from Tamil Nadu-An Economic Appraisal, Various Issues.

The following staked bar diagrams explain the consumption of power in various categories in Tamil Nadu for different periods.

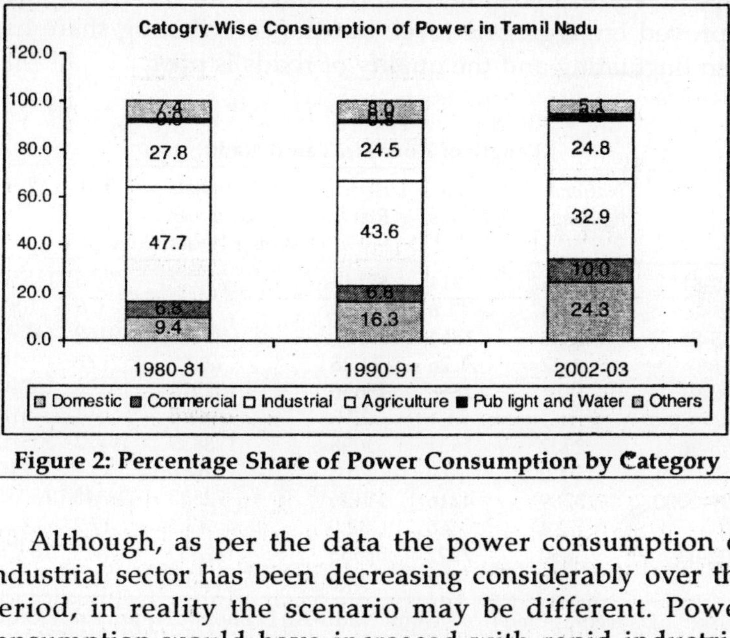

Figure 2: Percentage Share of Power Consumption by Category

Although, as per the data the power consumption of Industrial sector has been decreasing considerably over the period, in reality the scenario may be different. Power consumption would have increased with rapid industrial growth. There is no authentic data to support the view that industries evade payment of power tariff.

Transport and Communication

Transport and communication are playing a vital role in any economy as a whole and industrial sector in particular. The efficient network of transport helps to continuous availability of raw materials, fuel, and labour, marketing of finished products and their even distribution. It leads to improvement in productivity, reduction in cost of production and enlargement of the existing of market (DEAR, 2001-02).

In Tamil Nadu, out of the total roads 62 per cent are Panchayat union and village panchayath roads in 1980-81, followed by 28 per cent of District roads and 7 per cent of other roads. The State highways and National highways combindly accounted for only 3 per cent during the same period. The Panchayath Union and Village Panchayath roads came down to 44 per cent and it is increased during 2002-03; the District road and 'Other roads' registered 31 and 20 per cent respectively in the same period. Totally, all the roads have improved on aggregate level, but the contributing share has been fluctuating and the quality of roads is poor.

Table 5
Length of Roads in Tamil Nadu

Type of Roads	*National Highways*	*State Highways*	*District Roads*	*Panchayat Union & Village Roads*	*Others*	*Total*
1980-81	1865	1814	32146	71527	7956	115308
%	1.6	1.6	27.9	62.0	6.9	100.0
1985-86	1884	1864	35931	99112	9169	147960
%	1.27	1.26	24.28	66.99	6.20	100
1990-91	1884	1896	45656	102515	15156	167104
%	1.1	1.1	27.3	61.3	9.1	100
1995-96	2002	1934	53038	128859	19873	205706
%	1.0	0.9	25.8	62.6	9.7	100
1999-2000	3789	4216	51136	72523	28348	160012
%	2.4	2.6	32.0	45.3	17.7	100
2002-03	3850	7222	58533	82859	37319	189783
%	2.0	3.8	30.8	43.7	19.7	100

Source: Data computed from Tamil Nadu-An Economic Appraisal, Various Issues.

The following trend lines highlights that the share of Panchayath Union and Village roads has decreased dramatically. Ironically, due to contribution of public and private sectors the other roads and State highways have increased moderately.

Plan-Wise Expenditure in Tamil Nadu

It is necessary to probe the financial allocation for industrial sector in a study on the growth and structural changes in the industrial economy, as industrial development is directly linked with finance. Table 6 explains that the outlays on various sectors from first Five Year Plan to Tenth Five Year Plan. The allocation for industries and minerals formed 1.9 per cent of

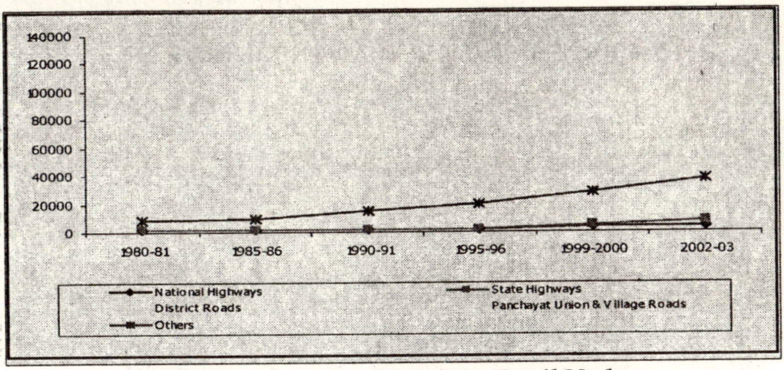

Figure 3: Length of Roads in Tamil Nadu

total plan expenditure in the first plan. This proportion suddenly jumped to 7.5 per cent between 1955 and 61. The outlays on industries and minerals fluctuated in the subsequent five year plans and sharply dwindled to 1.4 per cent during the latest five year plan [Tenth five year plan]. The deceleration of investment on industries and its related activities may directly affect the industrial growth and sophistication.

STRUCTURAL CHANGES

Structural Changes in the Economy of India and Tamil Nadu

It is generally observed that the economic development is accompanied by structural transformation. The term structural change is defined as the shift in the contribution of different sectors to total output and also the proportion of employment in agriculture, in favour of secondary and tertiary sectors (Kuznets.1972, & Clark, 1960). The structural changes in an economy may occur on two counts. They are inter-sectoral and intra-sectoral. The process of structural changes occurring within a sector naturally leads to a substantial changes in the sectoral composition of an economy (Thangamuthu, 1983).

In this regard the structural changes in the economy of India and Tamil Nadu are analyzed. The national and State income (GDP&NSDP), are used to study the structural changes taking place in the economy. There is general perception that

Table 6

Plan Wise Expenditure for Major sectors from First Plan to Tenth Five Year Plan

Sectors	*51-56*	*56-61*	*61-66*	*69-74*	*74-78*	*80-85*	*85-90*	*92-97*	*97-02*	*2002-07*
Agei & Allied Activities	9.57	30.62	74.53	103.75	93.28	707.88	938.14	2510.71	4851.36	7989.75
%	11.9	16.31	21.47	18.56	11.18	19.42	14.85	17.91	19.47	19.97
Co-operation	0.11	1.88	5.52	7.87	38.55	24.55	53.94	89.48	61.72	42.3
%	0.14	1	1.59	1.41	4.62	0.67	0.85	0.64	0.25	0.11
Irrigation & Flood Control	20.15	17.56	31.46	28.29	59.65	204.25	343.92	539.66	1846.92	2375
%	25.07	9.35	9.06	5.06	7.26	5.6	5.45	3.85	7.41	5.94
Power	30.28	79.15	119.2	210.05	259.82	967.57	1770.81	3115.95	4560.62	8029.65
%	37.67	42.15	34.34	37.58	31.17	26.55	28.04	22.23	18.3	20.07
Industries & Minerals	1.53	14.08	23.73	33	50.54	293.18	504.84	1160.24	864.59	555
%	1.9	7.5	6.84	5.9	6.06	8.04	7.99	8.28	3.47	1.39
Transport & Communication	2.7	5.52	11.74	30.73	86.06	291.42	342.13	1465.55	2959.4	6730
%	3.36	2.94	3.38	5.5	10.32	8	5.42	10.46	11.48	16.83
Social & Com.Services	16.05	37.96	80.25	142.82	237.68	1108.69	2293.29	5043.37	9481.14	13813.95
%	19.97	20.22	23.12	19.97	20.22	19.72	19.98	35.98	38.05	34.53
Economic Services	0	0.99	0.72	2.45	2.65	27.1	18.61	27.19	62.44	175.6
%	0	0.53	0.21	44	0.32	0.74	0.29	0.19	0.25	44
General Services	0	0	0	0	5.38	19.99	50.39	64.65	228.49	288.75
%	0	0	0	0	0.65	0.55	0.8	0.46	0.92	0.72
Grand Total	80.39	187.76	347.15	558.96	833.61	3733.92	6316.07	14116.8	24916.71	40000
	100	100	100	100	100	100	100	100	100	100

Source: Data computed from Tamil Nadu-An Economic Appraisal, Various Issues.

when an economy is in a state of underdevelopment, the primary sector (agriculture and allied activities such as forestry and logging, fishing, mining and quarrying), contributes the largest proportion to the national income. As the country grows and gets developed, the contribution of the industrial and service sector increases gradually.

It may be noticed from the following Table 7 that the structure of Tamil Naud's had experienced drastic changes over the four decades. The sectoral composition of the State income has undergone a sea change depending on the fact growth rate of a particular sector in relation to the other sectors. The structural transformation in the sectoral composition is perceptible from this table the share of primary sector in the Net State domestic product (NSDP), was 43.5 per cent in 1960-61, slipped down to 35 per cent by 1970-71 and further to 25, 23, 18 per cent respectively in 1980-81, 1990-91 and 2001-02. The reduction in the relative role of primary sector to the national and State economy was caused by the domination of the other sectors. In addition, it is cited that the gambling of monsoon and erratic water management are the causes for the poor performance of the primary sector.

The share of secondary sector revealed a mixed picture. It rose to 33.9 per cent by 1980-81 from 20.7 per cent and 26.9 per cent respectively in 1960-61and 1970-71. Thereafter, it decreased considerably while the tertiary sector had moved up steadily form 36 per cent to 50.2 per cent during the study periods.

Table 7
Structural Changes in Tamil Nadu and India

	Tamil Nadu (NSDP)			*All India (GDP)*		
Year	*Primary sector*	*Secondary sector*	*Tertiary sector*	*Primary sector*	*Secondary sector*	*Tertiary sector*
1960-61	43.51	20.27	36.22	54.7	16.6	28.7
1970-71	34.79	26.88	38.33	48.1	19.9	32.1
1980-81	25.92	33.49	40.59	41.8	21.6	36.6
1990-91	23.42	33.10	43.48	34.9	24.5	40.6
2001-02	18.25	29.27	52.30	24.3	26.7	49.0

Source: Source: Data computed from Tamil Nadu-An Economic Appraisal, Various Issues. Hansde(2001).

In the Indian scenario, during the process of growth there has been a change in the structure with a shift away from agriculture towards industry and service sector. The agricultural sector's share in the Indian economy particularly in GDP has dwindled from 55 per cent in 1960-61 to 41.8 per cent in 1980-81 and further it halved by 2001-02.

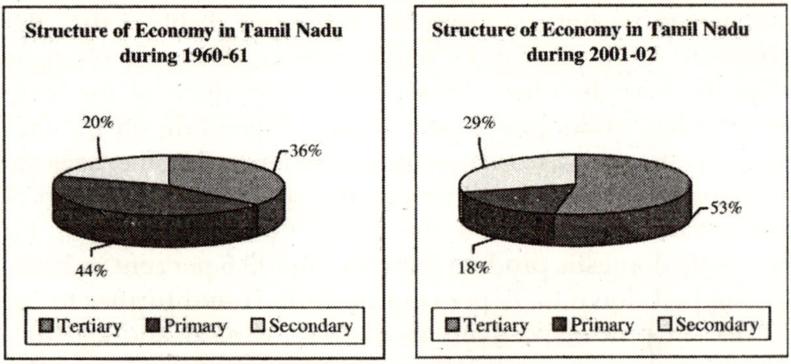

Figure 4: Structural transformations in Tamil Nadu (1960-61 and 2001-02)

At the same time, secondary sector revealed a gentle raise as it accounted for 16.6 per cent in 1960-61, increased to 21.6 per cent and 26.7 per cent respectively by 1980-81 and 2001-02. While, the tertiary sector recorded considerable up trend, i.e. the tertiary sector registered an increase of 28.7 per cent in 1960-61 and further it reinforced to 36.6 per cent and 49 per cent respectively in the period 1980-81 and 2001-02. The rapid rise in service sector to GDP in India is similar to the experience of other Asian countries like China, Korea, Philippines and Thailand (Highlight of Economic Survey, 2002-03).

It is observed from this analysis that the primary sector remained dominant during 1960's in the economy of both India and Tamil Nadu. Interestingly, during the latest decade the whole scenario changed subsequently in favour of industrial and service sector. The growing service sector is generally associated with economic development and is an indicator of change in demand for goods form necessaries to luxuries (Rajeshweri, 1989). It is to be mentioned here that within the tertiary sector, the income generation of Banking and Insurance, Communication, Real Estate and Business services and Public Administration are significant. Studies conducted by Joshi (2004), Dhingra (2003) and Sebastian (1989), reached the same conclusion that is observed in this present study. It appears that service sector is getting prominence even before the industrial sector is sufficiently developed. Much emphasis is being placed on information technology both at the national and at the state level, because of the availability of educated manpower in the country as well as in the State and the favorable exchange mechanism. In addition there is high external demand for IT service. As a result much emphasis is being laid on the IT sector. The structural change in the economy of both State and the nation is very transparent during the 2001-02; this is very clear from the following pie diagrams.

In the earlier phase the economy was encompassed by simple production technique-few skilled labour, weak transport and communication, lackadaisical fund allocation for development and the economy was closed one. As a result of above-mentioned reasons the economy relied on primary sector.

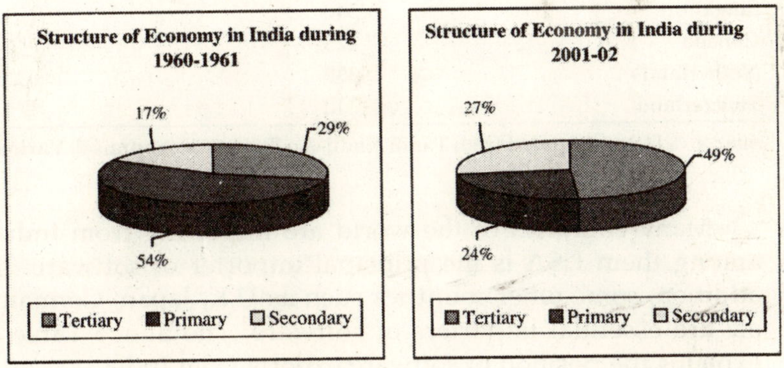

Figure 5: Structural transformations in India (1960-61 and 2001-02)

Thanks to the changes in the techniques of production, expansion of demand of IT sector, physical quality of labour, penetration of information technology, application of telecommunication in productive process through improved Human Resource Development, development–mindedness of the people, the economy has been transformed from primary dominated one to service sector (DEAR, 2001-02).

Information Technology

Information technology is a sunrise industry in Tamil Nadu, as it has accomplished the rapid economic growth. The prime beneficial impact of IT sector is cost-effective, pollution-free, timesaving and source of external economies. IT industry has acquired pronounced global dimensions. Indian software exports have been growing at a compound annual growth rate of more than 50 per cent for the last five years, the hardware exports have also picked up (*www,economywatch.com*). In India, Tamil Nadu is one of the leading States in the development of Information Technology.

Table 8

Export of Software from India in 2000-01

Countries	*Rs. in Crores*	*Percentage*
USA	17336	61.15
UK	3355	11.84
Japan	1021	3.6
Germany	900	3.2
Singapore	540	1.9
Canada	425	1.5
Netherlands	350	1.27
Switzerland	340	1.2

Source: Data computed from Tamil Nadu-An Economic Appraisal, Various Issues.

Many countries of the world are importing from India, among them USA is the principal importer of software. In addition, some other countries such as U.K, Japan, Germany etc are essential importers of software. The above Table 8 explains the position of software exports from India.

Status of IT industry in Tamil Nadu

At all India level, Tamil Nadu occupied second position in the software exports next only to Karnataka. Tamil Nadu achieved 14.7 per cent of all Indai's software exports. The number of software companies and value of exports have been increased dramatically over the past ten years. The number of registered software companies was just 10 in 1993-94, increased to 108 in 1997-98, and 934 in 2002-03. While, the value of export has increased sizably the value of export of Tamil Nadu IT industries was only 2 crores in 1993-94 jumped upto 393 crores in 1997-98 and reached 6316 crore in 2002-03. Where as, there is $ 485 million of Indian's export in 1994-95, it increased to $6300 million in 2000-01 (Kumar, 2001). Favorable policy and exports are the causative factors for this good performance.

Table 9
Growth Performance of Software Industries in Tamil Nadu.

Year	*No of Companies (Cumulative)*	*Value of Exports (in* Crores)
1993-94	10	2
1994-95	23	12
1995-96	34	37
1996-97	69	161
1997-98	108	393
1998-99	166	1246
1999-2000	601	1914
2000-01	766	3116
2001-02	865	5223
2002-03	934	6316

Source: Data computed from Tamil Nadu-An Economic Appraisal, Various Issues.

In Tamil Nadu, Chennai is playing a predominant role in software development, as the largest exporter of computer hard-discs, and it is the center for development of advanced multimedia applications, communications and software. Dun and Bradstrect, TCS, Pentafour, Ramco, Singapore Airlines, Citibank, etc are the major companies at Chennai. Recently the Government of Tamil Nadu announced an attractive Information Technology Policy for stimulating this industry *(www.smallindustryindia.com)*.

The establishment of Software Technology Park (TIDEL) at Taramani, in Chennai, Government Policy of favouring information technology revolution, computer literacy and global demand are the important factors responsible for the dramatic development of IT sector in Tamil Nadu. Software development is currently (2000) $100 million in Tamil Nadu with collaboration of some foreign companies. Today the proposals of Indian software are considered as best among the world proposals.

Per Capita Income of Tamil Nadu and India

Generally, per capita income is used to indicate the stage of development and main determinant of domestic demand. Hence, per capita income of Tamil Nadu and India for the last ten years is analysed using annual average growth rate. The per capita income of Tamil Nadu is higher than the National per capita income during the beginning of the period. During 1993-94 the per capita income of Tamil Nadu was higher with as 1254 more than the National level.

Based on this criterion, country overtook the State in 1996-97, which accounted for Rs. 1018 higher than that of the State. Thereafter this trend is continuing. The growth in per capita income reflects in a number of social indicators such as rise in the literacy rate, the availability of medical and health facilities, and expansion in education etc., (Rangarajan, 2000).

Considering the annual average growth rate of per capita income of Tamil Nadu and India, the growth rate was higher during the first half of the analyzed period, thereafter the growth rate had suffered a set back. The per capita income of Tamil Nadu surpassed the per capita income of India during 1993-94. But, this situation got reversed in 2002-03.

Index of Industrial Production in Tamil Nadu and India

The index of industrial production in Tamil Nadu and India increased considerably over the last two decades (despite some fluctuations). Here the index of industrial production of Tamil Nadu and India has been analyzed for the past twenty-one years (from 1982-83 to 2002-03). To have a meaningful result,

Table 10
Annual Average Growth Rate of Per Capita Income: Rs. [at 1993-94 Prices]

Year	*Tamil Nadu*	*AAGR*	*India*	*AAGR*
1993-94	8952	-	7698	-
1994-95	9944	11.1	8876	15.3
1995-96	10191	2.5	10160	14.5
1996-97	10583	3.8	11601	14.2
1997-98	11240	6.2	12772	10.1
Average	10182	5.9	10221	13.5
1998-99	11608	3.3	14712	15.2
1999-2000	12144	4.6	16047	9.1
2000-01	12944	6.6	16707	4.1
2001-02	13108	1.3	17978	7.6
2002-03	13003	-0.8	18912	5.2
Average	12561	3.0	16871	8.2

Source: Data computed from Tamil Nadu-An Economic Appraisal, Various Issues.

the indices of industrial production and sub sectors have been analyzed taking 1993-94 as base year. It is observed from the following Table 11 that the index of industrial production is fluctuating from year to year for both the State and country, this year to year fluctuation in the industrial production is mainly influenced by changes in the macro economic climate (DEAR, 93-94). The State has exhibited higher growth of industrial production based on the index of industrial production in three years viz, 1984-85, 1988-89 and 1999-2000. Whereas, the index number of industrial production of India was impressive at 1986-87 and 1995-96. Mention should be made that during the study periods, India has registered a positive growth in all sub sectors. However, Tamil Nadu shows negative growth by 1983-84, 1992-93, 1993-94, 1997-98 and 1998-99. The setback in index of industrial production is due to the deceleration of the sub sectors such as electricity and manufacturing. The negative growth of these sub sectors pulled down the general index of industrial production in Tamil Nadu.

Table 11
Index Numbers of Industrial Production of Tamil Nadu and India

[Base: 1993-94=100]

Year	*Tamil Nadu*	*% Variations as Compared to Previous years*	*India*	*% Variations as Compared to Previous years*
1982-83	63.8	–	48.6	–
1983-84	62.1	-2.66	51.9	6.79
1984-85	72.4	16.59	56.3	8.48
1985-86	78.0	7.73	61.3	8.88
1986-87	79.8	2.31	66.9	9.14
1987-88	85.2	6.77	71.7	7.17
1988-89	94.5	10.92	77.9	8.65
1989-90	97.8	3.49	84.7	8.73
1990-91	102.1	4.40	91.6	8.15
1991-92	106.2	4.02	92.2	0.66
1992-93	101.8	-4.14	94.4	2.39
1993-94	100.0	-1.77	100.0	5.93
1994-95	107.3	7.30	109.1	9.10
1995-96	112.4	4.75	123.3	13.02
1996-97	114.4	1.78	130.8	6.08
1997-98	113.8	-0.52	139.5	6.65
1998-99	109.7	-3.60	145.2	4.09
1999-2000	124.1	13.13	154.9	6.68
2000-01	125.5	1.13	162.6	4.97
2001-02	127.3	1.43	167.0	2.71
2002-03	130.3	2.36	176.6	5.75

Source: Data computed from Tamil Nadu-An Economic Appraisal, Various Issues, and CSO.

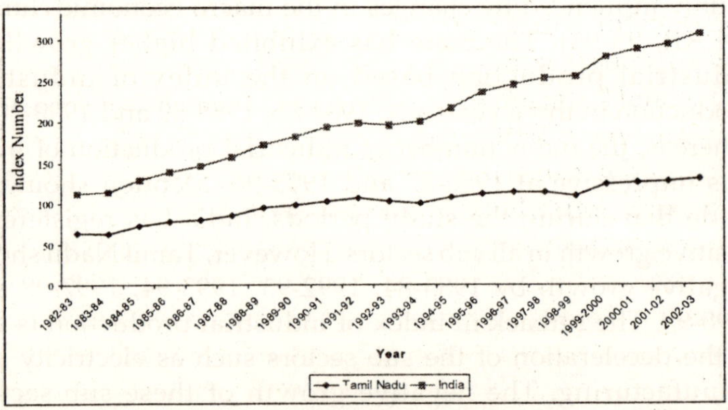

Figure 6: Index of Industrial Production (Tamil Nadu and India)

To understand the full spectrum of the Index of industrial production of Tamil Nadu, it is necessary to analyse each sub segments- Mining, Manufacturing and Electricity. To analyze the growth of these sub sectors annual average growth rates have been employed.

It is very clear from the following Table 12 that during 1988-89 to 1992-93 the mining sector has recorded an impressive growth of 10 per cent and negative growth rate of -0.62 per cent during 1998-99 to2002-03. Manufacturing and electricity registered a higher growth of 5.3 per cent and 10.5 per cent respectively during the first five years of the study period (1983-84 to 1987-88). Thereafter its growth rate slowed

Table 12
Sector wise Growth Rate of Index of Industrial Production of Tamil Nadu

Year	*Mining*	*Manufacturing*	*Electricity*	*General*
1983-84	17.90	-2.30	-2.39	-2.66
1984-85	-1.78	15.15	34.60	16.59
1985-86	0.49	6.90	-3.24	7.73
1986-87	-1.96	1.55	7.95	2.31
1987-88	1.67	5.41	15.31	6.77
Growth Rate	3.27	5.34	10.45	6.15
1988-89	16.91	10.04	17.31	10.92
1989-90	14.47	3.35	-1.43	3.49
1990-91	8.59	2.85	10.76	4.40
1991-92	3.28	4.10	4.99	4.02
1992-93	7.11	-5.68	13.25	-4.14
Growth Rate	10.07	2.93	8.97	3.74
1993-94	2.15	-2.82	10.38	-1.77
1994-95	21.30	6.40	17.00	7.30
1995-96	8.90	4.51	7.26	4.75
1996-97	4.31	1.53	5.58	1.78
1997-98	9.80	-0.97	1.28	-0.52
Growth Rate	9.29	1.73	8.30	2.31
1998-99	4.76	-4.56	5.66	-3.60
1999-2000	6.25	14.90	-3.24	13.13
2000-01	-19.54	0.98	8.24	1.13
2001-02	-0.89	0.89	8.08	1.43
2002-03	6.33	2.40	0.31	2.36
Growth Rate	-0.62	2.92	3.81	2.89

Source: *Data computed from Tamil Nadu-An Economic Appraisal, Various Issues.*

down considerably. The growth of general index of industrial production also showed the same trend, with 6 per cent growth during the above referred period and since then decreased considerably.

The deceleration in the manufacturing sector is due to slow down of agricultural production. Low level of agricultural production leads to a decline in the production of agro-based industries, which is reflected in the general industrial growth.

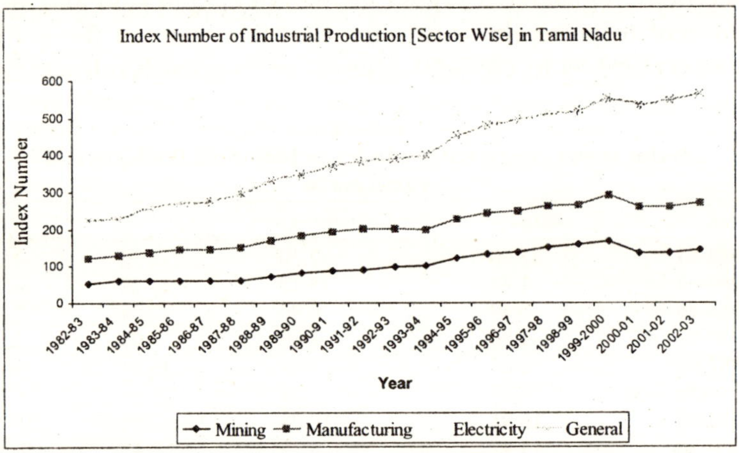

Figure 7: Sector wise Index of Production (Tamil Nadu)

Annual Compound Growth Rates of Index

The annual compound growth rates have been calculated for the index of industrial production of Tamil Nadu and India. It reveals the better performance of mining, manufacturing and electricity at all India level when compared to Tamil Nadu. During the pre-liberalisation period the annual compound growth rates of mining and electricity were more or less the same for both India and Tamil Nadu.

However, manufacturing sector of India registered significant growth in pre liberalization period, while Tamil Nadu has shown only a moderate growth. During the post liberalization period, Tamil Nadu registered perceptible increase in annual compound growth rate of mining and

Table 13
Growth Rates of Index of Industrial Production in Tamil Nadu and India

Period	Mining	Manufacturing	Electricity	General
Tamil Nadu				
82-83 to 86-87	2.5	4.1	6.5	4.6
87-88 to 91 92	8.5	4.0	6.1	4.5
92-93 to 96-97	7.1	1.9	7.9	2.4
97-98 to 2002-03	-0.95	2.3	3.1	2.3
82-83 to 90-91	6.0	4.6	8.2	5.4
91-92 to 2002-03	3.8	1.3	6.0	1.7
82-83 to 2002-03	4.9	2.9	7.2	3.5
India				
82-83 to 86-87	6.1	6.5	7.6	6.6
87-88 to 91 92	3.8	5.0	7.3	5.2
92-93 to 96-97	1.8	7.2	5.6	6.7
97-98 to 2002-03	1.7	4.3	3.9	4.0
82-83 to 90-91	5.9	7.4	8.2	7.3
91-92 to 2002-03	3.2	5.9	5.3	5.6
82-83 to 2002-03	4.3	6.5	6.9	6.3

Source: Data computed from Tamil Nadu-An Economic Appraisal, Various Issues, and CSO.

electricity, while the manufacturing sector of all India has shown a remarkable increase in the annual compound growth rate. Tamil Nadu has shown a marginal increase. It is to be mentioned, that the indices of industrial production of all the sub-sectors show a strong growth during the pre-liberalisation period. The same trend is observed in India also.

Foreign Trade

Foreign trade consists of exports and imports. The exports and imports of an economy have strongly influencing in all the economic activities. Kavoussi (1985), found that export expansion being associated with better economic performance of both low income as well as middle-income countries. Similarly Kindleberger(1962) shows that the expanded exports offer investment opportunities and induce cost reducing innovations and economies of large-scale production. Becarman(1962), reveals that the rapid growth will depend upon confident expectations concerning the future demand potentials both in the domestic and foreign market. It is understood that the export and import of any nation play a vital role. The following Table 14 shows the import and export of Tamil Nadu for the past ten years.

Table 14
Foreign Trade of Tamil Nadu (Exports and Imports)

Year	*Export*	*% Changes*	*Import*	*% Changes*
1991-92	5389.88	-	5359.21	-
1992-93	6884.23	27.73	7310.65	36.41
1993-94	9085.8	31.98	8111.8	10.96
1994-95	12460.09	37.14	12541.53	54.61
1995-96	15832.83	27.07	17416.72	38.87
1996-97	17596.27	11.14	14966.54	-14.07
1997-98	16529.64	-6.06	36877.89	146.40
1998-99	18771.28	13.56	23482.9	-36.32
1999-2000	26983.75	43.75	25600.16	9.02
2000-01	11736.96	-56.50	18821.37	-26.48
ACGR	8.1	-	13.4	-

Source: www.tn.gov.in.

It is observed that the higher growth of 13.4 per cent is revealed by import as against 8 per cent of export. The increasing trend shown by export up to first half of nineties, there after it registered a fluctuating trend. The same trend is observed in import also. The acceleration of import may be due to bringing in equipments and advanced machineries from abroad.

CONCLUSION

It may be concluded from the foregoing analysis that the industrial scenario of Tamil Nadu is kaleidoscopic. The endowment of mineral resources is very scanty and the plan wise allocation for industries and minerals has been decreasing from the First plan to the Tenth plan. In 1980, the hydro power dominated, and it is replaced by Thermal power in the recent period. With regard to percentage share the consumption of power of industrial sector has been diminished. In the economy, inter-sectoral changes are perceptible in both Tamil

Nadu and India and the structure of the industrial sector has changed over the period.

In the current scenario, IT sector is the sunrise industry. Even though the growth rate of power is appreciable its distribution and mode of use are erratic. Transport and communications have increased considerably but the quality is poor when compared to industrially developed states. The per capita income of Tamil Nadu was high for the first three years of the study period, there after the per capita income of India overtook that of Tamil Nadu. India has achieved higher growth rate of per capita income. The index of industrial production is fluctuating year to year for both the State and country. The index of industrial production with regard to growth had decreased. This setback in the industrial production is due to the poor performance of mining and manufacturing sector for certain periods. This poor performance of these sub sectors pulled down the general industrial production. Considering the trade of Tamil Nadu, the import revealed higher growth then that of exports.

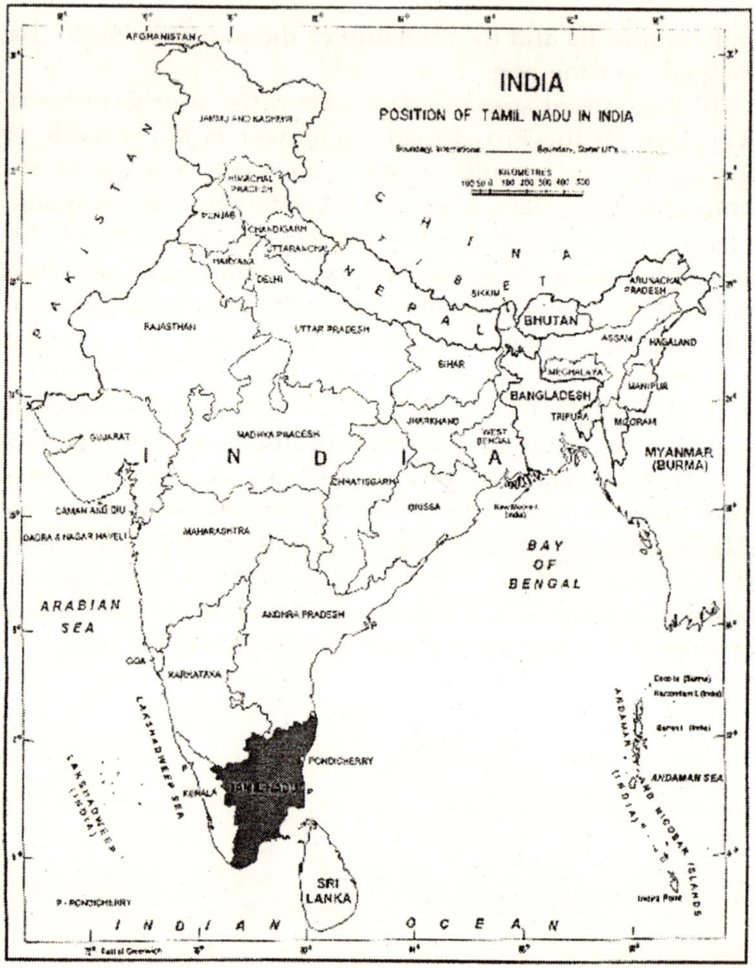

India Map–Indicating the Study State

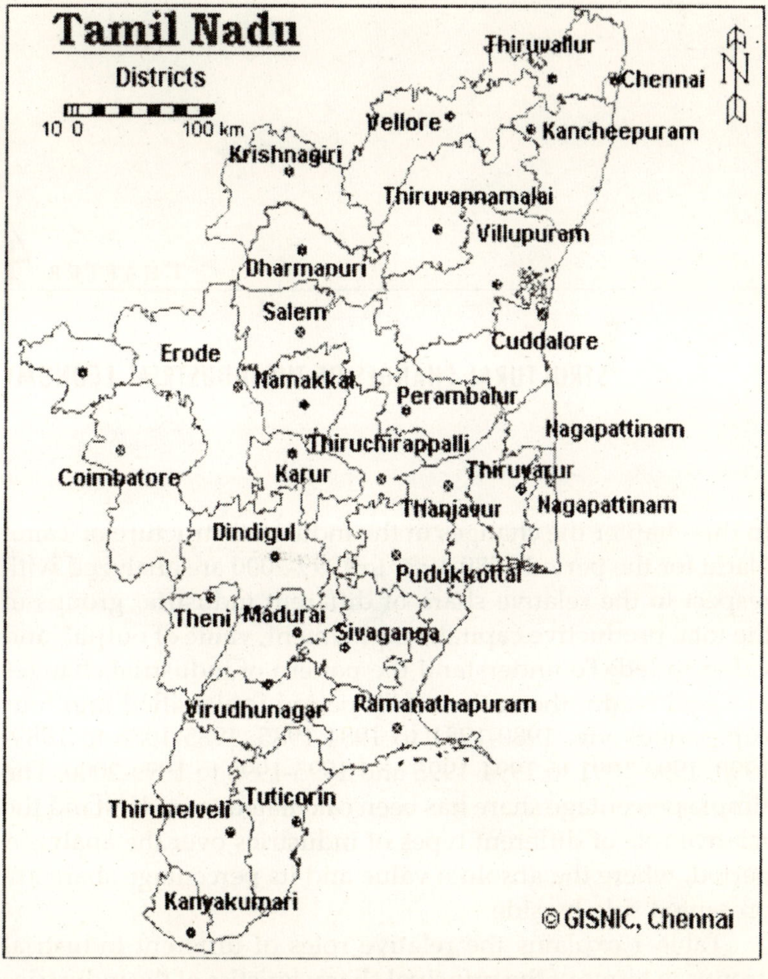

Map-Study State [Tamil Nadu]

CHAPTER 4

STRUCTURAL CHANGES OF THE INDUSTRIAL ECONOMY

In this chapter the changes in the industrial structure of Tamil Nadu for the period 1980-1981 to 1999-2000 are analyzed with respect to the relative share of different industrial groups in the total productive capital, employment, value of output, and value added. To understand the pattern of industrial changes in Tamil Nadu, the entire study period is classified into four sub-periods viz. 1980-1981 to 1984-1985, 1985-1986 to 1989-1990, 1990-1991 to 1994-1995 and 1995-1996 to 1999-2000. The simple percentage share has been calculated to understand the relative role of different types of industries over the analyzed period, where the absolute value and its percentage share are presented side by side.

Table 1 explains the relative roles of different industrial groups in terms of the principal characteristics of the industries in 1980-1981 at 1993-1994 prices. This highlights the performance of various industrial groups in terms of productive capital, employment, output and value added.

Textile industry group is dominant in terms of its relative share in productive capital and it is followed by chemical and chemical products, transport equipment and parts, machinery and machine tools. These groups put together contributed 58.82 per cent of the total productive capital. The industry groups such as wood and wood products, 'Other

Table 1

Principal Characteristics of the Industries in Tamil Nadu in 1980-81 at 1993-94 Prices. (Rs. in Lakhs]

Industry Group	*Productive Capital*	*P.C.S*	*Number of Persons Employed*	*P.C.S*	*Value of Output*	*P.C.S*	*Value Added*	*P.C.S*
Food Products	47275.52	8.29	260801	19.95	213202.90	13.30	23438.22	8.40
Beverages, Tobacco & Tobacco Products	4681.50	0.82	17967	1.37	14991.05	0.94	2187.26	0.78
Textiles	106142.20	18.60	354312	27.11	294292.70	18.36	69907.90	25.05
Wood & Wood Products	1245.84	0.22	10169	0.78	3341.01	0.21	826.30	0.30
Paper & Paper Products	25405.47	4.45	54191	4.15	48736.25	3.04	12494.24	4.48
Leather & LeatherProducts	14128.93	2.48	42498	3.25	69429.52	4.33	6965.98	2.50
Rubber, Plastic, Petroleum & Coal Products	26999.23	4.73	32905	2.52	234783.80	14.64	13837.30	4.96
Chemical & Chemical Products	100588.40	17.63	136130	10.42	211330.30	13.18	37505.76	13.44
Non-Metallic Mineral Products	30688.16	5.38	46145	3.53	53834.74	3.36	10892.81	3.90
Basic Metal & Alloy Products	49639.29	8.70	58038	4.44	78196.47	4.88	15205.94	5.45
Metal Products & Parts	16771.55	2.94	35924	2.75	29552.32	1.84	7805.07	2.80
Machinery & Machine Tools	63335.89	11.10	93698	7.17	150337.70	9.38	31414.68	11.26
Electrical Equipments & Parts	15464.31	2.71	36777	2.81	55653.62	3.47	12936.81	4.64
Transport Equipment & Parts	65587.11	11.49	119438	9.14	138994.60	8.67	32100.28	11.50
Other Manufacturing Industries	2637.50	0.46	7963	0.61	6497.83	0.41	1542.59	0.55
Total	*570590.90*	*100*	*1306956*	*100*	*1603175*	*100*	*279061.1*	*100*

Source: Annual Survey of Industries, 1980-81, C.S.O.

Note: Productive Capital, Output and Value Added are monetary terms Factories and Number of Persons Employed are in Numbers.

manufacturing industries' and beverages, tobacco and tobacco products are insignificant in their contribution to productive capital.

Textile group occupies the first place in respect of its relative share in employment also. The textiles, food products, chemical and chemical products and transport equipment and parts generated 66.6 per cent of the total employment, 53.5 per cent of the output and 58.39 per cent of value added. The industry groups such as wood and wood products and other manufacturing were insignificant in the generation of employment in the industries. The food product group, which occupies sixth position in its relative share of productive capital, stands second in terms of employment generation.

The share of the dominant groups namely textiles, rubber, plastics, food product and chemical towards the total output come to 59.48 per cent. The relative share towards value added of the major industry groups viz. textiles, chemicals and chemical products, machinery and machine tools and transport equipment and parts is around 61.25 per cent. Machinery and machine tool industry being capital intensive occupy fifth position in terms of employment and output generation. The textile group is in the predominant place with respect to all the principal characteristics. Traditional formation is the main reason for this; now it is well established and is reaping economies of scale.

The principal characteristics in terms of productive capital, number of persons employed value of output and value added by manufacture for 1985-1986 are presented in Table 2.

The industrial structure in 1985-1986 shows that the textile group, which occupied first position in the previous period is related to the second position in terms of productive capital. The change in structure is perceived by the relative role of chemical and chemical producing group, which has become dominant group in terms of its relative share in productive capital alone. This is due to expansion of internal and external demand of chemical products. Still textile occupies the predominant position in its relative roles of employment output and value added. Textiles, chemicals, transport,

Table 2

Principal Characteristics of the Industries in Tamil Nadu in 1985-86 at 1993-94 Prices [Rs in Lakhs]

Industry Group	*Productive Capital*	*P.C.S*	*Number of Persons Employed*	*P.C.S*	*Value of Output*	*P.C.S*	*Value Added*	*P.C.S*
Food Products	63226.37	6.09	189730	13.65	264448.10	11.40	34535.36	8.67
Beverages, Tobacco & Tobacco Products	5842.68	0.56	18100	1.30	28594.59	1.23	3852.04	0.97
Textiles	148246.20	14.27	385563	27.73	376649.00	16.23	69149.60	17.36
Wood and Wood Products	1899.53	0.18	9721	0.70	3463.47	0.15	777.81	0.20
Paper & Paper Products	35889.80	3.46	61838	4.45	69789.61	3.01	12988.18	3.26
Leather & Leather Products	14684.33	1.41	58676	4.22	95097.87	4.10	10696.66	2.69
Rubber, Plastic,Petroleum & Coal Products	110572.90	10.65	37010	2.66	360142.90	15.52	26034.89	6.54
Chemical & Chemical Products	230391.60	22.18	169301	12.18	294686.20	12.70	50192.03	12.6
Non-Metallic Mineral Products	55297.07	5.32	54544	3.92	102171.10	4.40	23622.64	5.93
Basic Metal & Alloy Products	88541.32	8.52	56327	4.05	131517.90	5.67	17738.68	4.45
Metal Products and Parts	25508.91	2.46	34446	2.48	39244.50	1.69	7794.92	1.96
Machinery& Machine Tools	129462.40	12.46	116465	8.38	256177.20	11.04	68442.90	17.18
Electrical Equipments & Parts	24856.57	2.39	42770	3.08	73726.49	3.18	19097.19	4.79
Transport Equipment &Parts	99000.96	9.53	148713	10.70	212533.10	9.16	50471.81	12.67
Other Manufacturing Industries	5188.20	0.50	7064	0.51	12232.02	0.53	2913.30	0.73
Total	1038609	100	1390268	100	2320474	100	398308	100

Source: Annual Survey of Industries, 1985-86, C.S.O.

Note: Productive Capital, Output and Value Added are monetary terms Factories and Number of Persons Employed are in Numbers.

machinery and machine tools contribute 58.41 per cent of the total productive capital during this period.

Textiles, food products, chemicals and chemical groups and transport equipment and parts contributed 64.26 per cent of total employment. There is a decline in employment generation in these groups during 1985-1986. This industry generated 66.6 per cent of total employment in 1980-1981.

In 1985-1986 textiles, rubber, plastics, petroleum, food products and chemical and chemical products contributed 55.85 per cent of output.

By 1985-1986 four industry groups viz. textiles, chemical and chemical products machinery and machine tools and transport equipment and parts accounted for 60 per cent of value added and 59 per cent of employment.

The comparative study of the industrial structure over the period 1980-1981 and 1985-1986 shows that chemical and chemical group, rubber group and machinery and machine tools are growing industries in terms of productive capital. Employment has grown at a snail's pace in chemical group, textile group, paper and paper products, leather and leather products, rubber group, non-metallic and mineral products, machinery and machine tools electrical equipment and parts and transport equipment and parts. The industry groups such as beverages, tobacco and tobacco products, rubber group, non-metallic and mineral products, basic metal and alloy products, machinery and machine tools, transport equipments and parts, and other manufacturing industries increased their relative share of output from 1980-1981 to 1985-1986.

Chemical group and metal products, textiles and basic metal and alloy had a declining share in the value added, while, rubber group machinery and machine tools, non-metallic and mineral and transport equipments had an increase in the relative share of value added from 1980-1981 to 1984-1985.

The contribution of all groups of industry in the manufacturing sector towards productive capital, employment, output and value added for the year 1990-1991 is presented in Table 3.

Table 3

Principal Characteristics of the Industries in Tamil Nadu in 1990-91 at 1993-94 Prices [Rs in Lakhs]

Industry Group	*Productive Capital*	*P.C.S*	*Number of Persons Employed*	*P.C.S*	*Value of Output*	*P.C.S*	*Value Added*	*P.C.S*
Food Products	105765.50	7.76	216535	13.24	397331.00	11.88	58877.91	8.85
Beverages, Tobacco & Tobacco Products	15950.97	1.17	21377	1.31	49104.00	1.47	8309.75	1.25
Textiles	226344.60	16.61	433105	26.48	628449.50	18.78	134756.50	20.27
Wood and Wood Products	1742.02	0.13	8120	0.50	5145.01	0.15	1014.24	0.15
Paper & Paper Products	65889.54	4.83	64394	3.94	136501.40	4.08	49448.39	7.44
Leather & Leather Products	45033.00	3.30	99216	6.07	179342.20	5.36	24601.05	3.70
Rubber, Plastic, Petroleum & Coal Products	112263.10	8.24	43904	2.68	378739.80	11.32	52319.60	7.87
Chemical & Chemical Products	230771.30	16.93	279308	17.08	390924.60	11.68	93790.13	14.11
Non-Metallic Mineral Products	69717.76	5.12	54290	3.32	122783.60	3.67	33937.16	5.10
Basic Metal & Alloy Products	95801.62	7.03	46213	2.83	169264.60	5.06	15214.12	2.29
Metal Products & Parts	39495.34	2.09	37753	2.31	66827.62	2.00	16409.77	2.47
Machinery& Machine Tools	138927.60	10.19	119048	7.28	346376.60	10.35	66419.69	9.99
Electrical Equipments & Parts	39899.99	2.93	42997	2.63	110495.80	3.30	23338.25	3.51
Transport Equipment & Parts	153254.30	11.25	154636	9.45	323621.20	9.67	76605.73	11.52
Other Manufacturing Industries	21987.69	1.61	14625	0.89	40827.32	1.22	9898.36	1.49
Total	1362844	100	1635521	100	3345734	100	664940.7	100

Source: Annual Survey of Industries, 1990-91, C.S.O.

Note: Productive Capital, Output and Value Added are monetary terms Factories and Number of Persons Employed are in Numbers.

From Table 3 it is found that in 1990-1991 the chemical group was in the top position in terms of its shares in investment. The industry groups such as textiles, chemicals and chemical products, transport equipments and parts and machinery and machine tools together contributed 54.98 per cent of productive capital.

In respect of relative share in employment, the textile group is in the top most position and the food producing industrial chemicals and chemical products, and transport equipment and parts combinedly contributed 66.25 per cent of employment in 1990-1991.

Textile group maintains the same place in the case of output. The other industrial group such as rubber, plastic, petroleum and coal products, food and chemical producing industrial groups with textiles contributed 53.66 per cent of value of output during this period.

In terms of value added also, textile industrial group continue to enjoy the first position. The industrial groups such as textiles, chemicals and chemical products, transport equipments and parts and machinery and machine tools have offered 55.89 per cent of value added.

By 1990-1991, wood and wood producing industries, beverages, tobacco and tobacco group and 'other manufacturing industries' make insignificant contribution to the analyzed characteristics.

In respect of productive capital, the textile group, food producing industries, leather producing industries, transport equipment and parts and 'other manufacturing industries' increased their contribution to total productive capital form 1985-1986 to 1990-1991. Chemical and chemical producing industries and leather and leather producing industries, increased their contribution to total employment. In the case of output industrial groups such as textile, paper, leather and 'other manufacturing industries' revealed slight progress from 1985-1986 to 1990-1991.

In respect of value added the industries such as textiles, paper and paper products, leather and leather products, chemical group, and rubber group have increased their contribution to the total value added. The relative share of value added of machinery and machine tools has nearly halved.

The structure of the manufacturing industries in Tamil Nadu is seen through their contribution towards the principal characteristics from the following Table 4.

It is understood that the food producing industry overtakes all the industry groups in terms of the relative share of productive capital. Owing to the lion's share contributed by food producing industry, there has been a decline in the productive capital of textiles, chemicals, transport, machinery and machine tools industries. They offered 55 per cent of productive capital in 1990-1991 decreased to 45.6 per cent in the year (1995-1996).

The textile group registered first place with huge share (30%) of total employment. The textiles, food products, chemical and chemical products. transport equipment and parts of industrial groups together put forward 62.3 per cent of total employment in 1995-1996.

The textile group contributes to enjoy the first position in respect of output, and value added. The four industrial group-textile, rubber, plastic, petroleum and coal products, food products and chemical producing industries have contributed 53.4 per cent of total output, which decreased marginally in 1995-1996.

In respect of relative share of value added, the four industrial groups such as textiles, chemical and chemical products, transport equipment and parts and machinery and machine tools together offered 53.5 per cent of value added in 1995-1996.

When compared to the industrial scenario of 1995-1996 with 1990-1991 it is obvious that among the fifteen industrial groups food-producing industry has more than doubled its relative share of productive capital. The other industrial groups such as textile, paper producing industry and rubber producing industrial groups have achieved considerable progress in respect of their relative share of productive capital.

Table 4

Principal Characteristics of the Industries in Tamil Nadu in 1995-96 at 1993-94 Prices [Rs in Lakhs]

Industry Group	*Productive Capital*	*P.C.S*	*Number of Persons Employed*	*P.C.S*	*Value of Output*	*P.C.S*	*Value Added*	*P.C.S*
Food Products	490299.70	18.65	241985	12.22	551404.50	11.04	65932.12	7.22
Beverages, Tobacco & Tobacco Products	39400.41	1.50	31227	1.58	125272.30	2.51	30638.20	3.35
Textiles	466631.60	17.75	604523	30.53	1143124.00	22.89	162676.50	17.81
Wood and Wood Products	2481.58	0.09	10488	0.53	5341.39	0.11	783.61	0.09
Paper & Paper Products	153221.60	5.83	78316	3.95	182998.90	3.66	45272.17	4.96
Leather & Leather Products	82009.20	3.12	169000	8.53	216899.60	4.34	31112.31	3.41
Rubber, Plastic,Petroleum & Coal Products	248189.80	9.44	60989	3.08	449259.30	9.00	84513.08	9.25
Chemical & Chemical Products	370248.30	14.08	238987	12.07	522779.80	10.47	115504.10	12.64
Non-Metallic Mineral Products	98741.13	3.76	64289	3.25	181328.10	3.63	53385.53	5.84
Basic Metal & Alloy Products	164395.40	6.25	66413	3.35	264256.10	5.29	30959.04	3.39
Metal Products & Parts	39425.10	1.50	45039	2.27	80072.71	1.60	16937.81	1.85
Machinery & Machine Tools	179845.00	6.84	163021	8.23	568589.00	11.39	106062.30	11.61
Electrical Equipments & Parts	59159.15	2.25	33749	1.70	158439.70	3.17	49796.55	5.45
Transport Equipment & Parts	183553.10	6.98	148648	7.51	480636.10	9.62	104803.30	11.47
Other Manufacturing Industries	51427.32	1.96	23556	1.19	63286.28	1.27	15098.41	1.65
Total	2629028.40	100	1980230	100	4993687.8	100	913475.03	100

Source: Annual Survey of Industries, 1995-96, C.S.O

Note: Productive Capital, Output and Value Added are monetary terms Factories and Number of Persons Employed are in Numbers.

In terms of employment generation the industrial groups viz. textiles, leather, rubber, basic metal, machinery and other manufacturing industrial groups have shown a little increase from 1990-1991 to 1995-1996. The employment contribution of chemical group, transport and electrical equipment groups has decreased considerably.

In the case of output, the beverages, tobacco and tobacco products, textiles, metal products and parts and machinery and machine tools industries has increased slightly. Similarly, in terms of value added the beverages group, rubber group, machinery group and electrical group exhibited meagre increase for the above referred period.

The relative position of fifteen industrial groups in the manufacturing sector of Tamil Nadu is given in Table 5. This shows that in 1999-2000 the chemical group emerged as a predominant one in terms of productive capital, while the textile group occupies the second position. The industrial groups such as textiles, chemical and chemical products, transport equipment and parts and machinery and machine tools have offered 61.6 per cent of the total productive capital.

But in the case of employment provision the industries such as textiles; chemical group, food group and transport equipment and parts have accounted for 64.85 per cent.

The textile group, chemical group, food products and rubber group contributed 63 per cent of the total output. The industrial group such as wood and wood products, beverages group and other manufacturing industrial group occupy insignificant place in respect of contribution of output.

The chemical group scored lion's share in terms of value added, while the textile group come in the second place. The industrial group such as textiles, chemicals, transport equipments and parts and machinery and machine tools offered 59 per cent of total value added. Here also the industrial groups, producing wood and wood products, beverage groups, basic metal and other manufacturing groups are meagre in respect of all the principal characteristics.

In respect of percentage change, the industrial group such as transport equipment, textile groups, chemical group and

Table 5

Principal Characteristics of the Industries in Tamil Nadu in 1999-2000 at 1993-94 Prices [Rs in Lakhs]

Industry Group	*Productive Capital*	*P.C.S*	*Number of Persons Employed*	*P.C.S*	*Value of Output*	*P.C.S*	*Value Added*	*P.C.S*
Food Products	193462.10	6.57	238380	14.12	813782.80	13.14	67214.29	5.71
Beverages, Tobacco &Tobacco Products	54607.87	1.86	18903	1.12	60982.51	0.98	14217.93	1.21
Textiles	598419.10	20.33	494425	29.29	1381974.00	22.32	225231.00	19.13
Wood and Wood Products	5041.55	0.17	4405	0.26	9849.85	0.16	1752.19	0.15
Paper & Paper Products	107298.10	3.65	91316	5.41	194041.50	3.13	51126.09	4.34
Leather & Leather Products	69928.57	2.38	98829	5.85	224271.90	3.62	43170.55	3.67
Rubber, Plastic, Petroleum & Coal Products	306185.90	10.40	62816	3.72	759858.60	12.27	112215.70	9.53
Chemical & Chemical Products	603946.10	20.52	280257	16.60	957640.70	15.47	249970.10	21.23
Non-Metallic Mineral Products	76263.85	2.59	63457	3.76	207118.10	3.34	55657.43	4.73
Basic Metal & Alloy Products	127480.30	4.33	23421	1.39	211716.50	3.42	20086.73	1.71
Metal Products & Parts	76264.58	2.59	63456	3.76	207118.80	3.34	55656.71	4.73
Machinery & Machine Tools	197211.40	6.70	97371	5.77	383357.90	6.19	93924.20	7.98
Electrical Equipments & Parts	66523.32	2.26	37390	2.21	161836.00	2.61	36749.27	3.12
Transport Equipment & Parts	420978.90	14.30	82292	4.87	544072.90	8.79	129378.30	10.99
Other Manufacturing Industries	39344.02	1.34	31390	1.86	74330.90	1.20	21076.53	1.79
Total	2942956	100	1688108	100	6191953	100	1177427	100

Source: Annual Survey of Industries, 1999-2000, C.S.O

Note: Productive Capital, Output and Value Added are monetary terms Factories and Number of Persons Employed are in Numbers.

metal group have increased their productive capital from 1995-1996 to 1999-2000. The relative share of food producing industry slipped down. The food producing industries, paper producing industries chemical, metal and electrical equipments producing industries increased with regard to percentage share in employment.

In the case of output, the industrial groups such as food products, rubber group and chemical and its related industries have exhibited a little progress. Where as, the textile group, chemical group and metal group revealed an increasing trend with respect to their value added from 1995-1996 to 1999-2000. Among the fifteen industrial groups wood and wood producing industries, metal products and other manufacturing industries are meagre groups in respect of all the principal characteristics over the analyzed period.

A hypothesis was framed to test the structural changes in the industrial economy of Tamil Nadu with regard to the contribution of value added. For this purpose the value added has been compared from the beginning year to the ending year (1980-81 to 1999-2000).

For this purpose the following are the null and alternative hypothesis.

Null hypothesis: There is no broad spectrum of industrial diversification with bias on chemical and its related industries in the recent periods, with regard to value added.

Alternative hypothesis: There is a broad spectrum of industrial diversification with bias on chemical and its related industries in the recent periods with regard to value added.

It is very clear from Table 6 that the textile industry has a dominant place with regard to value added in 1980-81 and it was replaced by chemical based industries in the industrial economy of Tamil Nadu. *Hence the null hypothesis has not gained support from this analysis.*

It is very transparent that the structural change is perceived. In the first phase the textile industry is in a dominating position with regard to all the principal characteristics. But in 1985-86, the chemical based industry came to a predominant place in terms of productive capital alone and all other characteristics are dominated by textile group. Surprisingly, the food producing industry was in the first place with regard to capital, while the textile group exists in the apex place with regard to employment, output and value added.

Table 6
Structural Changes in the Industrial Economy of Tamil Nadu

Year/Industry	*Capital*	*Employment*	*Output*	*Value added*
1980-81	Textiles	Textiles	Textiles	Textiles
1985-86	Chemicals	Textiles	Textiles	Textiles
1990-91	Chemicals	Textiles	Textiles	Textiles
1995-96	Food Products	Textiles	Textiles	Textiles
1999-2000	Chemicals	Textiles	Textiles	Chemicals

Source: Annual Survey of Industries, 1999-2000, C.S.O
Note: Productive Capital, Output and Value Added are monetary terms *Factories and Number of Persons Employed are in Numbers.*

The following scatter diagram explains that the changes in the relative shares of different types of industries in the manufacturing sector of Tamil Nadu in 1980-81 and 1999-2000.

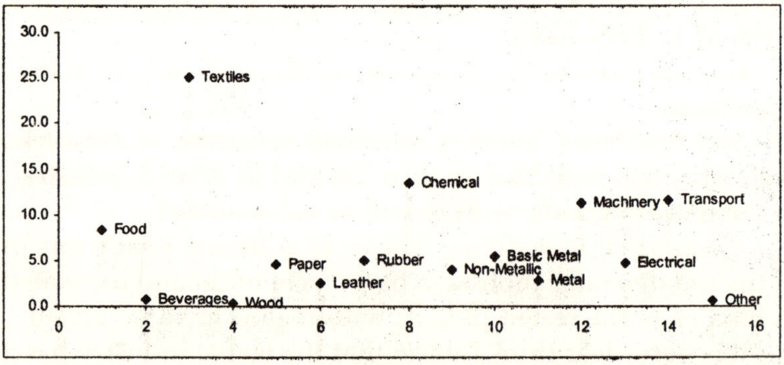

Figure 1: Industry-wise Percentage Shares of Value Added in 1980-81

During the course of industrialization the importance of some agro-based industries declined by contrast chemical and transport groups revealed relatively dominant position. Such trend exists not only in the manufacturing sector of Tamil Nadu but also in India. As the real per capital income increases, the demand for agro-based commodities decline. The Engals Law is held responsible for this. Haffman and Chennery discussed in their work that changes occur in the manufacturing sector as economic development takes place.

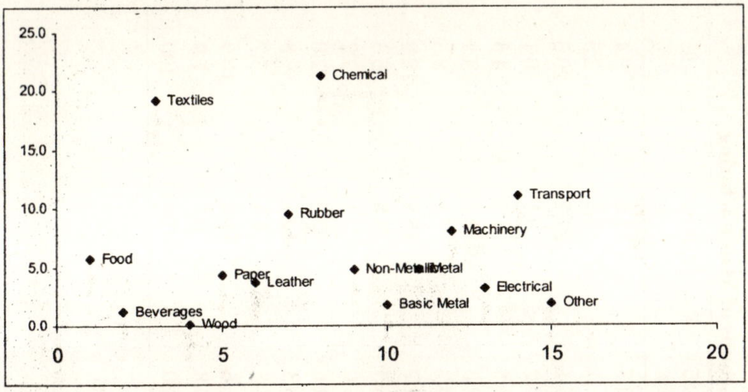

Figure 2: Industry-wise Percentage Shares of Value Added in 1999-2000

STRUCTURAL CHANGE IN TAMIL NADU BY VALUE ADDED [1980-81 TO 1999-2000]

Structural changes in the industrial economy of Tamil Nadu may be analyzed on the basis of the share of value added by manufacturing. Most of the previous studies considered the value added as a matter to examine the structural changes in an economy.

It is highlighted from Table 7 that the relative share of value added of the textile group, food products, rubber products, chemical and chemical products, non-metallic minerals and electrical equipments and parts indicated fluctuation over the study period. Mention should be made to the fact that the relative share of textiles though fluctuating is dominant throughout except in 1999-2000. In this period, the chemical group is dominant in its relative share in value added. The leather industry alone exhibited a continuous up trend in its relative share of value added. The relative share of value added of the transport equipments and parts remained more or less constant.

Table 7
Relative Share of Value Added by Different Groups of Manufacturing

Industry Group	*1980-81* %	*1984-85* %	*1989-90* %	*1994-95* %	*1999-2000* %
Food product	8.4	9.7	11.6	9.4	5.7
Beverages, Tobacco & Tobacco products	0.8	1.1	0.8	2.5	1.2
Textiles	25.1	15.1	21.2	20.5	19.1
Wood &Wood products	0.3	0.2	0.1	0.1	0.1
Paper &Paper products	4.5	3.8	4.3	4.8	4.3
Leather &Leather products	2.5	2.8	3.2	3.4	3.7
Rubber, Plastics, Petroleum &Coal products	5.0	9.7	7.8	8.5	9.5
Chemical &Chemical products	13.4	13.2	15.8	12.9	21.2
Non-Metallic &Mineral products	3.6	6.3	3.8	5.5	4.7
Basic Metal & Alloy products	5.4	3.0	2.4	2.2	1.7
Metal products & parts	2.8	2.6	2.7	2.0	4.7
Machinery & Machine Tools	11.3	16.3	10.1	9.8	8.0
Electrical Equipments & Parts	4.6	3.8	4.1	5.7	3.1
Transport Equipments & Parts	11.5	11.6	11.2	10.9	11.0
Other Manufacturing industries	0.6	0.8	0.7	1.9	1.8
Total	100	100	100	100	100

Source: Computed from ASI data.
Note: Productive Capital, Output and Value Added are monetary terms Factories and Number of Persons Employed are in Numbers.

Other manufacturing industries had less than 1 per cent of its relative share in value added, and it increased mildly to 1.8 per cent during 1999-2000. The industries producing metal and machinery and machine tolls exhibited a continuous declining trend in its relative share in the value added from the second half of the eighties.

STRUCTURAL RATIOS AT A GLANCE

For the purpose of analyzing structural change in industrial economy of Tamil Nadu, the ratio analysis is attempted. It is more appropriate to analyze the changes in these ratios, which will reflect the structural changes in the industry (Upendranadh *et. al.* 1994). This study gives us an idea of the pattern of industrialization in Tamil Nadu.

This analysis will answer the following specific questions: (i) what is the level of output per factory? (ii) what is the productive capital per employee? (iii) what is the productive capital and value added per factory? (iv) what is the position of employment per factory? and (v) what is the value added per employee?

It is observed from Table 8 that the structural ratios differ widely for different industrial groups with respect to size and nature of industries.

The principal ratios are insignificant during the first phase (1980-1981) for all the industry groups. Thereafter it increased in the following two phases, viz. 1985-1986, 1990-1991. The structural ratios for all the industries have increased significantly during 1999-2000.

The value of output per employee and productive capital per employee for all the industrial groups reveals an up trend during the study period. The value added per employee has increased moderately except in some industries. The industries which exhibit a deceleration in terms of number of employees per factory were (i) food producing industries (ii) textiles (iii) wood and wood products (iv) chemical and chemical products (v) non-metallic mineral (vi) basic metal and alloy (vii) machinery and machine tools (viii) electrical equipment and parts and (ix) transport equipment and parts.

Table 8(a)
Principal Ratios at a Glance in Tamil Nadu for Various Periods

Year	PC/ Fact	PC/ Emp	Emp/ Fact	Out/ Fac	Out/ Emp	Vad/ Fact	Vad/ Emp
Food Product							
1980-81	19.41	0.18	107	87.52	0.82	9.62	0.09
1985-86	21.95	0.33	66	91.82	1.39	11.99	0.18
1990-91	32.54	0.49	67	122.26	1.83	18.12	0.27
1995-96	137.15	2.03	68	154.24	2.28	18.44	0.27
1999-2000	56.26	0.81	69	236.63	3.41	19.54	0.28
Beverages, Tobacco							
1980-81	11.5	0.26	44	36.83	0.83	5.37	0.12
1985-86	30.75	0.32	95	150.5	1.58	20.27	0.21
1990-91	53.71	0.75	72	165.33	2.3	27.98	0.39
1995-96	102.07	1.26	81	324.54	4.01	79.37	0.98
1999-2000	157.37	2.89	54	175.74	3.23	40.97	0.75
Textiles							
1980-81	52.99	0.3	177	146.93	0.83	34.9	0.2
1985-86	54.2	0.38	141	137.71	0.98	25.28	0.18
1990-91	67.77	0.52	130	188.16	1.45	40.35	0.31
1995-96	69.74	0.77	90	170.84	1.89	24.31	0.27
1999-2000	134.54	1.21	111	310.7	2.8	50.64	0.46
Wood and Wood							
1980-81	5.51	0.12	45	14.78	0.33	3.66	0.08
1985-86	6.93	0.2	35	12.64	0.36	2.84	0.08
1990-91	5.36	0.21	25	15.83	0.63	3.12	0.12
1995-96	6.11	0.24	26	13.16	0.51	1.93	0.07
1999-2000	43.84	1.14	38	85.65	2.24	15.24	0.4
Paper and Paper products							
1980-81	37.75	0.47	81	72.42	0.9	18.56	0.23
1985-86	40.69	0.58	70	79.13	1.13	14.73	0.21
1990-91	67.72	1.02	66	140.29	2.12	50.82	0.77
1995-96	135.47	1.96	69	161.8	2.34	40.03	0.58
1999-2000	85.77	1.18	73	155.11	2.12	40.87	0.56

Note: Out/Fac = Output per Factory. PC/Emp = Productive capital per Employee, PC/Fa =Productive Capital per Factory, Vad/Fa = Value Added per Factory, Emp/Fa =Employment per Factory, Vad/Emp = Value Added per Employee, Out/Emp = Output per Employee.

Note: Productive Capital, Output and Value Added are monetary terms. Factories and Number of Persons Employed are in Numbers.

Source: Computed from ASI data, Various Issues.

Table 8(b)
Principal Ratios at a Glance in Tamil Nadu for Various Periods

Year	*PC/ Fact*	*PC/ Emp*	*Emp/ Fact*	*Out/ Fac*	*Out/ Emp*	*Vad/ Fact*	*Vad/ Emp*
Leather and Leather							
1980-81	36.04	0.33	108	177.12	1.63	17.77	0.16
1985-86	28.08	0.25	112	181.83	1.62	20.45	0.18
1990-91	53.87	0.45	119	214.52	1.81	29.43	0.25
1995-96	75.24	0.49	155	198.99	1.28	28.54	0.18
1999-2000	79.46	0.71	112	254.85	2.27	49.06	0.44
Rubber, Plastics							
1980-81	101.12	0.82	123	879.34	7.14	51.83	0.42
1985-86	288.70	2.99	97	940.32	9.73	67.98	0.70
1990-91	204.11	2.56	80	688.62	8.63	95.13	1.19
1995-96	401.60	4.07	99	726.96	7.37	136.75	1.39
1999-2000	450.27	4.87	92	1117.44	12.10	165.02	1.79
Chemical and Chemical							
1980-81	128.47	0.74	174	269.90	1.55	47.90	0.28
1985-86	218.38	1.36	160	279.32	1.74	47.58	0.30
1990-91	188.08	0.83	228	318.60	1.40	76.44	0.34
1995-96	229.83	1.55	148	324.51	2.19	71.70	0.48
1999-2000	305.02	2.15	142	483.66	3.42	126.25	0.89
Non-Metallic & Mineral							
1980-81	113.66	0.67	171	199.39	1.17	40.34	0.24
1985-86	114.72	1.01	113	211.97	1.87	49.01	0.43
1990-91	104.52	1.28	81	184.08	2.26	50.88	0.63
1995-96	128.07	1.54	83	235.19	2.82	69.24	0.83
1999-2000	96.9	1.2	81	263.17	3.26	70.72	0.88
Basic Metal							
1980-81	97.91	0.86	114	154.23	1.35	29.99	0.26
1985-86	144.2	1.57	92	214.2	2.33	28.89	0.31
1990-91	165.46	2.07	80	292.34	3.66	26.28	0.33
1995-96	262.61	2.48	106	422.13	3.98	49.46	0.47
1999-2000	400.88	5.44	74	665.78	9.04	63.17	0.86

Note: Out/Fac = Output per Factory. PC/Emp = Productive capital per Employee, PC/Fa =Productive Capital per Factory, Vad/Fa = Value Added per Factory, Emp/Fa =Employment per Factory, Vad/Emp = Value Added per Employee, Out/Emp = Output per Employee.

Note: Productive Capital, Output and Value Added are monetary terms Factories and Number of Persons Employed are in Numbers.

Source: Computed from ASI data, Various Issues.

Table 8(c)
Principal Ratios at a Glance in Tamil Nadu for Various Periods

Year	*PC/ Fact*	*PC/ Emp*	*Emp/ Fact*	*Out/ Fac*	*Out/ Emp*	*Vad/ Fact*	*Vad/ Emp*
Metal Product							
1980-81	36.15	0.47	77	63.69	0.82	16.82	0.22
1985-86	43.24	0.74	58	66.52	1.14	13.21	0.23
1990-91	57.32	1.05	55	96.99	1.77	23.82	0.43
1995-96	54.08	0.88	62	109.84	1.78	23.23	0.38
1999-2000	96.78	1.2	81	262.84	3.26	70.63	0.88
Machinery & Machine Tools							
1980-81	110.92	0.68	164	263.29	1.60	55.02	0.34
1985-86	141.03	1.11	127	279.06	2.20	74.56	0.59
1990-91	127.22	1.17	109	317.19	2.91	60.82	0.56
1995-96	159.01	1.10	144	502.73	3.49	93.78	0.65
1999-2000	169.86	2.03	82	330.20	3.94	80.90	0.96
Electrical Equipments and Parts							
1980-81	58.14	0.42	138	209.22	0.42	48.63	0.35
1985-86	73.11	0.58	126	216.84	0.58	56.17	0.45
1990-91	96.61	0.93	104	267.54	0.93	56.51	0.54
1995-96	38.27	1.75	22	102.48	1.75	32.21	1.48
1999-2000	133.31	1.78	75	324.32	1.78	73.65	0.98
Transport Equipments							
1980-81	237.63	0.55	433	503.6	1.16	116.31	0.27
1985-86	220	0.67	330	472.3	1.43	112.16	0.34
1990-91	326.77	0.99	330	690.02	2.09	163.34	0.5
1995-96	346.33	1.23	280	906.86	3.23	197.74	0.71
1999-2000	1349.29	5.12	264	1743.82	6.61	414.67	1.57
Other Manufacturing							
1980-81	31.03	0.33	94	76.45	0.82	18.15	0.19
1985-86	52.41	0.73	71	123.56	1.73	29.43	0.41
1990-91	161.67	1.5	108	300.2	2.79	72.78	0.68
1995-96	333.94	2.18	153	410.95	2.69	98.04	0.64
1999-2000	194.77	1.25	155	367.97	2.37	104.34	0.67

Note: Out/Fac = Output per Factory. PC/Emp = Productive capital per Employee, PC/Fa =Productive Capital per Factory, Vad/Fa = Value Added per Factory, Emp/Fa =Employment per Factory, Vad/Emp = Value Added per Employee, Out/Emp = Output per Employee.

Note: Productive Capital, Output and Value Added are monetary terms. Factories and Number of Persons Employed are in Numbers.

Source: *Computed from ASI data, Various Issues.*

There were two important reasons, which could be attributed to the fall in the employment per factory for the above-mentioned industrial groups. Firstly, (i) the total number of factories from 1980-1981 to 1999-2000 increased steadily. At the same time the number of employees exhibited down tern trend in the industrial groups. And secondly, most of the industries are capital intensive.

The output per factory increased noticeably and productive capital per factory too increased moderately for all the industrial groups in Tamil Nadu during the study period.

INDUSTRY WISE STRUCTURAL RATIO (1980-81 TO 1999-2000)

It is worthwhile to analyze the structural ratio for different types of industries. In the previous section, the structural ratio has been analyzed for different periods for different types of industries. Similarly, in this section, the value of the factors for entire period have been averaged and the principal ratios such as productive capital per factory, productive capital per employee, employment per factory, output per factory, output per employee, value added per factory and value added per employee have been computed.

Table 9 depicts that the structural ratios for different groups of industries in Tamil Nadu for the entire study period (1980-81 to 1999-2000). It is observed that the transport industry is the largest group of industry in respect of value added per factory, output per factory, employment per factory and productive capital per factory. Based on the productive capital per employee the chemical group stands first, regarding the output per employee also the chemical and chemical producing group occupies predominant position.

The other important industries are rubber group, 'other manufacturing' industries and chemical group in the case of value added per factory. In respect of value added per employee the industrial group producing chemical, 'other manufacturing' and electrical groups are important.

With regard to employment per factory the textile group including, cotton textiles, wool, silk and synthetic fibber textiles

Table 9

Principal Ratios at a Glance in Tamil Nadu (1980-81 to 1999-2000)

Industry Groups	*PC/FC*	*PC/EMP*	*EMP/FC*	*OUT/FC*	*OUT/EMP*	*VAD/FC*	*VAD/EMP*
Food Products	41.62	0.57	72.79	133.40	1.83	19.47	0.27
Beverages, Tobacco & Tobacco products	57.03	0.59	97.23	166.20	1.71	33.28	0.34
Textiles	72.84	0.59	112.84	195.53	1.59	35.78	0.29
Wood & Wood products	9.23	0.29	32.13	20.53	0.64	4.00	0.12
Paper & Paper products	95.46	1.17	81.72	123.46	1.51	27.86	0.34
Leather & Leather products	54.12	0.45	120.20	213.60	1.78	28.87	0.24
Rubber, Plastics, Petroleum & Coal products	199.58	1.24	160.87	323.99	2.01	72.22	0.45
Chemical & Chemical products	308.30	3.38	91.13	798.64	8.76	104.50	1.15
Non-Metallic & Mineral Products	120.69	1.18	102.53	206.18	2.01	57.23	0.56
Basic metal A& alloy products	247.32	2.42	102.34	325.69	3.18	34.18	0.33
Metal products & parts	123.73	1.92	64.54	109.54	1.70	26.55	0.41
Machinery A& Machine tools	163.63	1.27	128.34	349.78	2.73	64.21	0.50
Electrical Equipments & parts	115.64	1.13	102.42	294.32	2.87	62.15	0.61
Transport Equipments & parts	373.97	1.25	300.20	684.20	2.28	161.40	0.54
Other manufacturing industries	205.85	1.64	125.31	307.84	2.46	91.57	0.73

Note: Out/Fac = Output per Factory. PC/Emp = Productive capital per Employee, PC/Fa =Productive Capital per Factory, Vad/Fa = Value Added per Factory, Emp/Fa =Employment per Factory, Vad/Emp = Value Added per Employee, Out/Emp = Output per Employee.

Note: Productive Capital, Output and Value Added are monetary terms; Factories and Number of Persons Employed are in Numbers.

Source: Computed from ASI data, Various Issues.

and textile products is the second largest group of industry and followed by rubber machinery and machine tools and chemicals and chemical products.

In respect of output per factory and output per employee the other important industries are rubber group, chemical group, basic metal and alloy and machinery and machine tools. While, industries producing basic metal and alloy, chemical group and rubber group are other important industries in the case of productive capital per factory. Mention should be made that wood and wood producing industry registered the last position in all the analyzed principal characteristics.

The inferences of the foregoing structural analysis may be summarized as under: (a) The structural ratios differ widely for different types of industries and periods. (b) The structural ratios are relatively small during first phase and increased significantly for the subsequent phases; registered marked increase (c) The capital per factory and capital per worker had increased substantially, particularly in the 1990s. (d) The transport group is predominant industry with respect to value added per factory, output per factory, employment per factory and productive capital per factory for the study period of 1980-1981 to 1999-2000 (f) there had been a declining trend in the employment during the nineties. This conclusion confirms the results of the studies made by Burange (1999), Deb (2001), Upendranadh and *et. al* (1994) and Thangamuthu (2004) results.

PRINCIPAL RATIOS FOR DIFFERENT TYPES OF INDUSTRIES IN TAMIL NADU

The analysis in this section focuses on the principal ratios for different industries in Tamil Nadu. The principal ratios include capital-labour ratio, capital-output ratio and input-output ratio. The principal ratios for different types of industries for the industrial economy of Tamil Nadu are presented in the following Table 10. (These ratios for two comparative periods– 1980-81 and 1999-2000).

The capital labour ratio is defined as the value of capital employed per unit of labour. The capital-output ratio shows

Table 10

Principal ratios in Tamil Nadu for 1980-81 and 1999-2000 by industries.

Industry Group	*80-81* K/L	*80-81* K/O	*80-81* I/O	*99-2000* K/L	*99-2000* K/O	*99-2000* I/O
Food product	0.40	0.22	0.87	1.84	0.24	0.92
Beverages, Tobacco & Tobacco products	0.60	0.31	0.84	6.53	0.90	0.77
Textiles	0.64	0.36	0.74	2.61	0.43	0.84
Wood &Wood products	0.27	0.37	0.74	2.51	0.51	0.82
Paper &Paper products	1.07	0.52	0.65	2.68	0.55	0.74
Leather &Leather products	0.73	0.20	0.88	1.55	0.31	0.81
Rubber, Plastics, Petrole &Coal products	0.44	0.11	0.93	2.46	0.40	0.85
Chemical &Chemical products	7.26	0.48	0.79	23.23	0.63	0.74
Non-Metallic &Mineral products	1.50	0.57	0.76	2.92	0.37	0.73
Basic Metal & Alloy products	1.96	0.63	0.78	12.49	0.60	0.91
Metal products & parts	1.07	0.57	0.71	2.92	0.37	0.73
Machinery & Machine Tools	1.63	0.42	0.77	5.16	0.51	0.75
Electrical Equipments & Parts	0.99	0.28	0.75	3.61	0.41	0.77
Transport Equipments & Parts	1.27	0.47	0.74	12.19	0.77	0.76
Other Manufacturing industries	0.77	0.41	0.72	3.40	0.53	0.72
Total	0.97	0.36	0.80	3.95	0.48	0.81

Source: Computed from ASI data.

Note: K- Capital, L- Labour, I- Input, O- Output.

the value of capital used per unit of output. Similarly, the input-output ratio means the output obtained per unit of input.

An underdeveloped country is characterized by a large amount of labour in relation to capital and the low propensity to save. Ironically, a developed country exhibits higher rate of capital formation, because of the higher rate of savings and the limited availability of labour in relation to capital.

These principal ratios indicate the changes that take place in different groups of manufacturing sector in Tamil Nadu. Out of fifteen industrial groups the capital intensity in chemical and chemical products, basic metal and alloy products registered an increase, and also transport equipments and parts, beverages, tobacco and tobacco products and machinery and machine tools.

In respect of capital output ratio, the beverages group, leather group, rubber, plastics, petroleum and coal producing industries, chemical and chemical producing industries, transport equipment and parts has increased over the study period. The remaining industries mostly revealed a fluctuating trend in the case of capital output ratio.

The input output ratio reveals that the industry producing textiles, wood and wood products, basic metal and alloy, electrical equipments and parts and transport group showed an increase. The productivity of other manufacturing industries registered a constant at 0.72, while the beverages group and leather group revealed a decreasing trend. The rest of the industrial groups showed a fluctuating trend.

Similar analysis of structural ratio was conducted by Sharma R. (1982), V. Rajeswari (1989) and Rao A.V.V.S.K. (1989). Sharma found the increase in the capital-output ratio for chemicals and fertilizer, electrical machinery, metal products, cement, iron and steel etc. in Andhra Pradesh for the period 1960-1971. Rao found that there was the increasing trend of labour capital ratio in Andhra Pradesh during 1976-1977 to 1981-1982. Rajeswari traced that there was higher capital intensity in all the industrial groups (except sugar industries) and higher capital output ratio in food group, textiles, electrical machinery shipbuilding and chemical groups. Similarly Ahluwalia (1985) found an increase in the capital output ratio of Indian manufacturing during 1966-1967 to 1979-1980.

STRUCTURAL RATIOS–TAMIL NADU

The performance of the factory sector in Tamil Nadu over a long period appears quite impressive (except some dismal), while analyzing the aggregate structural ratios of Tamil Nadu, the study observed that, the productive capital per factory increased steadily from 1979-1980 to 1999-2000. It averaged 116 lakhs in the eighties and increased to 163 lakhs in the nineties.

Similarly the output per factory increased moderately for the referred period. The output per factory and value added per factory ranged between 202 and 38.7 lakhs respectively in the eighties and it increased to 284 and 53 lakhs in the nineties.

The employment (employment per factory) picture in Tamil Nadu shows a fluctuating trend during the period under review. During the eighties it averaged 127 and it reduced to 109 in the nineties. The reason behind the declaration is the technological upliftment in the manufacturing industries. The output per employee in below 2 lakhs upto 1988-1989, there after it increased slightly, which averaged 1.6 lakhs in the eighties and improved to 2.6 lakhs in the nineties. Similarly the value added per employee is below 1 lakh in the analysis period, and it averaged 0.3 and 0.48 lakhs for the above mentioned periods. In toto, the productive capital per factory, and output per factory have experienced appreciable progress over the period of study. This improvement may be attributed to performance of private sector in this state.

STRUCTURAL RATIOS–ALL INDIA

The fixed capital per factory was found below 2 crores up to 1989-1990. There after it increased to nearly 3 crores, while it averages 1.6 and 2.7 crores for the eighties and the nineties. The output per factory and value added per factory revealed

Table 11
Some Structural Ratios in Tamil Nadu, (1979-80 to 1999-2000)

Year	*PC/ Fac*	*Output/ Fac*	*Vad/ Fact*	*Emp/ Fact*	*Output/ Emp*	*Vad/ Emp*
1979-80	91.04	174.03	33.41	144.34	1.21	0.23
1980-81	84.88	164.91	30.56	139.33	1.18	0.22
1981-82	98.31	177.54	31.81	135.61	1.31	0.23
1982-83	86.11	187.27	35.27	130.55	1.43	0.27
1983-84	93.43	171.64	33.79	122.96	1.40	0.27
1984-85	140.87	176.06	37.28	121.09	1.45	0.31
1985-86	127.96	203.91	37.75	124.25	1.64	0.30
1986-87	120.11	212.41	39.79	121.06	1.75	0.33
1987-88	120.58	217.60	37.55	121.05	1.80	0.31
1988-89	152.46	239.63	46.08	123.36	1.94	0.37
1989-90	134.77	251.54	49.32	122.35	2.06	0.40
1990-91	139.92	251.71	52.73	118.28	2.13	0.45
1991-92	142.09	243.69	47.18	115.04	2.12	0.41
1992-93	127.20	231.34	44.47	107.98	2.14	0.41
1993-94	144.47	246.38	53.36	107.68	2.29	0.50
1994-95	176.52	286.64	55.58	110.45	2.60	0.50
1995-96	164.78	290.41	58.81	112.07	2.59	0.52
1996-97	182.52	310.46	61.09	116.15	2.67	0.53
1997-98	190.65	326.85	53.42	115.83	2.82	0.46
1998-99	164.72	280.90	49.96	99.76	2.82	0.50
1999-2000	169.98	340.50	53.26	98.39	3.46	0.54

Source: Computed from EPW data.
Note: Productive Capital, Output and Value Added are monetary terms Factories and Number of Persons Employed are in Numbers.

an increase and fluctuating trends respectively. However, the output per factory increased to 4 crores in nineties from 2.4 crores in eighties, it must be due to exploitation of labours through over duets and additional shifts. The value added per factory increased from 0.45 to 0.78 crore for the above mentioned periods. The employment scenario appears slightly gloomy. It registered 0.14 thousand during the eighties and decreased to 0.13 thousand in the nineties. The output per employee and value added per employee had undergone a phenomenal rise over these years at all India level.

Table 12
Some Structural Ratios in India, (1979-80 to 1999-2000)

Year	*PC/ Fac*	*Output/ Fac*	*Vad/ Fact*	*Emp/ Fact*	*Output/ Emp*	*Vad/ Emp*
1979-80	1.22	1.68	0.35	0.143	11.70	2.43
1980-81	1.14	1.62	0.32	0.143	11.35	2.22
1981-82	1.15	1.71	0.34	0.132	12.90	2.55
1982-83	1.45	2.17	0.42	0.154	14.15	2.74
1983-84	1.54	2.14	0.46	0.145	14.82	3.19
1984-85	1.65	2.25	0.45	0.144	15.65	3.10
1985-86	1.62	2.32	0.45	0.132	17.66	3.42
1986-87	1.71	2.56	0.49	0.135	18.90	3.63
1987-88	1.81	2.64	0.48	0.135	19.52	3.59
1988-89	1.79	2.84	0.53	0.132	21.49	4.04
1989-90	1.88	3.08	0.58	0.134	22.99	4.32
1990-91	2.13	3.27	0.62	0.131	24.88	4.74
1991-92	2.09	3.19	0.58	0.129	24.74	4.53
1992-93	2.30	3.33	0.64	0.128	25.88	5.00
1993-94	2.56	3.50	0.73	0.126	27.75	5.76
1994-95	2.64	3.75	0.79	0.131	28.72	6.02
1995-96	2.78	4.09	0.85	0.131	31.12	6.47
1996-97	2.97	4.14	0.85	0.127	32.53	6.72
1997-98	3.38	4.76	0.90	0.129	36.78	6.95
1998-99	2.81	4.45	0.83	0.114	39.23	7.28
1999-2000	2.80	4.97	0.86	0.110	45.28	7.81

Source: Computed from EPW data.
Note: Productive Capital, Output and Value Added are monetary terms Factories and Number of Persons Employed are in Numbers.

The output per employee was 17.17 crores in the eighties, and it reached 32.44 crores is nineties and the value added per employee showed a similar trend of from 3.3 crores to 6.3 crore increase for the above said periods. It is very clear that on account of the impact of globalization, privatization and liberalization process the investment and output experienced considerable improvement, but it is not reflected in the employment generation.

HIRSCHMAN HERFINDAHL INDEX [HHI]

In order to understand the concentration of principal characteristics in the industrial (manufacturing) economy of

Tamil Nadu, the Hirschman Herfindahl Index [HHI] is applied for the period of 20 years from 1980-81 to 1999-2000. Similar analysis was used by Hirschman, A.O. (1964), and it is followed by Burange L. G. (1999).

The HH index has been constructed for the principal characteristics, which include number of factories, productive capital, number of employed, value of output and value added.

Hirschman Herfindahl Index [HHI] has been used to calculate the concentration of different types of industries in Tamil Nadu.

$$HHI = \sum_{i=1}^{n} \frac{P_i^2}{100}$$

Where Pi = the percentage share of the industry in the manufacturing sector of Tamil Nadu. The HH index is calculated totally for all the two digit industrial groups. The absolute values have been deflated to constant price (at constant 1993-94 prices). The values of HH index have been presented in the following Table 13 The HH criterion is that the HHI is greater than 6.6 it means that the variable is concentrated in some industries; i.e minimum value of HHI is 6.6. The maximum value of HHI is 100 when the entire variable is concentrated in one industry only in the manufacturing sector.

The result depicts that all the indices have fluctuating trend over the study period. Considering the productive capital, it fluctuates between 10.6 and 13.2 points. This trend implies that the fixed capital has shows less concentration in some industries.

It is noted that the degree of concentration of employment decreased up to 1992-93. Thereafter, it increased at a snail's pace. That means the contribution of employment is distributed several industries. In respect of output, the degree of concentration is more or less stagnant up to 1996-97, and after that it increased slightly. The concentration of value added of Tamil Nadu's manufacturing sector has been slowly accelerating during the study period.

Table 13
HH Index for the Manufacturing Sector of Tamil Nadu.

Year	*Factories*	*Capital*	*Employment*	*Output*	*Value Added*
1980-81	13.47	11.51	14.61	11.45	12.64
1981-82	13.53	11.24	14.37	10.92	11.20
1982-83	13.14	11.05	13.88	11.06	11.03
1983-84	12.84	11.18	13.48	10.88	13.17
1984-85	12.97	10.79	13.67	10.84	10.85
1985-86	13.18	12.20	13.83	10.93	11.35
1986-87	12.82	10.84	13.84	10.69	18.47
1987-88	11.82	10.77	14.14	10.85	11.44
1988-89	13.05	11.84	13.21	10.92	11.77
1989-90	13.01	10.96	13.74	10.81	12.00
1990-91	12.80	10.52	14.04	10.62	11.05
1991-92	13.14	10.68	14.14	10.85	11.28
1992-93	13.22	10.63	14.14	10.94	10.94
1993-94	13.78	11.21	15.38	11.53	11.50
1994-95	14.55	10.70	14.72	12.03	10.78
1995-96	16.87	11.56	14.83	11.53	10.10
1996-97	14.76	12.29	16.56	11.82	11.48
1997-98	14.68	10.65	15.89	13.12	14.00
1998-99	13.81	13.21	13.42	13.31	13.95
1999-2000	14.03	12.97	15.07	12.42	12.19

Source: Computed from ASI data.
Note: Productive Capital, Output and Value Added are monetary terms Factories and Number of Persons Employed are in Numbers.

Here it is to be noted that the industries producing textiles, chemical and chemical products, transport equipment and parts and machinery and machine tools contributed to 62 per cent of capital in 1999-2000. Output the manufacturing of textiles, chemicals machinery and machine tools, and transport equipment and parts contribute 54 per cent of value of output in the same period.

In the case of employment, in 1999-2000, only four industries, such as textiles, chemicals, food producing industries, and transport equipments and parts accounted for 65 per cent of employment. The manufacturing of textiles, chemicals, transport equipment and parts and machinery and machine tolls contributed 59 per cent of the total value added in 1999-2000.

However, in 1980-81 the industries producing textiles, chemicals and chemical products, machinery and machine tools and transport equipments and parts together contributed 59 per cent of productive capital, and 54 per cent of employment, 50 per cent of value of output and 61 per cent of value added. It is observed from this analysis that no one industry has contributed to all the values.

USE-BASED AND INPUT BASED ANALYSIS

Use-based

In this section, an attempt has been made to know the structural changes in the industrial economy of Tamil Nadu between 1980-81 and 1999-2000, using use-based and input-based classification.

Under the use-based classification the industries are grouped as Basic goods, Capital goods, Intermediary good, Consumer durable goods and Consumer-non durable goods. In the basic good industries, the industries producing (1) Iron and Steel, (2) Cement, lime and plaster, (3) Fertilizers and pesticides, (4) Generation and transmission of electric energy and distribution of electric energy to house hold, industrial and commercial use, are the important industries.

Under the Capital good industries (1) hand tools and general hardware, (2) Manufacture of prime movers, boilers and steam generating plants such as diesel engines and parts (3) Machinery for food and textiles industries (4) Electrical machinery apparatus (electrical motors, generators, transformers, electromagnetic clutches and brakes etc) and (5) Manufacture of transport equipment and parts are the important industries.

In the Intermediary group, (1) Cotton spinning, wearing shrinking, sanforizing, mercerising and finishing of cotton textiles in mills, (2) Spinning, weaving and finishing of other textiles, synthetic fibers, rayon, nylons etc, (3) Manufacture of leather and leather products, (4) Tyre and tube industries and (3) manufacture of photochemical, sanctioned films and papers are important industries.

In the Consumer durable industrial group (1) Fabricated metal products, (2) Electrical apparatus, appliances and other parts such as lamps, bulbs, tubes, sockets, switches, fans, insulators (3) Manufacture of motor cycles and scooters and parts, (4) Manufacture of medical surgical and scientific equipments are important industries.

Similarly, in the Consumer non-durable group, (1) Manufacture of food and food products (2) Beverages tobacco and tobacco products (3) Manufacture of drugs and medicines, (5) Manufacture of matches and (6) All the cosmetic items are important industries in Tamil Nadu.

These use-based industries have been analysed using simple percentage share of principal characteristics including number of factories, productive capital, employment, value of output and value added.

Table 14
Percentage Share of Number of Industries by Manufacturing Sector of Tamil Nadu (U.B)

Industrial Group/Year	*1980-1981*	*1985-1986*	*1990-1991*	*1995-1996*	*1999-2000*
Basic Goods	6.73	7.66	5.38	5.28	5.76
Capital Goods	11.58	14.17	15.09	16.78	18.38
Intermediary Goods	23.78	23.06	20.45	21.17	20.40
Consumer Durable Goods	10.63	11.13	9.45	7.44	5.69
Consumer Non Durable Goods	47.29	43.99	49.63	49.33	49.77
Total	100	100	100	100	100

Source: Computed from ASI data.

The percentage share of different industrial groups is presented in Table 14 for the five different periods viz. 1980-81, 1985-86, 1990-91, 1995-96 and 1999-2000. The relative share of number of factories of consumer-non durable goods had upsurged from 47 per cent to 50 per cent; expansion of market for this commodity influenced new industries to emerge. The relative role of capital goods increased steadily during the study period. At the same time, the percentage share of consumer durable goods, in terms of number of factories has been shrinking and all other groups registered fluctuating trend.

In the case of productive capital, the basic goods had a stagnant position in 1980-81 and 1985-86, there after decreased sharply, this may be due to the reduction in the number of factories. The share of capital goods has fluctuating trend up to 1990-91. Thereafter increased sharply. This is due to many branches of this sector undergoing modernization and expansion in the scale of production. But the relative share of intermediary goods decreased considerably up to 1995-96 and it increased in 1999-2000.

Table 15
Percentage shares of Productive Capital by Manufacturing Sector of Tamil Nadu (U.B)

Industrial Group/Year	*1980-1981*	*1985-1986*	*1990-1991*	*1995-1996*	*1999-2000*
Basic Goods	49.26	49.50	42.74	31.03	23.65
Capital Goods	16.90	19.32	18.86	22.10	29.45
Intermediary Goods	20.31	19.20	12.33	11.77	18.60
Consumer Durable Goods	3.69	4.06	3.87	3.17	2.65
Consumer Non Durable Goods	9.82	7.89	22.21	31.93	25.65
Total	100	100	100	100	100

Source: Computed from ASI data.

The percentage share of consumer durable goods hovered around 3 to 4 per cent over the study period. The contribution of consumer non-durable goods in respect of productive capital increased noticeably upto 1995-96, there after it decreased.

Table 16
Percentage Share of Employment by Manufacturing Sector of Tamil Nadu (U.B)

Industrial Group/Year	*1980-1981*	*1985-1986*	*1990-1991*	*1995-1996*	*1999-2000*
Basic Goods	15.24	12.53	12.27	14.29	22.56
Capital Goods	17.72	21.29	19.39	17.76	15.41
Intermediary Goods	29.46	31.36	20.95	19.38	20.64
Consumer Durable Goods	6.53	7.41	5.32	5.04	3.83
Consumer Non Durable Goods	31.05	27.42	42.07	43.53	37.56
Total	100	100	100	100	100

Source: Computed from ASI data.

The relative share of employment of consumer non-durable is the highest during the study period except for the year 1985-86, and the intermediary goods industry got first place by providing maximum employment in 1985-86, and in that year the group belonging consumer non-durable slipped to second position. Capital goods industry group and consumer durable registered a continuous fall in the provision of employment since 1985-86 the reason behind is that the growth in manufacturing export and GDP share has not been matched by growth of manufacturing employment (Nagaraj, 2003). There has been a steady increase in the generation of employment in basic goods industries from 1990-91 to 1999-2000. The dominant position of basic goods in the case of generation of employment may be due to expansion of market and increase of the number of factories.

The percentage share of basic goods, in the case of output had been fluctuating over the study period. It decreased from 20.6 per cent in 1980-81 to 14.7 per cent in 1995-96; it tended to increase to 19 per cent in 1999-2000. The contributing share of output by capital goods has registered 23 per cent in 1980-81 and it increased to 25 per cent and 27 per cent respectively for the following two periods.

Table 17
Percentage Share of Output by Manufacturing Sector of Tamil Nadu (U.B)

Industrial Group/Year	*1980-1981*	*1985-1986*	*1990-1991*	*1995-1996*	*1999-2000*
Basic Goods	20.60	21.68	18.92	14.70	18.95
Capital Goods	22.94	24.61	26.92	30.82	34.34
Intermediary Goods	29.79	28.39	21.19	16.02	17.83
Consumer Durable Goods	4.99	5.71	5.47	4.36	4.71
Consumer Non Durable Goods	21.67	19.60	27.50	34.10	24.18
Total	100	100	100	100	100

Source: Computed from ASI data.

Its contribution was more than 30 per cent by 1995-96 and 1999-2000. Owing to economic liberalization a heavy dose of capital has been accumulating and high technology has been employed. They improve the output.

The contribution of intermediary goods was maintained nearly 30 per cent during 1980-81 and 1985-86. It decreased sharply for the following three phases. The relative role of consumer durable goods with respect to output had been around 4 to 6 per cent. The contributing share of consumer non-durable good has a fluctuating trend over the study period with regard to output.

Considering value added the capital goods sector is in a dominant position. The contribution of capital goods improved in 1990-91 from the previous period and it declined by 1995-96, after this period its contribution increased appreciably. At the same time, the relative share of basic goods in respect of value added in the manufacturing sector of Tamil Nadu increased in 1995-96 over 1980-81 and it slipped down to 18 per cent by 1999-2000.

Table 18
Percentage share of Value Added by Manufacturing Sector of Tamil Nadu (U.B)

Industrial Group/Year	*1980-1981*	*1985-1986*	*1990-1991*	*1995-1996*	*1999-2000*
Basic Goods	21.06	23.36	26.24	27.39	18.65
Capital Goods	24.25	30.89	32.94	29.89	34.64
Intermediary Goods	31.62	25.31	10.51	11.38	17.80
Consumer Durable Goods	9.12	9.67	5.84	4.10	4.75
Consumer Non Durable Goods	13.94	10.77	24.47	27.25	24.16
Total	100	100	100	100	100

Source: Computed from ASI data.

There has been a steady decline in the intermediary goods in the case of percentage share of value added up to 1990-91, which improved to 17.8 per cent by 1999-2000. Where as, the percentage share of consumer-durable goods decreased over the analyzed periods. The relative share of consumer non-durable goods with respect of value added increased in 1990-91 from 1980-81. Its contribution had been fluctuating by 1995-96 and 1999-2000. Economist very often cited that the value added is the mater to be analyzed in the industrial economy. From their point of view, the industrial economy of Tamil

Nadu has been dominated by capital goods industries with regard to value added.

It is realized in the industrial economy of Tamil Nadu that the capital goods industry has dominated in this state in 1999-2000, but up to 1970 consumer goods industry dominated in the industrial sector of the state (Vijayalakshmi, 1994) this is in conformity with *W.G. Hoffmann's hypothesis(1958) of the patterns of development of manufacturing industries. He addressed that, whatever be the relative amount of the factors of production, whatever be the relative amount of the factors, whatever be the stage of technology, the structure of the manufacturing sector of the economy has always followed an uniform pattern- the consumer goods industries develop first and the capital goods industries dominant in the last stage in the course of industrialization.*

Input Based

The manufacturing industries are classified on the basis of input used by the industries. Under the classification of input-based, industries are grouped in to three fold viz (I) Agro-based industries (II) Metal-based industries and (III) Chemical-based industries. These categories covered more than 75 per cent of industries of the State.

In Tamil Nadu, the agro-based industries are in a dominating position in terms of number of industries during the study period. In the agro-based industries (i) Manufacturing of cotton textiles (ii) Leather and leather products, (iii) Food producing industries (iv) Tyre and tube producing industries and rubber producing industries are important.

In the metal-based industries, the (i) Fabricated metal products (such as metal cans from tin-plate, enameled sheet metal, metal shipping containers barrels, drums, kegs, pails, safes, vaults, enamelled sanitary and all other fabricated metal products) (ii) Manufacture of structural metal products (iii) Manufacture of electrical industrial machinery and apparatus and parts (such as electrical motors, generators, transformers, electromagnetic clutches and brakes etc) (iv) Transport equipments and parts and (v) Manufacture of medical surgical and scientific equipments) are the important industries.

Similarly, in the chemical-based industries (i) Petroleum products and petroleum refineries (ii) Chemical and chemical products such as basic industrial organic and in organic chemicals, gases and manufacture of fertilizers and pesticides (iii) Manufacture of paints, varnishes and lacquers (iv) Manufacture of drugs and medicines (v) Manufacture of cosmetic items (such as lotions, hair dressings, tooth pastes, soap in any form, synthetic detergents, shampoos, shaving products, cleaners, washing and scoring products and other toilet preparations) are important industries.

Here the relative share of these three groups in respect of the number of industries, productive capital, employment, value of output and value added has been analyzed.

Table 19
Percentage share of Number of Factories by manufacturing sector of Tamil Nadu (I.B)

Industrial Group/Year	*1980-1981*	*1985-1986*	*1990-1991*	*1995-1996*	*1999-2000*
Agro-Based	67.22	66.88	67.92	67.25	67.12
Metal-Based	16.58	16.61	18.53	15.85	15.57
Chemical-Based	16.20	16.50	13.55	16.90	17.32
Total	100	100	100	100	100

Source: Computed from ASI data.

Based on the criterion of the number of factories, agro-based group is dominating throughout the study period. The climatic condition of this state is suitable to start the agro based industries, particularly in some industrially developed districts. The position of chemical-based industries and metal-based industries are changing from second position to the third position and vice versa. The relative share of metal-based industries has increased by 1991-91, there after it decreased. The contribution of relative share of chemical-based industry is 16 per cent for the first two phases, which decreased in 1991, and increased sharply during 1999-2000. This sharp increase in the number of chemical industry is due to emerging of drugs and fire based industries in this state.

Table 20
Percentage share of Productive Capital by manufacturing sector of Tamil Nadu (I.B)

Industrial Group/Year	*1980-1981*	*1985-1986*	*1990-1991*	*1995-1996*	*1999-2000*
Agro-Based	45.09	40.42	43.51	46.32	35.85
Metal-Based	25.21	26.79	31.92	20.30	24.67
Chemical-Based	29.70	32.79	24.57	33.38	39.48
Total	100	100	100	100	100

Source: Computed from ASI data.

There has been a remarkable change in the structure of industries in terms of input based classification. Based on the criterion of productive capital, industrial sector shows continuous changes during the study period. The percentage share of agro-based industries was dominated in 1980-81. That was replaced by chemical-based industries in 1999-2000. For the four phases viz 80-81, 85-86, 90-91 and 95-96 the agro-based industries were in dominant position. By 1999-2000, the chemical-based industries emerged as an important industrial group in terms of productive capital. The appreciable performance of chemical based industries was attributed to starting of many new industries and expansion of already existing industries in this state.

Table 21
Percentage Share of Employment by Manufacturing Sector of Tamil Nadu (I.B)

Industrial Group/Year	*1980-1981*	*1985-1986*	*1990-1991*	*1995-1996*	*1999-2000*
Agro-Based	61.08	56.83	60.87	63.74	58.92
Metal-Based	21.67	23.15	24.39	23.73	17.52
Chemical-Based	17.26	20.02	14.74	12.53	23.56
Total	100	100	100	100	100

Source: Computed from ASI data.

Of the total employment, the agro-based industries have got sizable amount of employment over the study periods. In the agro-based industries, food and food products, and cotton textiles are a major contributor of employment (CII, 2003). The relative share of metal-based industries with regard to employment increased from 21.6 per cent in 1980-81 to 24 per cent in 1990-91, there after it decreased. The chemical-based industries amplified its contribution from 17 per cent by 1980-81 to 20 per cent in 1985-86, since then it shrank for the following two phases and upsurged to nearly 22 per cent in 1999-2000. The reason behind this is the emergence of new industries during the nineties.

Table 22
Percentage Share of Output by Manufacturing Sector of Tamil Nadu (I.B)

Industrial Group/Year	*1980-1981*	*1985-1986*	*1990-1991*	*1995-1996*	*1999-2000*
Agro-Based	52.18	52.21	51.36	49.57	41.70
Metal-Based	21.56	22.09	25.35	22.81	24.50
Chemical-Based	26.27	25.70	23.29	27.62	33.80
Total	100	100	100	100	100

Source: Computed from ASI data.

It is observed form Table 22 that the agro- based industrial group is the largest single group in terms of output. However, the output of agro-based industry dwindled from 1980-81 to 1999-2000. The proportion of output of metal-based industries increased gradually up to second phase of 1990s. Thereafter it decreased slightly. The relative share of chemical-based industries with regard to output increased from 26 per cent in 1980-81 to 33.8 per cent in 1999-2000. It is very obvious that the use of chemical in all the productions increased sharply, in particular the use of chemicals in agriculture, medical field and textile industries increased tremendously in the recent periods. Owing to the above mentioned reasons the output of chemical-based industries recorded maximum amount of 34 per cent in 1999-2000.

Considering value added, agro-based industries, played a major role up to 1995-96. There after the chemical-based industry emerged as an important industry in respect of value added. The manufacturing sector of the state has experienced a progressive structural change in favor of chemical based

Table 23
Percentage Share of Value Added by Manufacturing Sector of Tamil Nadu (I.B)

Industrial Group/Year	*1980-1981*	*1985-1986*	*1990-1991*	*1995-1996*	*1999-2000*
Agro-Based	50.91	47.21	51.25	46.90	34.02
Metal-Based	26.10	29.18	30.07	31.90	28.91
Chemical-Based	22.99	23.62	18.68	21.20	37.07
Total	100	100	100	100	100

Source: Computed from ASI data.

industries. The proportion of chemical-based industry ranged from 19 to 23 per cent during 1980-81 to 1995-96 with regard to value added. Since then it recorded considerable progress of 37 per cent. The progresses made by chemical based industry was due to contribution of the industries producing basic chemicals, fertilizers, pharmaceuticals, medicinal chemicals, cosmetic items, and manufacture of other chemicals such as matches and photochemical. The metal-based industry increased its share gradually up to 1995-96, since then it has diminished.

THE CHANGING TRENDS IN THE INDUSTRIAL PRODUCTIVITY OF THE STATE AND THE MAGNITUDE OF INDUSTRIAL GROWTH IN THE STATE SINCE 1980

In this section, an attempt is made to analysis the productivity trends of manufacturing industries in Tamil Nadu. The term productivity is defined by ILO (1954), as the ratio between the output of wealth and the input of resources used up in the production process. In addition, it gives room to improve the productivity so that the higher productivity levels can be obtained by making more efficient use of all resources in employment to produce as much of goods and services as possible at the lowest possibilities of real cost. In addition Fenske (1968), defines productivity as the average amount of goods and services produced by an unit of productive factor in a specified period of time.

It is well-known that productivity has been a major factor in economic growth. The world famous *Vardoon's law* shows that there has been a positive linear relationship between productivity growth and output growth, and it is realized by a number of other studies. One of the main aims of New Economic Policy of India is to achieve sustained growth in productivity.

Fast growth of economy is achieved by upliftment of industrial productivity in this world. For instance, Japan from the end of the world war II and the United State of America from the 1970's have achieved higher productivity, which is reflected in their economic development.

Hong Kong, South Korea, Singapore, Philippines, India, Mexico and Brazil are considered as middle-income countries. They have embraced increasing productivity schemes as an integral part of their national planning and now a days they exhibit significant status in the global industrial market *(www.cenbank.org)*.

The importance of productivity has been conceptually and empirically enriched by a number of economists. The analysis of industrial productivity is necessary one because, the higher productivity led to boostingup of economic growth and raising the standard of living of the people *(www.cenbank.org)*. In addition, (A) the study on productivity is useful to make comparison between firms with in an industry, (B) comparison with other countries, (C) measure the degree of development achieved by the industry and (D) to ensure the efficient use of inputs in the production process.

Partial factor productivity is defined as the average ratio of output to one or more of the inputs used in the production process.

(i) The labour productivity is measured in terms of output per unit of labour.

(ii) Other partial productivities such as capital productivity and material productivity are similarly defined.

The total factor productivity is the ratio of output to the aggregate measures of the inputs of all the factors of production (Anyanwu, 2000). Theoretically, this is the true measurement of productivity as it incorporates the contribution of all the factor inputs. In other words, the total factor productivity is defined as the ratio between real product or output and real factor or input. The total factor productivity is measured as a difference between the rate of growth in value added and the rate of growth in total factor inputs.

In the productivity studies Solow(1957), has made a systematic pioneering work and it is followed by a number of studies. There are three major studies on the productivity of industrial economy of India, which were conducted by Brahamananda, P. R. (1982), Goldar, B. N. (1985), and Ahluwali, I. J. (1986).

Among them Brahamananda observes that the productivity performance during 1971-81 was worse than in the earlier two decades.

In Goldar's work showed that there was improvement in productivity performance in the post 1965 period over the pre 1965 period. The TFP growth was being positive in both the periods. Very recently (during nineties) he compared the productivity the pre and post reform periods and found slow down in the trend of the TFP growth of India's manufacturing sector in the post reform period (Golder, 2004).

Ahluwalia's concentration shows that the annual average growth of TFP changed over the period 1959 to 80, for the aggregate manufacturing range between -0.2 and 0.3 and for total intensity range between -0.3 and 0.6.

Partial Factor Productivity

Here, the partial factor productivity is analysed for the manufacturing economy of Tamil Nadu in the major fifteen industrial groups. Generally, the partial factor productivity is examined in terms of capital-output ratio and labour-output ratio.

Mathematically these are known as

$$\text{Labour Productivity} = \frac{O}{L}$$

$$\text{Capital Productivity} = \frac{O}{K}$$

Table 24 shows that the capital output ratio for different periods on various industrial groups. This table highlights that the capital productivity is fluctuating for all the industrial groups over the period under analysis. In 1980-81 the industry producing rubber, plastics, petroleum and coal was predominant in respect of capital productivity. It was replaced by leather group for the following two periods, this is due to expansion of leather and its related products in Tamil Nadu, particularly in Chennai. The beverage group was in first place with regard to capital productivity in 1995-96, it is dominated by food producing industries in 1999-2000, this could be due to rise in population and technological improvement. The four industries, such as food group, beverages, leather and textiles were holding the principal places over the study period. The industry producing basic metal, wood and wood based industry and 'other manufacturing industry' have been holding the bottom position in the capital productivity over the study period.

It is seen from Table 25 that out of fifteen manufacturing industrial groups in Tamil Nadu, the industry producing chemical and chemical products were in the apex place with respect to labour productivity over the study period. Based on the labour output ratio, the other important industries are machinery and machine tools, electrical equipments and parts, basic metal and alloy. Particularly in 1999-2000, four industry groups such as chemical and chemical products, transport equipment and parts, basic metal and alloy and machinery occupy dominant places with regard to labour productivity.

Mention should be made that the transport equipments and parts producing industry had come to a significant place (second place) from an insignificant place, This noticeable performance is revealed by the transport industry group emerging with new industries for the purpose of producing consumer care and two wheelers in and around Chennal, Salem and Namakkal. It must be noted that among the fifteen industrial groups, the industry producing wood and wood product had shown meagre labour productivity during the

Table 24

Capital Productivity of Different Types of Industry Groups in Tamil Nadu for Various Periods

Industry Group	*1980-81 Out/Cap*	*1985-86 Out/Cap*	*1989-90 Out/Cap*	*1995-96 Out/Cap*	*1999-2000 Out/Cap*
Food product	4.51	4.18	3.76	1.12	4.21
Beverages, Tobacco & Tobacco products	3.20	4.89	3.08	3.18	1.12
Textiles	2.77	2.54	2.78	2.45	2.31
Wood & Wood products	2.68	1.82	2.95	2.15	1.95
Paper & Paper products	1.92	1.94	2.07	1.19	1.81
Leather & Leather products	4.91	6.48	3.98	2.64	3.21
Rubber, Plastics, Petroleum &Coal products	8.70	3.26	3.37	1.81	2.48
Chemical & Chemical products	2.10	1.28	1.69	1.41	1.59
Non-Metallic & Mineral products	1.75	1.85	1.76	1.84	2.72
Basic Metal & Alloy products	1.58	1.49	1.77	1.61	1.66
Metal products & parts	1.76	1.54	1.69	2.03	2.72
Machinery & Machine Tools	2.37	1.98	2.49	3.16	1.94
Electrical Equipments & Parts	3.60	2.97	2.77	2.68	2.43
Transport Equipments & Parts	2.12	2.15	2.11	2.62	1.29
Other Manufacturing industries	2.46	2.36	1.86	1.23	1.89

Source: Computed from ASI data.
Note: Out-Output, Cap-Capital.

Table 25

Labour Productivity of Different Types of Industry Groups in Tamil Nadu for Various Periods

Industry Group	*1980-81 Out/Lab*	*1985-86 Out / Lab*	*1990-91 Out / Lab*	*1995-96 Out / Lab*	*1999-2000 Out / Lab*
Food product	1.82	3.09	4.06	5.05	7.74
Beverages, Tobacco & Tobacco products	1.91	3.44	5.24	9.05	7.29
Textiles	1.76	2.05	3.07	4.04	6.03
Wood & Wood products	0.73	0.77	1.39	1.11	4.90
Paper & Paper products	2.05	2.56	5.14	5.38	4.84
Leather & Leather products	3.60	3.48	3.86	2.87	4.98
Rubber, Plastics, Petroleum &Coal products	3.81	4.69	3.08	4.15	6.10
Chemical & Chemical products	15.25	18.26	21.02	20.04	36.83
Non-Metallic & Mineral products	2.64	4.25	5.11	6.39	7.94
Basic Metal & Alloy products	3.08	5.40	8.61	9.11	12.75
Metal products & parts	1.89	2.59	4.39	4.09	7.94
Machinery & Machine Tools	3.87	5.29	7.22	10.01	10.03
Electrical Equipments & Parts	3.55	4.07	6.20	6.55	8.78
Transport Equipments & Parts	2.69	3.29	4.85	7.54	15.75
Other Manufacturing industries	1.89	4.11	6.61	6.21	6.42

Source: Computed from ASI data

Note: Out- Output, Lab- Labour.

study period. This may be due to technological upliftment in the wood and its related industries.

To understand the year to year growth of both labour and capital productivity in the industrial economy of Tamil Nadu, annual average growth rate has been calculated for the study period of 20 years and the result is presented in the following Table 26.

Table 26

Annual Average Growth Rates of Partial Factor Productivities in Tamil Nadu

Year	*O/L*	*AAGR*	*O/K*	*AAGR*
1980-81	2.736	0.000	2.810	0.000
1981-82	3.029	10.704	2.757	-1.863
1982-83	3.232	6.714	2.924	6.048
1983-84	2.968	-8.153	2.044	-30.097
1984-85	3.352	12.913	2.297	12.364
1985-86	3.703	10.479	2.234	-2.722
1986-87	3.965	7.070	2.394	7.145
1987-88	4.056	2.290	2.412	0.775
1988-89	4.419	8.973	2.195	-8.995
1989-90	4.720	6.811	2.348	6.958
1990-91	4.596	-2.641	2.455	4.549
1991-92	4.983	8.424	2.259	-7.990
1992-93	4.949	-0.672	2.353	4.168
1993-94	4.969	0.396	2.274	-3.360
1994-95	5.390	8.477	2.212	-2.705
1995-96	5.631	4.464	1.899	-14.145
1996-97	5.918	5.089	1.864	-1.847
1997-98	6.499	9.822	2.150	15.336
1998-99	5.989	-7.843	1.283	-40.314
1999-2000	8.308	38.717	2.104	63.935
X	4.671	6.423	2.264	0.381

Source: Computed from ASI Data.
Note: O-Output, L-Labour, K-Capital and AAGR-Annual Average Growth Rate.

In Table 26 output-labour ratio and output-capital ratio have been presented. It is observed that the output labour ratio in the industrial economy of Tamil Nadu had increased from 1980-81 to 1999-2000 with an average of 4.7 for this period. In contrast, the output capital ratio had been fluctuating over the same period with the value of 2 to 3 and it averaged 2.3. Here, it should be mentioned that the labour productivity is higher than the capital productivity. Similar inference was found by Rao (1989) at Andhra Pradesh, Vysaulu & Kumar(1997) at Orissa and Goldar (1985), Chaudhrui (2002) at all India level. The good performance in the labour productivity is could be attributed by technological improvements, introduction of process and product innovation and managerial skills (DEAR, 1997-98). Considering the annual average growth rate, the labour productivity recorded 6.4 per cent of growth over the study period, while capital productivity revealed a scanty growth of 0.38 per cent for the same period.

Out of twenty-year period, the labour productivity showed a negative growth for just four years, but the capital productivity revealed the negative growth for ten year period. This negative growth for the number of years may be due to the fluctuating role played by the industry groups like paper and paper products and leather and its related industry.

The following trend lines clearly pronounce the productivity of both labor and capital for the study period.

Total Factor Productivity

The partial factor productivity is computed to understand the nature of factor use pattern in the industrial economy of Tamil

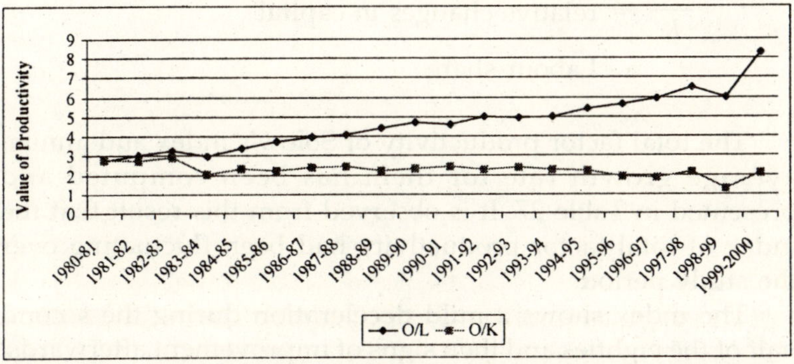

Figure 3: Trend of Labour and Capital Productivity over the Study Period

Nadu during 1980-81 to 1999-2000. But these partial productivity ratios may exhibit diverse movements over time and it is often necessary to have a composite measure (Subramanian, 1992). Total factor productivity is one such measure.

Economists like Ahluwalia, Golder, Brahamananda, Burange, Balakrishnan, have used a number of models to assess the total factor productivity in the industrial economy.

Solow has given a pioneering and systematic work and a number of studies have followed this method. Hence Solow's index of total factor productivity has been constructed for this study by using the formula.

$$\left(\frac{\Delta A}{A}\right)_t = \left(\frac{\Delta V}{V}\right)_t - at\left(\frac{\Delta L}{L}\right)_t - (1 - at)\left(\frac{\Delta K}{K}\right)_t$$

where $\frac{\Delta A}{A}$ = relative changes in productivity

$\frac{\Delta V}{V}$ = relative changes in value added

$\frac{\Delta L}{L}$ = relative changes in labour

$\frac{\Delta K}{K}$ = relative changes in capital

a = Labour share

The total factor productivity of Solow's index and annual average growth rate for them has been computed and presented in Table 27. It is observed from this result that the index of total factor productivity had been fluctuating over the study period.

The index shows a mild deceleration during the second half of the eighties and then signs of improvement afterwards. Where as, during second part of nineties it exhibited fluctuations. The index of total factor productivity averaged 99 over the study period.

Table 27
Solow's Index of Total Factor Productivity in Tamil Nadu

Year	*Solow's Index*	*AAGR*
1980-81	100.00	0.00
1981-82	102.20	2.20
1982-83	108.21	5.88
1983-84	81.59	-24.60
1984-85	90.66	11.12
1985-86	92.13	1.62
1986-87	98.26	6.65
1987-88	99.50	1.26
1988-89	96.89	-2.62
1989-90	103.16	6.47
1990-91	105.37	2.15
1991-92	103.07	-2.19
1992-93	105.67	2.53
1993-94	103.49	-2.07
1994-95	104.55	1.03
1995-96	96.76	-7.45
1996-97	97.25	0.50
1997-98	109.16	12.25
1998-99	74.57	-31.69
1999-200	104.30	39.87
X	98.84	1.21

Source: Computed from ASI Data.
Note: AAGR-Annual Average Growth Rate.

Considering the annual average growth rate, maximum growth was witnessed in 1999-2000, and it revealed negative growth for six years period. The Solow's index of industrial economy of Tamil Nadu showed 1.2 per cent annual average growth for the study period of 1980-81 to 1999-2000. Here it should be mentioned that the growth rate of total factor productivity in the manufacturing sector of other countries (both developed and developing) are above 2 per cent (Goldar, 1985). But in case of Tamil Nadu the growth rate is very meagre, it should be improved.

The reason for the above mentioned trend that the under utilization of capacity, shortages of fuels, materials, spares of power, inadequacies of network of transport and communication, and disturbed industrial relations. The above mentioned factors was gained support from the study done by Golder (1985), he underlined that the these factors are significant in affecting industrial productive.

The following trend line clearly pronounces the total factor productivity for the study period.

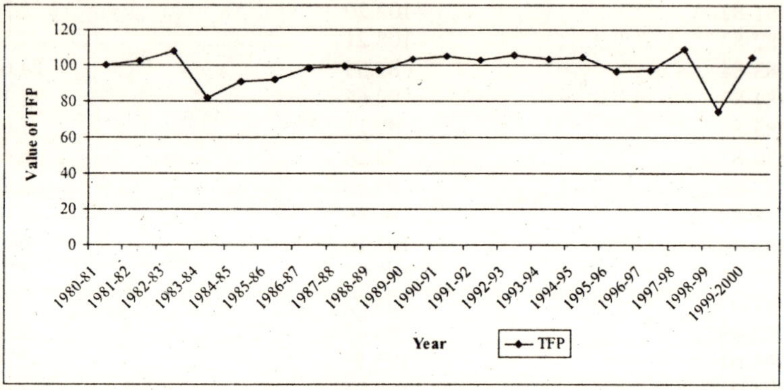

Figure 4: Trend Total Factor Productivity over the Study Period

Growth Performance of Industrial Economy of Tamil Nadu

Studies on the industrial economy of India and various states have been conducted by a number of authors and they concentrated on several dimensions. Most of the studies have used the growth rate as an indicator to understand the performance of industrial economy. In addition to this UNCTAD (2001), underlined that there is a strong correlation between the industrial growth and industrial structural changes.

From the light of the previous studies the growth rate has been computed to understand the performance of the industrial economy of Tamil Nadu for the period from 1980-81- to 1999-2000. The annual compound growth rates have been worked out for different types of industries (15 two digit industrial groups). For this intension the principal factors include number of factories, productive capital, number of persons employed, value of output and value added have been taken. The result of the different types of industries has been presented in the following Table 28.

It is observed from Table 28 that the non-metallic mineral industry attained predominant increase in terms of number of factories, followed by rubber, plastics, petroleum and coal products, chemical and chemical producing industries and 'other manufacturing industries'. In the case of investment the 'other manufacturing industry' is in dominating position. The other industries such as beverages, tobacco and tobacco products, rubber, plastics, petroleum and coal products and transport equipments and parts have important places with regard to investment.

Table 28
Compound Growth Rate of Different Types of Industries for the Entire Period [1980-81 to 1999-2000]

Industry Groups	*Number of Factories*	*Productive Capital*	*Employ-ment*	*Value of Output*	*Value Added*
Food Products	1.7	7.3	-0.4	6.9	5.4
Beverages, Tobacco & Tobacco Products	-0.8	13.1	0.3	7.3	9.8
Textiles	4.1	9.0	1.7	8.0	6.0
Wood & Wood Products	-3.3	7.2	-4.1	5.6	3.8
Paper & Paper Products	3.1	7.5	2.6	7.2	7.3
Leather & Leather products	4.1	8.3	4.3	6.0	9.5
Rubber, Plastic, Petroleum & Coal Products	4.8	12.9	3.2	6.0	11.0
Chemical & Chemical Products	4.7	9.4	3.7	7.8	9.9
Non-Metallic Mineral Products	5.5	4.7	1.6	6.9	8.5
Basic Metal & Alloy Products	-2.3	4.8	-4.4	5.1	1.4
Metal Products & Parts	2.7	7.9	2.9	10.0	10.3
Machinery & Machine Tools	3.6	5.8	0.2	4.8	5.6
Electrical Equipments & Parts	3.2	7.6	0.1	5.5	5.4
Transport Equipment & Parts	0.6	9.7	-1.8	7.1	7.2
Other Manufacturing Industries	4.4	14.5	7.1	12.96	13.9

Source: Calculated from ASI data, Various Issues
Note: Productive Capital, Output and Value Added are monetary terms Factories and Number of Persons Employed are in Numbers.

During the study period, the industrial groups producing food and food products, wood and wood products, basic metal and alloy products and transport equipments and parts registered negative growth in respect of employment. Only the other manufacturing industries revealed higher growth of 7 per cent.

Among the fifteen-industry groups, other manufacturing industry experienced the significant growth in the case of output, followed by metal products and parts, textiles and chemical and chemical producing industries.

With regard to value added also, other manufacturing industry registered a predominant place. The industries producing rubber, plastics, petroleum and coal products, metal products and parts chemical and chemical products, beverages tobacco and tobacco products, leather and leather products achieved noticeable (10%) growth. In addition the inter-industry difference with respect to growth does exist. Similar result was reached by Balakrishana,P & M.Sureshbabu(2003) in the two digit groups at all India level during 1973-74 to 1999-2000.

Agro and Non-Agro related Industries

The manufacturing industries are classified under the two heads viz agro and non-agro related industries. In the two digit groups, the agro related industries covered from 20-21 to 29 where as, the non-agro related industries are embodied remaining all industries (30 to 38). The annual average growth rates have been used to understand the growth of these industries for the pre and post reform periods.

In 1980-81 the agro-related industrial group registered 46.5 per cent of value added, the modern industries accounted for 53.5 per cent of value added. In 1999-2000, the proportion of agro-related industries declined to 43.7 per cent and the proportion of modern groups improved to 56.3 per cent with respect of value added. Considering the employment generation, the agro-related industries accounted for 59 per cent and modern industries provided 40.9 per cent in 1980-81. It is to be mentioned that in 1999-2000 also the employment generation of agro related and non-agro related industries are more or less static in the same place (They are reported in Table 4.1 and 4.5). A similar study was conducted by Burange(1999), and he underlined that the share of agricultural related industries with regard to fixed capital, employment, value of output and value added decreased substantially over the study period of 1979-80 to 1994-95. Ironically, the non-agro related industries went up; this is a common phenomenon that during the course of economic development the non-agro based industries came forward with regard to principal characteristics.

Table 29
Annual Average Growth Rates of Agro and Non-Agro Industries in Tamil Naud During 1980-81 to 1999-2000

Characteristics	*Agro-Based*	*Non-Agro-Based*
Factories	3.25	3.62
Productive Capital	10.07	10.90
Employment	1.98	1.85
Value of Output	8.14	7.95
Value Added	7.96	23.57

Source: Computed from ASI data.
Note: Productive Capital, Output and Value Added are monetary terms Factories and Number of Persons Employed are in Numbers.

Considering the result of annual average growth rate, the criterion viz number of factories, productive capital and employment are nearly the same for both agro and non-agro related industries. Surprisingly, the growth rate of output of agro-related industries is slightly higher than that of non- agro related industries. But in respect of value added the non- agro related industries revealed dramatic growth. This growth is aided by the hastening growth of chemical and chemical producing industries, transport equipment and parts and metal producing industries.

Growth Rates of Productive Capital and Employment for Different Periods in Manufacturing of Tamil Nadu

After analyzing the growth pattern of different group of industries in Tamil Nadu, it is necessary to assess the growth rate of two important variables such as productive capital and employment. For this intension, the annual compound growth rates for these two characteristics are computed for different periods.

Table 30
Compound Growth Rates of Productive Capital and Employment

Year	*Productive Capital*	*Employment*
1980-81 to 1984-85	9.74	0.69
1985-86 to 1989-90	5.37	1.45
1990-91 to 1994-95	9.1	5.4
1995-96 to 1999-2000	2.8	-3.14
1980-81 to 1999-2000	8.55	1.28

Source: Calculated from ASI data, Various Issues.

Table 30 shows that there is a fluctuating trend in the growth of productive capital for four different phases. The growth of employment has been increased up to the third phase, since then it slipped down. During the last phase, the productive capital registered 2.8 per cent and the employment growth reveled negative value of -3.14 per cent for the same period. The negative growth in the employment for the second half of the nineties is definitely due to the impact of new economic policy. After the introduction of economic reform, in most of the industries the concentration of labour is replaced by the accumulation of capital. Similarly, the same result was realized by Nagaraj and Balakrishnan at all India level.

The annual compound growth rate for entire period accounted 8.5 per cent in respect of productive capital and 1.28 per cent in the case of employment.

These two variables such as capital and employment are normalized (calculated capital per unit and employment per unit) and the hypothesis is framed to test the relationship between the growth of capital per unit and employment per unit and to find out the dominant factor in respect of growth.

The following are null and alternative hypothesis:

Null hypothesis: There is no significant difference between the growth of capital and employment.

Alternative hypothesis: There is a significant difference between the growth of capital and employment.

First of all, the correlation co-efficient is calculated for capital and employment, which yields the result that both the variables are correlated at 47 per cent. That means when the capital increases at 100 per cent employment increases at 47 per cent.

Table 31
Correlation and 't'-test Results-Growth Difference Between Employment and Capital

	Correlation Co-efficients GEMPL
GCAPIT	.4788 (19) P = .038

't'- test for independent samples

Variable	*Number of Cases*	*Mean*	*SD*	*SE of Mean*
GCAPIT GR Capital P/U				
GR capi P/U	19	6.9232	16.361	3.753
GR employer P/U	19	-1.2211	10.235	2.348

Mean Difference = 8.1442
Levene's Test for Equality of Variances: F= 5.947 P= .020.

To test the significance between these two variables the independent sample 't' test has been applied, which shows that there is significant difference between these two variables at 5 per cent level of significance. This implies that the factor capital have experienced higher growth than that of employment. Hence *this experiment dose not supports the null hypothesis*. This trend clearly explains that the industrial structure switched over from labour intensive to capital intensive.

GROWTH PERFORMANCE OF USE AND INPUT BASED INDUSTRIES

Use-based Industries

The growth and structural changes in the factory sector of Tamil Nadu may be advocated on the basis of use and input based classification. For this purpose the three digit (four digits after 1998) level data are classified on the basis of use-based and input based categories.

The annual compound growth rate has been treated to understand the nature of growth performance in the different groups of industries such as Basic goods, Capital goods, Intermediary goods, Consumer-durable goods and Consumer non-durable goods. With regard to the number of factories the capital good industries recorded a steady growth for all the sub periods. The consumer durable good industries revealed negative growth after first half of 1980s.

Table 32
Annual Compound Growth Rate of Number of Factories (U.B)

Year	*Basic*	*Capital*	*Inter-mediary*	*Consumer Durable*	*Consumer Non-Durable*
1980-81 to 1984-85	5.13	6.49	2.14	3.92	3.33
1985-86 to 1989-90	-0.61	8.68	-2.28	-5.47	2.76
1990-91 to 1994-95	6.42	12.18	3.13	-1.62	5.79
1995-96 to 1999-2000	6.19	18.45	3.63	-1.04	1.85
1980-81 to 1990-91	-1.15	5.31	1.40	1.72	3.44
1991-92 to 1999-2000	7.91	2.01	4.35	1.04	4.26
1980-81 to 1999-2000	2.77	6.01	2.79	0.41	3.84

Source: Computed from ASI data.

While comparing the industrial growth from the eighties in to the nineties the basic goods industry surged forward, intermediary and consumer durable industries shown moderate growth. The capital good industries registered a higher growth during the 20 year study period. This appreciable growth is due to the starting up of some basic industries such as organic and inorganic chemicals and generation and transmission of electric energy for house hold, industries and commercial centers.

Table 33 shows the changes in the growth of productive capital by manufacturing of major industry groups in 1980s and 1990s. Considering the four sub periods, all the industries have shown the fluctuating trend of growth, except the capital good industries. The capital good industries revealed a steady growth with respect to productive capital; this is due to the emerging of new industries during this period. During the second phase of 1990s the industrial groups such as basic goods, consumer durable and non-durables exhibited negative growth due to dominant growth recorded by the other industry group such as capital and followed by intermediate goods.

Table 33
Annual Compound Growth Rate of Productive Capital (U.B)

Year	*Basic*	*Capital*	*Inter-mediary*	*Consumer Durable*	*Consumer Non-Durable*
1980-81 to 1984-85	-1.72	9.14	14.55	10.09	4.54
1985-86 to 1989-90	3.02	9.92	-8.18	-3.39	12.38
1990-91 to 1994-95	5.74	12.13	17.37	3.62	16.12
1995-96 to 1999-2000	-5.39	21.47	9.47	-3.67	-9.89
1980-81 to 1990-91	5.61	8.08	-0.32	7.46	16.57
1991-92 to 1999-2000	-1.09	4.32	14.76	1.67	2.65
1980-81 to 1999-2000	2.79	9.63	6.19	4.86	11.87

Source: Computed from ASI data

During the eighties the consumer non-durable good industries recorded impressive growth of nearly 17 per cent. But in the nineties it was replaced by intermediary groups, which exhibits maximum growth of 15 per cent. Considering all through the study period, the consumer non-durable industrial group has shown higher growth in productive capital. In the consumer non-durable group industries producing drugs and medicines, food and food products, beverages, tobacco and tobacco products and cosmetic items have recorded relatively higher growth.

The behavior of employment growth is usually a matter of interest second only to that of output (Balakrishnal, P. & Suresh Babu, 2003). Based on the employment generation, no one industrial group reveals continuous growth during the period of study. The growth of employment in the manufacturing sector of Tamil Nadu has been highly fluctuating for the sub periods of 1980s and 1990s.

When the eighties are compared with the nineties, the consumer non-durable good industry exhibits higher growth during the eighties and it got replaced by basic goods in the nineties. The growth of basic goods was influenced by the growth of industries such as cement, lime and plastic, generation and transmission of electric energy, fertilizer and pesticides. The other important industry is intermediary group, which showed 6 per cent growth during the nineties. The growth of capital good industries is negative with regard to employment during the same period. This is due to the fact that the industries under this group were capital intensive. The basic good industries exhibit higher growth of 6.44 per cent for the entire study period also. Even though, the employment in basic goods has grown much high when compared to capital goods, considering the growth of productive capital the employment generation is low.

Table 34
Annual Compound Growth Rates of Employment (U.B)

Year	*Basic*	*Capital*	*Inter-mediary*	*Consumer Durable*	*Consumer Non-Durable*
1980-81 to 1984-85	-0.68	3.51	1.91	2.71	-1.39
1985-86 to 1989-90	1.81	-5.72	-10.43	-8.39	9.65
1990-91 to 1994-95	-1.52	8.67	2.88	-2.29	3.77
1995-96 to 1999-2000	8.3	1.43	6.09	-6.62	-4.88
1980-81 to 1990-91	-0.63	2.81	-4.15	-0.53	5.52
1991-92 to 1999-2000	16.41	-3.52	6.37	-2.44	-0.1
1980-81 to 1999-2000	6.44	1.06	0.67	-1.71	2.39

Source: Computed from ASI data.

In terms of the value of output, the basic goods industries reveal 7 per cent growth during the first phase of 1980s, but it exhibits negative growth of 8 per cent in the second phase, while the consumer-non durable group showed an appreciable growth of nearly 13 per cent during this period. Considering the first half of the nineties the basic good was in dominating position with regard to output growth, but in the second half the intermediary group revealed higher growth of 17 per cent. The improvement in the output during the 1990s has been attributed to improvement in public sector investment and public sector performance during the second phase of 1980s.

The consumer non-durable group was in a predominant place with respect to the growth of output during the eighties. But in the nineties, the intermediary group had shown an impressive growth of 13 per cent. This is due to reduction in import duties leading to better access of capital equipments; it led to phenomenal growth during the post reform period.

Table 35
Annual Compound Growth Rates of Value of Output (U.B)

Year	*Basic*	*Capital*	*Inter-mediary*	*Consumer Durable*	*Consumer Non-Durable*
1980-81 to 1984-85	7.01	5.32	5.42	4.63	3.68
1985-86 to 1989-90	-7.72	5.52	-10.88	-7.66	12.61
1990-91 to 1994-95	17.99	13.13	12.99	1.67	7.99
1995-96 to 1999-2000	6.74	10.82	16.98	5.22	-0.13
1980-81 to 1990-91	4.02	7.53	-6.87	6.92	15.05
1991-92 to 1999-2000	6.87	4.07	13.19	10.39	3.59
1980-81 to 1999-2000	5.86	8.15	5.27	6.56	10.19

Source: Computed from ASI data.

The growth of output of consumer non-durable group was relatively high in the study period, followed by capital, consumer non-durable and basic goods industries. They hasten the growth of sub groups of consumer non durable goods such as food and food products, beverages, tobacco and tobacco products and cosmetic items (such as perfumes, lotions, hair dressings, tooth pastes, soap in any form, synthetic, detergents, shampoos, cleaners, washing and scoring products and others) was the reason for an impressive growth of consumer non-durable goods.

The Growth of industrial sector of India was calculated by Uma Kapila for the period of twenty years starting from 1980-81, she underlined that the consumer durable goods industries have experienced higher growth of nearly eleven per cent during the pre reform period and it was maintained in the post reform period also.

Table 36
Compound Growth Rate in the Industrial Sector 1980-2000.(U.B)
[AAGR for Index of Industrial Production]

Industry Groups	*1980-81 to 1991-92*	*1992-93 to 1999-2000*
Basic	7.4	6.1
Capital	9.4	5.9
Intermediate	4.9	9.1
Consumer Durable	10.8	11.2
Consumer Non-Durable	5.3	5.1

Source: Uma Kapila, p. 362.

But the trend in this state of Tamil Nadu is different with regard to output. In Tamil Nadu, the consumer non-durable goods recorded higher growth during the pre-reform period and this group is dominated by intermediary during the post reform period (See Table 36).

Table 37

Annual Compound Growth Rates of Value Added (U.B)

Year	*Basic*	*Capital*	*Inter-mediary*	*Consumer Durable*	*Consumer Non-Durable*
1980-81 to 1984-85	7.54	9.64	2.84	3.23	6.99
1985-86 to 1989-90	-2.01	0.51	-9.72	-11.32	13.42
1990-91 to 1994-95	12.32	14.51	8.44	-0.29	5.06
1995-96 to 1999-2000	5.89	13.47	12.38	5.62	4.17
1980-81 to 1990-91	4.47	7.24	-3.33	2.71	18.36
1991-92 to 1999-2000	9.48	6.40	11.26	9.07	4.61
1980-81 to 1999-2000	6.36*	8.81	3.91	3.45	9.91

Source: Computed from ASI data.

Considering the value added, by use-based groups, the capital goods recorded nearly10 per cent growth of value added from 1980-81 to 1985-86. During the second half of the eighties, the consumer-non durable registered 13 per cent growth. But, over the 1990s the capital goods group was in a dominant position. Similar study carried out by Chaudhuri (2002) found that more than half the growth is contributed by consumer goods between 1990-91 and 1997-98. The contribution of consumer durable alone is 16.09 per cent. Basic and intermediate goods have accounted for only 16.34 per cent and capital goods 11.8 per cent. Further he observed during the 1980s, that the contribution of capital goods was somewhat higher than that of consumer durable.

Comparing the eighties with the nineties, the consumer non-durable group registered the highest growth in the eighties, but the intermediary group registered considerable growth in nineties. The consumer durable goods revealed meagre growth in the nineties. This was due to the reduction in the value added of fabricated metal products (such as metal cans from tin-plate, terne plate or enameled sheet metal, containers barrels, drums, kegs, pails, safes, vaulets, enameled sanitary and all other fabricated metal products).

Considering the overall growth of the industrial groups, the consumer non-durable registered 10 per cent growth. This considerable growth was due to higher growth of the sub sector of consumer non-durable group such as food and food products, drugs and medicines cosmetic items and matches.

Input Based Industries

The annual compound growth rate has also been obtained to understand the growth of input-based manufacturing sector in Tamil Nadu during 1980s and 1990s. The input based industry has been classified in to three sub-groups such as agro based, metal based and chemical based. It is observed from Table 38 that during the first phase of 1980s the agro-based and chemical-based industries accounted for equal growth (nearly 4 per cent) in respect of the number of factories and the metal-based industries accounted for less than 2 per cent growth.

Owing to restriction on hazardous chemicals in the second part of 1980s, chemical-based industries revealed negative growth of 7.6 per cent. But it reached higher growth-during the period 1995-96 to 1999-2000. The chemical-based industries recorded 13.4 per cent growth. This is due to improvement of matches industry in the southern districts. Moreover, sizable amount of petrochemicals and other chemicals are used for textiles, paper, leather and allied industries.

Table 38
Annual Compound Growth Rate of Number of Factories (I.B)

Year	*Agro-Based*	*Metal-Based*	*Chemical-Based*
1980-81 to 1984-85	3.81	1.20	3.71
1985-86 to 1989-90	1.09	0.99	-7.56
1990-91 to 1994-95	7.52	4.16	1.58
1995-96 to 1999-2000	1.75	3.20	13.50
1980-81 to 1990-91	1.92	2.87	0.81
1991-92 to 1999-2000	2.78	2.93	8.78
1980-81 to 1999-2000	3.43	3.12	3.78

Source: Computed from ASI data.

Considering the eighties and nineties, the chemical-based industries recorded nearly 9 per cent growth in the nineties. There has been a constant growth of 3 per cent (little higher in chemical-based) recorded by the input based industries during the study period with respect to the number of factories.

Based on the productive capital, chemical-based industries recorded 7 per cent growth in the first phase of 1980s, but it slipped down in the second phase of 1980s by -6.32 per cent of growth, because the chemical-based industries lost a (hazard chemicals) number of industries, which led to a decrease in its productive capital also. For the following two sub periods of 1990s all the industrial groups have recorded positive growth. This growth rate is higher in the chemical-based industries. This positive trend of chemical-based industries is mainly due to increase in particular industries such as petrochemicals, photochemical, and chemicals used to pharmaceuticals.

Table 39
Annual Compound Growth Rates of Productive Capital (I.B).

Year	*Agro-Based*	*Metal-Based*	*Chemical-Based*
1980-81 to 1984-85	4.60	4.60	6.80
1985-86 to 1989-90	5.02	-5.33	-6.32
1990-91 to 1994-95	1.60	9.30	15.50
1995-96 to 1999-2000	6.01	7.02	14.94
1980-81 to 1990-91	7.42	8.63	1.32
1991-92 to 1999-2000	2.91	8.49	16.21
1980-81 to 1999-2000	6.18	8.32	9.28

Source: Computed from ASI data.

Looking at the period of eighties and nineties, the chemical-based industries recorded higher growth in the nineties towards the productive capital. It has shown 9 per cent growth over the study period. At the same time, 8 per cent and 6 per cent growth rates were recorded by metal-based and agro-based industries respectively.

The employment picture has been very dismal for the 80s and 90s in the industrial economy of India. This is also true in the case of manufacturing sector in Tamil Nadu for the study period of 1980s and 1990s.

In the industrial sector, the chemical-based industries registered nearly three per cent growth of employment for the study period. The agro-based industries show 1.22 per cent of growth, but the metal-based industries exhibit -0.44 per cent growth during the same period. The agro-based and metal-based industries accounted for less than 2 per cent growth during nineties but the chemical-based industry exhibits the negative growth of 7 per cent for the same period. During the nineties the chemical-based industries achieved nearly 16 per cent growth of employment; this is mainly due to remarkable increase in the number of chemical and related industries.

Table 40

Annual Compound Growth Rate of Employment (I.B).

Year	*Agro-Based*	*Metal-Based*	*Chemical-Based*
1980-81 to 1984-85	0.38	1.98	3.09
1985-86 to 1989-90	0.03	-1.89	-12.90
1990-91 to 1994-95	3.75	2.40	6.70
1995-96 to 1999-2000	0.34	-6.12	14.50
1980-81 to 1990-91	0.09	1.69	-7.52
1991-92 to 1999-2000	1.92	-2.13	15.61
1980-81 to 1999-2000	1.22	-0.44	2.82

Source: Computed from ASI data.

In the four sub-periods, the chemical-based industries revealed 3 per cent growth of employment during the first half of the 1980s. All the industrial groups exhibit poor performance during the second phase of 1980s. The agro-based and metal-based industries have shown fluctuating trend during 1990s, but the chemical-based industries achieved steady growth. This considerable growth is due to strong growth of sub groups of chemical industries such as petroleum products, gases, fertilizer and pesticides, drugs and medicines inedible oils and matches.

All the industrial groups-agro-based, metal-based and chemical-based have registered a positive growth over the period with respect to output. While the chemical-based industry had dominated during the first half of 1980s and in the second phase of 1980s, all the input based groups witnessed appreciable growth. This growth is aided by the change of import restriction from quotas to tariffs at very high level.

Table 41
Annual Compound Growth Rate of Value of Output (I.B).

Year	*Agro-Based*	*Metal-Based*	*Chemical-Based*
1980-81 to 1984-85	0.70	3.35	6.80
1985-86 to 1989-90	6.47	6.59	4.74
1990-91 to 1994-95	10.36	6.92	0.52
1995-96 to 1999-2000	2.96	0.94	17.10
1980-81 to 1990-91	6.23	7.92	5.23
1991-92 to 1999-2000	3.62	8.12	11.92
1980-81 to 1999-2000	5.66	7.53	8.21

Source: Computed from ASI data.

The agro-based industries exhibit 10 per cent growth in the first phase of 1990s. This growth was mainly due to the important role played by a number of industries -textile groups, food products, leather and leather products. The growth of agro-based industry was replaced by the chemical-based industry, which exhibits 17 per cent growth in the second phase of 1990s due to expansion of demand.

Comparing the periods of the eighties and the nineties, the metal-based industries exhibit higher growth during the eighties. The input based sector was dominated by chemical-based industries with 12 per cent growth during the nineties. The chemical-based industries recorded 8 per cent growth for the entire study period and metal and agro-based industries were falling subsequently. The growth of agro-based industries has been declining over the periods. *This result is corroborated by Ahluwalia, I.J. (1985),where she analyzed the industrial structure of India based on input classification and reached a conclusion that the relative share of agro-based industries had declined during the study period 1960s to 1980s, while the share of metal and chemical-based industries had been rising. This is true in the case of Tamil Nadu also.*

The pattern of industrial change has also been analyzed with respect to value added by manufacturing industries in Tamil Nadu. There had been a fluctuating growth revealed

Table 42
Annual Compound Growth Rate of Value Added (I.B).

Year	*Agro-Based*	*Metal-Based*	*Chemical-Based*
1980-81 to 1984-85	1.40	5.40	10.69
1985-86 to 1989-90	9.58	4.82	2.64
1990-91 to 1994-95	5.60	5.96	4.80
1995-96 to 1999-2000	1.89	2.29	17.91
1980-81 to 1990-91	6.49	8.19	4.82
1991-92 to 1999-2000	4.15	9.82	16.40
1980-81 to 1999-2000	4.89	7.12	9.17

Source: Computed from ASI data.

by all the industrial groups (agro based, metal based and chemical based industries) with respect to the value added. During the second phase of 1990s both the agro and metal-based industries had shown very meagre growth, while the chemical-based industries exhibited strong growth of 18 per cent with regard to value added. But during the first half of1980s the chemical industry exhibited predominant growth and it got replaced by agro-based industries during the second half of the eighties.

Here also, the growth of agro-based industries had declined from the eighties to the nineties. The other industrial groups such as metal and chemical-based industries have been recorded 9 and 7 per cent growth respectively.

The chemical-based industries exhibited remarkable growth in respect of value added during the study period. This is due to the internal and external demand and considerable growth contributed by the sub groups of chemical and chemical products such as petroleum refinery products, fertilizer and nitrogen compounds, drugs, medicines, pharmaceutical chemicals, matches and inedible oils.

EFFECT OF NEW ECONOMIC POLICY ON THE INDUSTRIAL ECONOMY OF TAMIL NADU

In the Indian economy, the introduction of New Economic Policy is considered a milestone. Economists often underlined that the effect of new economic policy on several counts on the Indian economy. It is well known that the impact occurred in the Indian economy, in a sporadic manner in all the states. The new economic policy was introduced on 24th July 1991 with special emphasis on industrial economy. The quintessence of new economic policy are (a) the importance of public sector gradually got reduced, (b) free entry of the private sector, (c) free entry of foreign capital and technology (d) no upper limit for monopoly business, and so on.

The liberalization process, in which the devaluation of rupee has enhanced the demand for exports thereby boosting the industry, the capital market reforms lead to the greater inflow of foreign exchange, the reduction in import duties led to improved access to capital equipment, dismantling of controls led to better capacity utilization, which have all a positive impact on the Indian industries. In the above context, the present section of this study seeks to answer the questions that what has been the effect of economic liberalization on industry in Tamil Nadu? and has it helped to accelerate the industrial growth?

To find answers for these questions the ASI data for the period of twenty years is divided into two parts viz. 1980-1981 to 1990-1991 to 1991-1992 to 1999-2000. The simple statistical tools like percentage share, annual compound growth rate, ratios, and total and partial factor productivities have been used.

Structural Change in Tamil Nadu (Pre and Post Reform Comparison)

It is worthwhile to compare the industrial structure from pre reform to the post reform periods in Tamil Nadu. For this purpose, the principal characteristics include number of factories, productive capital, number of persons employed, value of output and value added has chosen. All the values are available in monetary terms (except employment). These available values are averaged for two phases; the first phase covered the period form 1980-81 to 1990-91 that is pre reform period. Where as, the post reform period covered are nine years from 1991-92 to 1999-2000.

Industry wise, simple percentage shares have calculated for these different types of industry groups and the result is (separately for pre and post reform periods) presented in the following Tables 43.

The relative share of the industrial groups in the total productive capital, persons employed, value of output and value added of the industrial sector of the state of Tamil Nadu is analysed in Table 43.

Table 43
Structure of Industry in Tamil Nadu (Pre-reform Period)

Industry Group	*Factories*	*Capital*	*Employ-ment*	*Output*	*Value Added*
Food product	21.9	7.0	14.7	12.0	9.0
Beverages, Tobacco & Tobacco products	2.8	0.7	1.5	1.4	1.0
Textiles	23.6	14.8	27.3	17.4	17.8
Wood & Wood products	2.3	0.2	0.7	0.2	0.2
Paper & Paper products	6.8	5.3	4.5	3.4	3.7
Leather &Leather products	4.4	2.0	4.6	4.4	2.7
Rubber, Plastics, Petroleum & Coal products	3.1	9.0	2.6	13.8	7.3
Chemical & Chemical products	8.3	17.2	12.4	12.4	12.3
Metallic & Mineral products	3.8	5.8	3.9	3.9	4.7
Basic Metal & Alloy products	4.4	8.3	4.0	5.3	3.1
Metal products & parts	4.5	2.4	2.4	1.8	2.1
Machinery & Machine Tools	7.1	13.5	8.0	10.6	15.7
Electrical Equipments & Parts	2.8	2.8	3.0	3.4	4.9
Transport Equipments & Parts	3.3	10.2	9.7	9.2	14.4
Other Manufacturing industries	0.8	0.9	0.7	0.7	1.0

Source: Calculated from ASI data.

It is seen that textile industry is the largest group of industry in terms of number of factories, employment, value of output and value added in the pre reform period, While, with regard to productive capital alone the industry producing chemical and its sub group in a leading place. The prime reason for the distinguishing performance of the chemical based industry is due to the increase in the number of factories (in 1980-81 the number of industries producing chemical and chemical products were 783 and it increased to 1227 in 1990-91). The increase in the number of factories led to accumulate the huge amount of capital.

The other important industries are machinery and machine tools and transport equipment and parts producing industries. The above mentioned four industries alone contributed 60 per cent of value added in the factory sector during the pre liberalization period.

The contribution of all groups of industry in the manufacturing sector towards number of factories, productive capital, number of persons employed, value of output and value added for the period of post liberalization is shown in Table 44.

Table 44
Structure of Industry in Tamil Nadu (Post-reform Period)

Industry Group	*Factories*	*Capital*	*Employ-ment*	*Output*	*Value Added*
Food product	19.8	8.4	13.4	12.0	9.8
Beverages, Tobacco & Tobacco products	1.7	1.3	2.3	1.6	2.1
Textiles	28.6	17.8	29.9	23.8	23.7
Wood & Wood products	1.6	0.2	0.4	0.2	0.2
Paper & Paper products	6.3	5.7	5.1	3.4	4.5
Leather &Leather products	5.8	2.7	6.5	4.8	3.9
Rubber, Plastics, Petroleum & Coal products	3.5	9.3	2.9	9.9	8.5
Chemical & Chemical products	8.9	14.4	12.6	11.4	15.3
Metallic &Mineral products	4.2	3.6	3.6	3.3	5.7
Basic Metal & Alloy products	3.0	7.9	2.8	4.8	2.7
Metal products & parts	4.0	5.8	2.5	2.1	2.9
Machinery & Machine Tools	6.3	7.9	7.6	9.5	6.0
Electrical Equipments & Parts	2.5	2.7	2.0	3.2	3.0
Transport Equipments & Parts	2.9	10.4	7.2	8.8	9.5
Other Manufacturing industries	0.9	1.9	1.2	1.3	2.3

Source: Calculated from ASI data.

Based on the criterion of productive capital, employment, value of output and value added, textile group of industry was the foremost group in the period of post liberalization period also. The basic reasons for the dominant role played by the textile industry are the favorable climatic condition, availability of raw materials, cheep labour and internal and external demand.

The industry manufacturing chemical and chemical products and food producing industries are the other biggest industries in the post reform period. With regard to employment the industry producing textiles, food products, and chemical and chemical groups together generated 56 per cent during the same period.

Eight industry groups such as, food products, wood products, non-metallic minerals, basic metal and alloy, machinery and machine tools, electrical equipments and parts, transport and other manufacturing industry provided 45 per cent of employment during the pre reform period and it down turned to 38 per cent during the post reform period. It is globally accepted that in the third world countries like India the employment generation plays a vital role in all walks of human life. But in the case of Tamil Nadu, employment trend has come down, this is not only due to technological upgradation in these industries but also the closing down of many polluting industries to save the environment (take for example the basic metal and alloy industry accounted for 568 in 1991-92 and it decreased to 318 in 1999-2000).

Structural Ratio for Pre and Post Reform Periods in Tamil Nadu

A comparative study of the structural ratio during the pre-liberalization and post-liberalization periods shows marked up trend in the value added per factory and value added per employee in all groups except machinery and machine tools, electrical equipments and rubber group. Output per factory and output per employee have increased significantly in all industries except rubber group. The productive capital per factory has increased in all the groups. Its increase is significant in the case of beverages, paper, chemical, basic metal and alloy, metal products, electrical equipments, transport equipment and other manufacturing industries.

With regard to employment per factory, no single industry exhibited continuous up trend over the study period. In the industrial composition, most of the industries had declining employment per factory during post liberalization period.

It is observed from the (industry wise comparison between pre and post reform periods) structural analysis that there are some noticeable differences across the industries over the study periods. It is found that the structural ratios are relatively meager during the pre reform periods and increased significantly for the post reform period and registered a

Table 45
Ratio Analysis for Pre and Post Reform Periods [A]

Industry Group	*OUT/ FAC*	*PC/ EMP*	*PC/ FA*	*VAD/ FA*	*EMP/ FA*	*VAD/ EMP*	*OUT/ EMP*
Food product							
Pre-Reform	99.70	0.35	24.00	14.64	73.70	0.22	1.46
Post-Reform	165.08	0.82	58.47	23.86	72.68	0.32	2.28
Beverages, Tobacco							
Pre-Reform	113.56	0.36	24.42	15.60	64.86	0.23	1.67
Post-Reform	255.47	1.23	102.10	58.45	134.15	0.69	3.08
Textiles							
Pre-Reform	155.13	0.38	55.00	30.45	147.26	0.21	1.06
Post-Reform	235.85	0.77	91.80	42.26	117.51	0.36	2.01
Wood & Wood products							
Pre-Reform	14.43	0.17	5.92	3.21	34.77	0.09	0.43
Post-Reform	38.27	0.49	18.40	7.64	33.33	0.18	1.05
Paper & Paper products							
Pre-Reform	93.66	0.82	60.29	20.36	74.64	0.28	1.27
Post-Reform	148.81	1.43	127.18	34.40	89.71	0.45	1.96
Leather & Leather products							
Pre-Reform	189.58	0.30	34.91	21.81	116.52	0.19	1.63
Post-Reform	227.81	0.55	66.20	33.40	121.45	0.28	1.90
Rubber, Plast, Petr & Coal pro							
Pre-Reform	853.43	2.34	223.26	84.01	98.43	0.88	8.74
Post-Reform	763.60	4.18	366.51	115.69	87.89	1.33	8.73
Chemical& Chemical products							
Pre-Reform	286.97	0.97	162.32	56.84	169.12	0.34	1.71
Post-Reform	350.10	1.45	223.66	82.23	155.41	0.53	2.27

Note: Out/Fac = Output per Factory. PC/Emp = Productive capital per Employee, PC/Fa =Productive Capital per Factory, Vad/Fa = Value Added per Factory, Emp/Fa =Employment per Factory, Vad/Emp = Value Added per Employee, Out/Emp = Output per Employee.

Note: Productive Capital, Output and Value Added are monetary terms Factories and Number of Persons Employed are in Numbers.

Source: Computed from ASI data, Various Issues.

marked increase. In particular, capital per factory and capital per employee have increased significantly during the post reform period more than that of pre reform period, this trend is witnessed the capital intensity in the industrial economy of Tamil Nadu. In the industrial composition, the transport group is predominant industry with respect to output per factory, productive capital per factory, value added per factory and value added per employee for the study period. In most of the

Table 46
Ratio Analysis for Pre and Post Reform Periods [B]

Industry Group	*OUT/ FAC*	*PC/ EMP*	*PC/ FA*	*VAD/ FA*	*EMP/ FA*	*VAD/ EMP*	*OUT/ EMP*
Non-Metallic & Mineral products							
Pre-Reform	199.28	1.04	119.76	47.16	123.94	0.40	1.70
Post-Reform	211.65	1.57	120.75	64.88	90.95	0.77	2.41
Basic Metal & Alloy products							
Pre-Reform	242.35	1.49	155.44	27.95	105.87	0.26	2.34
Post-Reform	460.83	3.99	417.29	46.49	101.59	0.47	4.69
Metal products & parts							
Pre-Reform	74.55	0.68	41.18	17.27	62.16	0.28	1.22
Post-Reform	142.26	2.46	204.27	34.95	67.29	0.49	2.00
Machinery & Machine Tools							
Pre-Reform	284.29	1.18	147.95	80.19	129.53	0.64	2.24
Post-Reform	409.47	1.37	174.68	46.21	129.27	0.45	3.17
Electrical Equipments & Parts							
Pre-Reform	231.28	0.67	79.01	65.49	121.66	0.55	1.93
Post-Reform	356.98	1.75	150.14	57.96	86.20	0.72	4.18
Transport Equipments & Parts							
Pre-Reform	540.73	0.74	250.91	164.75	346.47	0.48	1.60
Post-Reform	866.79	2.09	532.06	167.54	267.07	0.64	3.29
Other Manufacturing							
Pre-Reform	164.01	0.83	84.07	49.24	98.51	0.50	1.63
Post-Reform	410.09	2.06	293.35	118.24	143.45	0.82	2.86

Note: Out/Fac = Output per Factory. PC/Emp = Productive capital per Employee, PC/Fa =Productive Capital per Factory, Vad/Fa = Value Added per Factory, Emp/Fa =Employment per Factory, Vad/Emp = Value Added per Employee, Out/Emp = Output per Employee.

Note: Productive Capital, Output and Value Added are monetary terms Factories and Number of Persons Employed are in Numbers.

Source: Computed from ASI data, Various Issues.

industries the employment generation revealed a decelerating trend, particularly in the post reform periods. Similar result is observed by studies conducted by Nagaraj, Venkataramaiah, Burange Deb, Upendranadh and *et. al*, and Thangamuthu at all India level and various states.

Growth Rate of Principal Characteristics in Tamil Nadu

To understand performance of industrial economy, a number of studies have been handled, among them Nagarag, Chautheri, Burange, Kalipada Deb, Deepak Nayyar, Venkataramaiah, calculated the growth rate for different types of industries of various regions.

In the light of their research work, the annual average growth rate has been computed to understand the growth performance of different types of industries in Tamil Nadu. It is very clear that the analysis of annual average growth varied widely for different principal characteristics in Tamil Nadu. The number of industries reveals 3.78 per cent of growth over 21 years ending with 1999-2000, which registered 3.76 per cent in pre liberalization period and increased marginally in the post liberalization period. The productive capital and employment accounted for 8.2 and 1.8 per cent growth respectively by 1979-1980 to 1999-2000. They decreased to 6.39 and 1.73 in post liberalization period from 9.68 and 1.87 to the pre-reform era respectively.

The value of output and value added registered 7.46 and 6.57 per cent respectively for the study period. The sum of value of output was 7.35 per cent during pre-liberalization period and decreased marginally in the post-liberalized period. The value added slipped down from 8.45 per cent to 4.26 per cent for the above referred periods. To sum up, all the characteristics revealed a down turn trend in the post reform period, except a marginal increase shown by the number of factories and value of output with regard to annual average growth rate.

Growth Rate of Principal Characteristics in India

It is relevant to calculate the annual average for the principal characteristics in the industrial economy of all India too.

Table 47
Growth Rates of Some Principal Characteristics in Tamil Nadu

Year	*Num. of Fac.*	*Pro. Cap.*	*Employment*	*Output*	*Value add*
1979-80	0	0	0	0	0
1980-81	4.90	-2.19	1.26	-0.59	-4.05
1981-82	6.22	23.03	3.39	14.35	10.58
1982-83	3.39	-9.44	-0.47	9.06	14.63
1983-84	5.44	14.41	-0.69	-3.36	1.00
1984-85	9.72	65.42	8.05	12.54	21.06
1985-86	-4.95	-13.66	-2.47	10.09	-3.76
1986-87	1.50	-4.72	-1.10	5.74	6.99
1987-88	4.57	4.98	4.57	7.13	-1.32
1988-89	-0.71	25.54	1.18	9.34	21.86
1989-90	5.35	-6.87	4.49	10.59	12.76
1990-91	5.92	9.96	2.40	5.99	13.23
Growth rate	3.76	9.68	1.87	7.35	8.45
1991-92	6.05	7.70	3.14	2.67	-5.11
1992-93	14.19	2.23	7.19	8.40	7.64
1993-94	4.63	18.84	4.34	11.44	25.54
1994-95	1.26	23.72	3.86	17.81	5.48
1995-96	6.08	-0.98	7.63	7.47	12.23
1996-97	-3.48	6.91	0.04	3.19	0.27
1997-98	2.83	7.40	2.54	8.26	-10.08
1998-99	3.48	-10.59	-10.88	-11.07	-3.21
1999-2000	-0.91	2.26	-2.26	20.12	5.63
Growth rate	3.79	6.39	1.73	7.59	4.26
Growth rate for entire periods	3.78	8.20	1.81	7.46	6.57

Source: Computed from EPW data
Note: Productive Capital, Output and Value Added are monetary terms Factories and Number of Persons Employed are in Numbers.

Table 4.6 shows that the annual average rate of growth of principal characteristics such as number of factories, productive capital, employment, value of output and value added on India. The number of industries revealed 1.73 per cent of growth; while it showed 1.47 per cent growth during pre liberalization period and it increased by 2.05 per cent in the post liberalization period. The productive capital revealed nearly 7 per cent of growth during the pre liberalization period and it came down to 5.7 per cent in post liberalization period, which registered 6.32 per cent growth for 21 years of the study period. This trend reveals that, even though the financial liberalization adopted in the reformed regime, its accumulation in the manufacturing economy of Tamil Nadu is not noticeable.

Employment also shows a dismal picture in India during the study period, which accounted for 0.42 per cent growth in the overall study period. The growth of employment was 0.59 per cent in the pre-liberalization period and it decreased to 0.21 per cent during the post-liberalization period. The output has grown 7.8 per cent and marginally decreased in the liberalized period, and it recorded 7.5 per cent of growth for

Table 48
Growth Rates of Some Principal Characteristics in India

Year	*Num. of Fac.*	*Pro. Cap.*	*Employment*	*Output*	*Value add*
1979-80	0	0	0	0	0
1980-81	1.45	-4.65	0.89	-2.07	-8.01
1981-82	8.84	9.70	0.89	14.65	15.99
1982-83	-11.30	11.31	3.16	13.10	10.68
1983-84	3.80	10.35	-2.37	2.24	13.84
1984-85	0.25	7.46	-0.14	5.48	-3.06
1985-86	4.20	2.59	-4.81	7.42	5.12
1986-87	-3.03	2.26	-0.32	6.68	5.82
1987-88	4.74	11.10	4.52	7.97	3.45
1988-89	1.44	0.33	-0.57	9.46	11.76
1989-90	3.76	8.72	5.09	12.42	12.51
1990-91	2.03	15.42	0.10	8.20	9.56
Growth rate	1.47	6.78	0.59	7.78	7.06
1991-92	1.91	0.18	-0.15	-0.62	-4.35
1992-93	6.42	17.24	6.16	11.08	17.16
1993-94	1.76	13.16	-0.09	7.14	15.13
1994-95	1.16	4.41	4.77	8.44	9.37
1995-96	9.40	15.04	9.99	19.15	18.23
1996-97	-0.01	6.92	-3.19	1.21	0.58
1997-98	0.74	14.54	2.44	15.84	5.93
1998-99	-2.84	-19.32	-14.71	-9.03	-10.63
1999-2000	-0.11	-0.31	-3.34	11.56	3.74
Growth rate	2.05	5.76	0.21	7.20	6.13
Growth rate for entire periods	1.73	6.32	0.42	7.52	6.64

Source: Computed from EPW data.
Note: Productive Capital, Output and Value Added are monetary terms Factories and Number of Persons Employed are in Numbers.

the entire period. The value added dwindled to 6.13 per cent in liberalized period from 7.06 per cent during the pre liberalization period and it accounted for 6.6 per cent growth for the entire study period. It is found out form this analysis that even though the principal factors increased at an aggregate level, its year to year growth decreased during the liberalized regime more than that of pre-liberalized period.

Industry wise Growth between Pre and Post Liberalization Periods

The annual compound growth rates have been worked out to analyze the growth of different types of industries in Tamil Nadu.

Table 49
Compound Growth Rate for Pre-Liberalisation Period
[1980-81 to 1990-91]

Industry Groups	*Number of Factories*	*Productive Capital*	*Employ-ment*	*Value of Output*	*Value Added*
Food Products	2.7	7.6	-1.7	5.8	8.7
Beverages, Tobacco & Tobacco Products	-2.8	11.8	1.6	11.4	12.9
Textiles	4.8	7.1	1.8	7.1	6.1
Wood & Wood Products	3.4	3.1	-2.0	4.0	1.9
Paper & Paper Products	3.4	9.1	1.6	9.8	13.3
Leather & Leather products	7.1	11.1	5.7	9.0	12.2
Rubber, Plastic, Petroleum & Coal Products	6.7	13.8	2.6	4.8	12.8
Chemical & Chemical Products	4.2	7.8	6.7	5.4	8.7
Non-Metallic Mineral Products	8.6	7.8	1.5	7.8	10.9
Basic Metal & Alloy Products	1.2	6.2	-2.0	7.3	0.4
Metal Products & Parts	3.7	8.1	0.5	7.7	6.9
Machinery & Machine Tools	6.1	7.4	2.2	7.9	7.0
Electrical Equipments & Parts	4.1	8.9	1.4	6.4	5.5
Transport Equipment & Parts	4.9	8.1	2.4	7.9	8.2
Other Manufacturing Industries	4.4	21.3	5.7	18.2	18.4

Source: Calculated from ASI data, Various Issues.
Note: Productive Capital, Output and Value Added are monetary terms Factories and Number of Persons Employed are in Numbers.

The annual compound growth rate for all the industries on principal characteristics such as (number of factories, productive capital, employment, value of output and value added) are presented in Table 49. During the pre-liberalization period the 'other manufacturing' industries registered the highest growth rate in respect of productive capital value of output and value added. The chemical group achieved first place in respect of employment growth.

With regard to value added paper and paper products, beverages tobacco and tobacco products, leather and leather products, and rubber, plastic, petroleum and coal producing industries revealed more than ten per cent growth. At the same time, growth of metal producing industry with regard to employment was just 0.5 per cent. There had been a negative growth rate in employment revealed by food products, wood and wood products and basic metal product.

It should be mentioned that, only wood and wood products show minor growth of output, which was less than 5 per cent, and the basic metal group had the least growth rate with regard to value added.

During the post liberalization period (1991-92 to 1999-2000) the other manufacturing industry registered first place in respect of growth of number of factories. Based on the same criterion, the industrial units, which produced wood and wood products, leather and leather products, basic metal and alloy and transport equipments and parts, registered a negative growth. The basic reason for this negative growth is the closure of many industrial units in this state. In terms of investment, beverages, tobacco and tobacco producing industries, metal producing industries, and transport equipment and parts producing industries have revealed a significant growth. Owing to increase of demand for the above said commodities these industries observed the huge amount of capital.

The employment growth is not appreciable during the post liberalization period. Among the fifteen industrial groups the other manufacturing industry exhibits satisfactory growth of 10 per cent, followed by metal products and parts, and rubber group. Due to globalization, liberalization and privatization

Table 50
Compound Growth Rate for Post-Liberalisation Period
[1991-92 to 1999-2000]

Industry Groups	*Number of Factories*	*Productive Capital*	*Employ-ment*	*Value of Output*	*Value Added*
Food Products	0.7	5.4	1.03	7.3	-0.4
Beverages, Tobacco & Tobacco Products	2.8	18.1	0. 04	4.9	12.1
Textiles	2.9	9.8	0.8	7.8	7.3
Wood & Wood Products	-11.2	3.3	-8.7	4.2	7.6
Paper & Paper Products	3.4	6.4	2.9	4.9	7.8
Leather & Leather products	-0.3	4.8	-1.2	1.5	2.9
Rubber, Plastic, Petroleum & Coal Products	-2.7	8.9	4.4	8.0	9.1
Chemical & Chemical Products	5.4	10.4	3.3	9.6	12.3
Non-Metallic Mineral Products	1.9	-1.1	-0.04	3.7	3.9
Basic Metal & Alloy Products	-6.2	1.5	-9.1	-0.22	-3.5
Metal Products & Parts	3.0	12.9	7.9	15.1	10.7
Machinery & Machine Tools	1.1	-1.3	-2.3	-0.09	3.3
Electrical Equipments & Parts	3.2	3.4	-1.2	3.5	0.2
Transport Equipment & Parts	-4.6	12.4	-5.7	6.9	18.5
Other Manufacturing Industries	6.3	1.8	9.9	5.9	7.4

Source: Calculated from ASI data, Various Issues
Note: Productive Capital, Output and Value Added are monetary terms Factories and Number of Persons Employed are in Numbers.

process most of the industries transformed from labour intensive to capital intensive, which lead to diminish the employment generation. Taking into account the factor output, the metal producing industry is in the leading position, while, based on the value added the transport group chemical and chemical products, and beverage, tobacco and tobacco products revealed phenomenal growth, it could be attributed to growth of these sub groups in the industrial economy.

It is realized from the analysis of compound growth rate that the 'other manufacturing industries' underwent phenomenal growth in respect of value added in the pre reform periods and it was replaced by transport group industries during the post reform period. In addition, the inter-industry difference with respect to growth does exist. Similar result was obtained by Balakrishana,P & M.Sureshbabu(2003) in the two digit groups at all India level during 1973-74 to 1999-2000.

Growth Rates of Productive Capital and Employment

After analyzing the growth pattern of different groups of industries in Tamil Nadu, it is necessary to assess the growth rate of two important variables such as productive capital and employment. For this purpose, the annual compound growth rate for these two characteristics is computed for different periods.

Table 51
Comparison of Important Variables From Pre-Reform to the Post Reform

Variables/ Periods	*Pre-Liberalization*	*Post-Liberalization*	*Entire Periods*
Productive Capital	8.2	7.4	8.55
Employment	2.1	0.57	1.28

Source: Calculated from ASI data, Various Issues.

Table 51 shows that the productive capital grew at the rate of 8.2 per cent during pre-liberalization period and decreased at a snail's pace (7.4%) in the period of post liberalization. The employment growth exhibited very meager amount of 2.1 per cent during the pre liberalization period and it decreased further to 0.5 per cent during the post liberalization period.

It is understood from this analysis of compound growth rate for productive capital and employment that the growth of employment lagged behind when compared to the growth of capital investment to a rising trend in capital intensity.

Comparison of Growth between Pre and Post Reform Periods (Use-Based)

The annual compound growth rate has been worked out to analyse the progress of industries. The growth rate calculated for the use-based groups includes, basic goods, capital goods, intermediary goods, consumer durable and consumer non-durable goods. The results of the growth have been presented in Table 52.

Table 52

Comparison of Growth between Pre and Post Reform Periods (Factories)

Industry Groups/Periods	*Pre-reform Period*	*Post-reform Period*
Basic Goods	-1.15	7.91
Capital Goods	5.31	2.01
Intermediary Goods	1.40	4.35
Consumer Durable Goods	1.72	1.04
Consumer Non-Durable Goods	3.44	4.26

Source: Computed from ASI data.

Out of five use-based groups, there are three- basic goods, intermediary goods and consumer non-durable goods have experienced increasing trend from pre-reform period to the post reform period. It is to be mentioned that the Basic good industry revealed the highest growth during the post reform period. The share of basic goods in the state was primarily influenced by the share of electricity generating industry, cement industry, iron steel and casings industries. All other industries revealed decelerating trend from the pre-reform period to the post-reform period with regard to growth of factories.

Even though, the improvement is made in absolute terms, in the number of industries in the manufacturing economy of Tamil Nadu, the year to year growth has not revealed the appreciable trend.

The growth of different types of industry groups towards productive capital in the industrial economy of Tamil Nadu is presented in Table 10.

Table 53

Comparison of Growth between Pre and Post Reform Periods (Capital)

Industry Groups/Periods	*Pre-reform Period*	*Post-reform Period*
Basic Goods	5.61	-1.09
Capital Goods	8.08	4.32
Intermediary Goods	-0.32	14.76
Consumer Durable Goods	7.46	1.67
Consumer Non-Durable Goods	16.57	2.65

Source: Computed from ASI data.

There has been a marked increase in the growth of productive capital of consumer non-durable goods in the pre reform periods and it is replaced by the intermediary goods during the post reform periods. This sector has assumed much importance in the state because cotton ginning, spinning and weaving were the important sources of income for many persons of the state, and it increased in the investment of cotton yarn in the post reform period (Vijayalakshmi, 1994). In addition, the industries producing leather and leather products and photochemical, and tyre and tube producing industries have undergone considerable spatial expansion during the post reform period.

Table 54
Comparison of Growth between Pre and Post Reform Periods (Employment)

Industry Groups/Periods	*Pre-reform Period*	*Post-reform Period*
Basic Goods	-0.63	16.41
Capital Goods	2.81	-3.52
Intermediary Goods	-4.15	6.37
Consumer Durable Goods	-0.53	-2.44
Consumer Non-Durable Goods	5.52	-0.1

Source: Computed from ASI data.

Heavy investment in the consumer non-durable industries in the pre reform period led to increase in certain amount of employment generation in this group. But during the post reform period the industry producing basic goods reveals more than 16 per cent growth in terms of employment, it may be due to the expansion of chemical and chemical based industries in this state during the post reform periods (the chemical and chemical based industries alone generated employment for 136130 persons in 1980 to 81 and it increased to 280257 in 1999-2000). The industries producing consumer durable goods reveal negative growth in both pre and post reform periods due to the fact that the industries under this group (electrical apparatus, appliances and other parts such as lamps, bulbs, tubes, sockets, switches, fans, insulators, manufacture of medical surgical and scientific equipments are important industries) were capital intensive.

Table 55
Comparison of Growth between Pre and Post Reform Periods (Output)

Industry Groups/Periods	*Pre-reform Period*	*Post-reform Period*
Basic Goods	4.02	6.87
Capital Goods	7.53	4.07
Intermediary Goods	-6.87	13.19
Consumer Durable Goods	6.92	10.39
Consumer Non-Durable Goods	15.05	3.59

Source: Computed from ASI data.

Out of these use-based industry groups, consumer non-durable group revealed phenomenal growth in output during the pre reform period and it is replaced by the intermediate goods during the post reform period. It could be due to the improvement of investment in these industries. It is very transparent from the growth of capital (Table 10) that the consumer-non durable goods revealed nearly 17 per cent growth in the pre reform period and it is replaced by the intermediate goods during the post reform periods. The other industries such as basic and consumer durable revealed increasing trend when compared to pre-reform period to the post reform period.

The relative growth of different types of use-based industries with regard to value added is presented in Table 56.

Table 56
Comparison of Growth between Pre and Post Reform Periods (Value Added)

Industry Groups/Periods	*Pre-reform Period*	*Post-reform Period*
Basic Goods	4.47	9.48
Capital Goods	7.24	6.40
Intermediary Goods	-3.33	11.26
Consumer Durable Goods	2.71	9.07
Consumer Non-Durable Goods	18.36	4.61

Source: Computed from ASI data.

In terms of value added also the consumer-non durable goods industry underwent significant growth during the pre reform period and it is replaced by the intermediary goods in the post reform period. The same causes may have played a role in the improvement of value added. Here also the industries which produce basic and consumer durable goods revealed perceptible improvement with regard to growth. The improvement is more in the consumer durable sector. The reason behind this is the considerable improvement in the sub-sectors such as medical surgical and scientific equipments.

Comparison of Growth between Pre and Post Reform Periods (Input-Based)

Three digit level data have been classified in the context of input based classification also. The detailed note on use and input based classification has been given in the characteristics analysis. Here the comparison between pre and post reform periods in the input-based classifications with regard to principal characteristics has been made.

Table 57

Comparison of Growth between Pre and Post Reform Periods (Factories)

Industry Groups/Periods	*Pre-reform Period*	*Post-reform Period*
Agro-Based	1.92	2.78
Metal-Based	2.87	2.93
Chemical-Based	0.81	8.78

Source: Computed form ASI data.

It is observed from Table 57 that the metal based industry revealed nearly 3 per cent growth during the pre reform period and it is replaced by the chemical based industries during the post reform periods. Owing to expansion of demand for fertilizers, medicinal chemicals, and cosmetic items the industry has increased during the post reform period.

Owing to the structural transformation the growth of investment of agro-based industry dwindled during the post-reform period but its growth was high during the pre-reform period. Due to improvement in the number of industries in

Table 58
Comparison of Growth between Pre and Post Reform Periods (Capital)

Industry Groups/Periods	*Pre-reform Period*	*Post-reform Period*
Agro-Based	7.42	2.91
Metal-Based	8.63	8.49
Chemical-Based	1.32	16.21

Source: Computed form ASI data.

the chemical based industries (medicinal chemicals and matches) the capital growth of this industry group revealed perceptible growth during the post reform period, while the metal based industry revealed the stagnant position with regard to growth of productive capital.

Table 59
Comparison of Growth between Pre and Post Reform Periods (Employment)

Industry Groups/Periods	*Pre-reform Period*	*Post-reform Period*
Agro-Based	0.09	1.92
Metal-Based	1.69	-2.13
Chemical-Based	-7.52	15.61

Source: Computed from ASI data.

Considering the number of persons employed in the use-based groups, the agro-based industry groups revealed a marginal improvement and the chemical based industry expressed an extraordinary growth of nearly 16 per cent during the post reform period. The improvement in the number of industries has absorbed a number of workers during the post reform period. While viewing the entire manufacturing sector of Tamil Nadu the decelerating trend is evident in the employment generation.

Table 60 noticed that the growth of different types of industry group during pre and post reform periods. It is observed that the agro based industry revealed a down trend from pre reform period to the post reform period. In the agro-based industries the industry producing wood and wood products lost their share over the period. At the same time, the chemical based industry showed a phenomenal growth in the post reform period when compared to the pre reform period.

Table 60
Comparison of Growth between Pre and Post Reform Periods (Output)

Industry Groups/Periods	*Pre-reform Period*	*Post-reform Period*
Agro-Based	6.23	3.62
Metal-Based	7.92	8.12
Chemical-Based	5.23	11.92

Source: Computed from ASI data.

This perceptible improvement of chemical-based industry is not only in the growth of output but also in the value added.

Table 61
Comparison of Growth between Pre and Post Reform Periods (Value Added)

Industry Groups/Periods	*Pre-reform Period*	*Post-reform Period*
Agro-Based	6.49	4.15
Metal-Based	8.19	9.82
Chemical-Based	4.82	16.40

Source: Computed from ASI data.

Above Table 61 revealed that the agro based industry had meager growth during the post reform period when compared to the pre reform period. The metal based industry also revealed a marginal improvement with regard to growth of value added. But the growth of chemical based industry has jumped from nearly 5 per cent during the pre reform period to 16 per cent during the post reform period. This considerable progresses was due to the increase in the internal and external demand of industries producing basic chemicals, fertilizers, pharmaceuticals, medicinal chemicals, cosmetic items, and manufacture of other chemicals such as matches and photochemical.

Mean Differences

The 't'-test is administered in order to compare the pre and post reform periods. Mean value of factories, productive capital, employment, value of output and value added between pre and post reform periods have been calculated. The 't' value for the mean difference in the number of factories with respect to beverages, wood and wood products, leather and leather products, and basic metal and alloy products are found to be statistically not significant at 5 per cent level. It means that the liberalization has not brought about any significant increase in the mean value of the factories in these industrial groups, but the 't' values for the mean differences in the number of factories of food products, textiles, paper and paper products, rubber group, non-metallic minerals, metal products machinery and machine products, electrical equipment, transport equipments and parts, and 'other manufacturing industries' are found to be statistically significant at 5 per cent level. It showed that the mean values increased significantly after the liberalization in these industrial groups. Owing to economic liberalization the industrial licensing was more or less abolished, the door was opened to the private entrepreneurs to invest; this led to the increase in the number of industries during the post reform period. Here it should be mentioned that the economic impact is uneven across the industries.

Table 62 shows that the mean difference of the number of factories between pre and post liberalization periods.

Table 63 distinguished the mean difference of productive capital from the pre and post liberalization periods. It is observed that all the industrial groups except wood and wood products in Tamil Nadu manufacturing have statistically significant difference between the pre and the post liberalization periods. This implies that the liberalization process has impacted on the productive capital of manufacturing sector of Tamil Nadu.

Among the industrial groups the metal producing industries underwent maximum amount of increase (513%) from pre liberalization to the post liberalization period. The

Table 62
'T'-Test Results for Number of Factories

Industry Groups	*Mean Number in Pre-Liberalisation*	*Mean Numbers in Post-Liberalisation*	*Mean Differences*	*|t| Values*	*Significant with t 0.95 18 d-o-f*
Food Products	2845	3526	681	7.4	P<0.001
Beverages, Tobacco & Tobacco Products	346	305	-41	1.00	P>0.05
Textiles	2806	5081	2275	4.2	P<0.001
Wood & Wood Products	280	290	10	0.28	P>0.05
Paper & Paper Products	647	1115	468	5.9	P<0.001
Leather & Leather products	548	1025	477	0.89	P<0.001
Rubber, Plastic, Petroleum & Coal Products	388	629	241	6.5	P<0.001
Chemical & Chemical Products	1032	1576	544	5.9	P<0.05
Non-Metallic Mineral Products	474	749	275	6.9	P<0.001
Basic Metal & Alloy Products	550	527	-23	0.5	P>0.05
Metal Products & Parts	561	705	144	5.1	P<0.001
Machinery & Machine Tools	880	257	-623	3.5	P<0.01
Electrical Equipments & Parts	349	1317	968	6.2	P<0.001
Transport Equipment & Parts	406	523	117	3	P<0.01
Other Manufacturing Industries	95	160	65	5.4	P<0.001

Source: Calculated from ASI data, Various Issues.
Note: Productive Capital, Output and Value Added are monetary terms Factories and Number of Persons Employed are in Numbers.

Table 63
't'- Test Results for Productive Capital

Industry Groups	*Mean Number in Pre-Liberalisation*	*Mean Numbers in Post-Liberalisation*	*Mean Differences*	*ItI Values*	*Significant with t 0.95 18 d-o-f*
Food Products	69033	207075	138042	3.7	P<0.01
Beverages, Tobacco & Tobacco Products	7382	32493	25111	3.9	P<0.001
Textiles	147205	439970	292765	4.7	P<0.001
Wood & Wood Products	1649	3820	2171	5.0	P>0.001
Paper & Paper Products	52333	141250	88917	2.1	P<0.01
Leather & Leather products	19688	67656	47968	5.8	P<0.001
Rubber, Plastic, Petroleum & Coal Products	89141	231001	14186	7.5	P<0.001
Chemical & Chemical Products	170858	357466	186608	4.9	P<0.05
Non-Metallic Mineral Products	57417	90233	32816	5.1	P<0.001
Basic Metal & Alloy Products	82819	195619	112800	2.6	P<0.05
Metal Products & Parts	23383	143431	120048	1.2	P<0.05
Machinery & Machine Tools	133953	196482	62529	2.3	P<0.05
Electrical Equipments & Parts	28250	66605	38355	4.3	P<0.001
Transport Equipment & Parts	101564	257029	155465	4.3	P<0.001
Other Manufacturing Industries	8589	46682	38093	9.7	P<0.001

Source: Calculated from ASI data, Various Issues.
Note: Productive Capital, Output and Value Added are monetary terms
Factories and Number of Persons Employed are in Numbers.

very good performance in the increase of investment during the post reform period could be attributed to internal and foreign investors. In the metal products the sub-groups, which used to computer, deviser and official equipments have undergone phenomenal growth during the above referred period. The other major manufacturing industries are, beverages tobacco and tobacco products, 'other manufacturing industries' leather and leather products, and food products. The industry producing machinery and machine tools is the meager group in respect of increase of productive capital (47%) from pre liberalization to the post liberalization period.

Employment is one of the important indicators of growth performance. The number of persons employed in the manufacturing industries of Tamil Nadu has been analysed in Table 64. It is observed that the employment generation is poor in the manufacturing sector of Tamil Nadu during the period.

It is highlighted from Table 64 that out of fifteen industrial groups, six industries viz beverages tobacco and tobacco products, wood and wood products, non-metallic mineral, basic metal and alloy electrical equipments and parts and transport equipments and parts producing industries are not having statistically significant difference between the pre and post liberalization period (there is no improvement). All the remaining industrial groups showed statistically significant difference between the above-referred periods with regard to employment, which means the liberalization process, has negative impact on these industries. It may be due to perceptible improvement in the capital, and the technological improvement. Both led to negative impact on employment generation.

The output of manufacturing sector has been analysed for pre and post liberalization periods. The 't' values for different types of industries are presented in Table 65 't' value for all the industry groups is found to be statistically significant. Among the fifteen industrial groups the 'other manufacturing industries' have undergone maximum (296%) increase from pre liberalization to the post liberalization period. The other

Table 64
't'- Test Results for Employment

Industry Groups	*Mean Number in Pre-Liberalisation*	*Mean Numbers in Post-Liberalisation*	*Mean Differences*	*ltl Values*	*Significant with t 0.95 18 d-o-f*
Food Products	206939	256812	49873	2.6	P<0.05
Beverages, Tobacco & Tobacco Products	20953	45175	24222	1.0	P>0.05
Textiles	384775	575123	190348	6.0	P<0.001
Wood & Wood Products	9563	8621	-942	1.3	P>0.05
Paper & Paper Products	62822	98908	36086	1.7	P<0.005
Leather & Leather products	64564	124789	60225	6.6	P<0.001
Rubber, Plastic, Petroleum & Coal Products	37302	54898	17596	6.7	P<0.01
Chemical & Chemical Products	175010	242564	67554	4.5	P<0.05
Non-Metallic Mineral Products	55447	68511	13064	1.3	P>0.05
Basic Metal & Alloy Products	56465	53818	-2647	0.54	P>0.05
Metal Products & Parts	34421	47650	13229	3.6	P<0.01
Machinery & Machine Tools	112148	145445	33297	2.8	P<0.01
Electrical Equipments & Parts	41811	38471	-3340	1.8	P>0.05
Transport Equipment & Parts	136693	138901	2208	0.24	P>0.05
Other Manufacturing Industries	9486	23213	13727	6.7	P<0.001

Source: Calculated from ASI data, Various Issues.
Note: Productive Capital, Output and Value Added are monetary terms
Factories and Number of Persons Employed are in Numbers.

Table 65 't'-Test Results for Output

Industry Groups	*Mean Number in Pre-Liberalisation*	*Mean Numbers in Post-Liberalisation*	*Mean Differences*	*ltl Values*	*Significant with t 0.95 18 d-o-f*
Food Products	286355	584224	297869	5.8	P<0.001
Beverages, Tobacco & Tobacco Products	34223	79169	44946	4.2	P<0.001
Textiles	413865	1158177	744312	6.8	P<0.001
Wood & Wood Products	4027	8056	4029	4.5	P<0.001
Paper & Paper Products	81210	166156	84946	6.7	P<0.001
Leather & Leather products	105942	232499	126557	8.4	P<0.001
Rubber, Plastic, Petroleum & Coal Products	327581	480262	152618	3.7	P<0.001
Chemical & Chemical Products	296073	557429	261356	4.5	P<0.01
Non-Metallic Mineral Products	55447	68511	13064	3.8	P<0.01
Basic Metal & Alloy Products	126932	235761	108829	6.6	P<0.001
Metal Products & Parts	42105	100829	58724	2.6	P<0.05
Machinery & Machine Tools	252813	460993	208180	4.4	P<0.001
Electrical Equipments & Parts	81384	157933	76549	4.6	P<0.001
Transport Equipment & Parts	219708	428823	209115	5.6	P<0.001
Other Manufacturing Industries	16509	65333	48824	8.9	P<0.001

Source: Calculated from ASI data, Various Issues.
Note: Productive Capital, Output and Value Added are monetary terms
Factories and Number of Persons Employed are in Numbers.

manufacturing industries consist of the following industries viz., medical, surgical and scientific equipment, photographic and optical goods, manufacture of watches, jewellery, sports goods, musical instruments, stationary articles and costumes etc. These sub-groups experienced maximum growth, which led to achieve the highest growth of 'other manufacturing industries'.

The industries producing non-metallic mineral, rubber plastics, petroleum and coal products and machinery and machine tools exhibited very meager increase from the pre liberalization to the post liberalization period.

The value added is one of the important indicators to identify the industrial growth of an economy. In Tamil Nadu, the mean difference between the pre and post liberalization period of value added has been analysed and the 't' test is computed. The result of mean difference and 't' test have presented in Table 66.

With regard to the value added, the industries producing wood and wood products, machinery and machine tools, electrical equipments and parts and transport equipment and parts exhibited statistically not significant difference between the pre and the post liberalization period. All the remaining industries revealed significant difference between pre and post liberalization period with respect to value added.

Out of fifteen industry groups the 'other manufacturing industry' achieved noticeable increase form pre liberalization to the post liberalization period. The industries producing beverages tobacco and tobacco products, leather and leather products, and metal products are the major groups in respect of the growth of value added.

Agro and Non-Agro related Industries:

It is worthwhile, to compare the growth between pre and post reform period on principal characteristics such as number of factories, productive capital, number of persons employed, value of output and value added in the agro and no-agro based industries.

While comparing the pre reform period to the post reform period, in agro-based industries, the productive capital and

Table 66
't'- Test Results for Value Added

Industry Groups	*Pre-Liberalisation*	*Post-Liberalisation*	*Mean Differences*	*ltl Values*	*Significant with t 0.95 18 d-o-f*
Food Products	42335	84628	42293	4.1	P<0.01
Beverages, Tobacco & Tobacco Products	4692	18492	13800	3.8	P<0.01
Textiles	81569	204781	123212	5.1	P<0.001
Wood & Wood Products	892	1439	547	1.6	P>0.05
Paper & Paper Products	17504	38509	21005	4.4	P<0.001
Leather & Leather products	12467	33679	21212	8.0	P<0.001
Rubber, Plastic, Petroleum & Coal Products	34099	73548	39449	4.2	P<0.001
Chemical & Chemical Products	59649	132002	72353	3.9	P<0.05
Non-Metallic Mineral Products	22241	48887	26646	5.7	P<0.001
Basic Metal & Alloy Products	14402	23418	9016	3.8	P<0.01
Metal Products & Parts	9709	25041	15332	2.9	P<0.01
Machinery & Machine Tools	73447	51569	-21878	0.57	P<0.05
Electrical Equipments & Parts	23161	26048	2887	0.2	P>0.05
Transport Equipment & Parts	67318	82226	14908	0.69	P>0.05
Other Manufacturing Industries	4757	19622	14865	4.0	P<0.001

Source: Calculated from ASI data, Various Issues.
Note: Productive Capital, Output and Value Added are monetary terms
Factories and Number of Persons Employed are in Numbers.

employment increased their growth from pre liberalization period to the post liberalization period, the value of output is revealed the stagnant position and all other characteristics decreased for the above mentioned period.

Table 67
Growth Rates of Agro and Non-Agro Tamil Nadu

	Agro-related		*Non-Agro-related*	
Characteristics	*Pre-Reform*	*Post-Reform*	*Pre-Reform*	*Post-Reform*
Factories	3.97	2.45	5.38	1.67
Productive Capital	9.21	11.03	10.69	11.13
Employment	1.70	2.29	3.66	-0.17
Value of Output	8.08	8.20	7.70	8.22
Value Added	9.82	5.90	21.92	25.40

Source: Computed from ASI data.
Note: Productive Capital, Output and Value Added are monetary terms Factories and Number of Persons Employed are in Numbers.

Based on the non-agro based industries, productive capital and value of output increased at a snail's phase and the value added increased nearly 4 per cent form pre to post reform period. Conversely, the number of factories revealed sharp decline. A mention should be made that the growth of employment has shown a negative sign during the reform period. This jobless growth was also observed by Venkataramaiah and Burange (2003) and Chaudhuri (2002) at all India level.

A hypothesis was framed to test the difference in the growth between the agro-based industries and non-agro-based industries between pre and post reform periods.

For this purpose the following are the null and alternative hypotheses.

Null hypothesis: There is no significant difference between the output growths of agro-based industries between pre and post reform periods.

Alternative hypothesis: There is a significant difference between the output growths of agro-based industries between pre and post reform periods.

To understand the ground reality of the trend of output the values are normalized (output per unit have computed). To examine this hypothesis also 't' test is used and the result is presented below.

Table 68
't'-test Result-Difference in Growth between Pre and Post Reforms (Agro)

Variable	*Number of Cases*	*Mean*	*SD*	*SE of Mean*
AGRO GR for agro p/U				
Pre lib.	10	5.6760	13.268	4.196
Pos lib.	9	4.7378	22.175	7.392

Mean Difference = .9382.
Levene's Test for Equality of Variances: F = 3.282 P = .088

This experiment yielded the result that there is statistically significant difference between the pre and post reform period in agro based industries at 5 per cent level of significance. Hence the null hypothesis has not gained support.

Table 69
't'-test Result-Difference in Growth between Pre and Post Reforms (Non-Agro)

Variable	*Number of Cases*	*Mean*	*SD*	*SE of Mean*
NONAGRO GR for Non agro p/U				
pre lib.	10	16.6920	62.504	19.766
pos lib.	9	23.5144	75.832	25.277

Mean Difference = -6.8224
Levene's Test for Equality of Variances: F = .118 P = .735

But considering the non agro-based industries, there is a difference between the growth of pre and post reform period with regard to output, but it is not statistically significant difference.

Productivity Analysis between Pre and Post Reform Periods

Productivity is considered as one of the indicators of development in an economy. Number of studies have been made on industrial economy of India and various states for different periods of time. But very few studies have concentrated on the comparison between pre and post reform periods. Based on the previous studies made by some economists, the productivities (partial and total) are calculated and it is compared between for pre and post reform periods.

Here, a comparison between pre and post reform period has been made with respect to partial factor productivity in the industrial economy of Tamil Nadu. The result is presented in Table 70. It depicts that the labour productivity has been increased in both pre and post reform periods. On the other hand, the capital productivity is suggested in the pre reform period and it was fluctuating during the post reform period. The average of labour-output ratio for the pre reform period was lower than that of post reform period. But the average capital output ratio in the pre reform period was nearly the same as compared to pre reform period.

Table 70
Annual Average Growth Rates of Partial Factor Productivity in Tamil Nadu for Pre and Post Liberalisation Periods

	Pre-Reform Period					*Post-Reform Period*			
Year	*O/L*	*AAGR*	*O/K*	*AAGR*	*Year*	*O/L*	*AAGR*	*O/K*	*AAGR*
1980-81	2.736	0.000	2.810	0.000	-	-	-	-	-
1981-82	3.029	10.704	2.757	-1.863	-	-	-	-	-
1982-83	3.232	6.714	2.924	6.048	1991-92	4.983	0	2.259	0
1983-84	2.968	-8.153	2.044	-30.097	1992-93	4.949	-0.67	2.353	4.17
1984-85	3.352	12.913	2.297	12.364	1993-94	4.969	0.40	2.274	-3.36
1985-86	3.703	10.479	2.234	-2.722	1994-95	5.390	8.48	2.212	-2.70
1986-87	3.965	7.070	2.394	7.145	1995-96	5.631	4.46	1.899	-14.15
1987-88	4.056	2.290	2.412	0.775	1996-97	5.918	5.09	1.864	-1.85
1988-89	4.419	8.973	2.195	-8.995	1997-98	6.499	9.82	2.150	15.34
1989-90	4.720	6.811	2.348	6.958	1998-99	5.989	-7.84	1.283	-40.31
1990-91	4.596	-2.641	2.455	4.549	1999-00	8.308	38.72	2.104	63.94
X	3.707	5.015	2.443	-0.584	X	5.848	6.495	2.044	2.341

Source: Computed from ASI data.
Note: O-Output, L-Labour and AAGR-Annual Average Growth Rates.

Based on the average annual growth rates, labour productivity recorded 5 per cent growth in the pre reform period and it increased to 6.5 per cent during the post reform period. The capital productivity revealed a negative growth (-0.58) during the pre reform period, it has enhanced to 2.3 per cent during the post reform period. The above results imply that the reform process had encouraged the partial factor productivity of both labour and capital. This may be due to better utilization of available factors of production and managerial skill.

The study of secondary data has clearly delineated that there is an increase in labour productivity, but the ground reality dose not approve of it since the fact is to the effect of globalization, liberalization and privatization, which paved avenues for temporary projects, outsourcing and contracts, there is tremendous change in our industrial economy. The available secondary data doesn't support this fact.

Total Factor Productivity

The comparative study has been made for the pre and post reform periods on the basis of Solow's index of total factor productivity in Tamil Nadu. Solow's method is noted for productivity analysis. Number of studies has followed this method to calculate total factor productivity for different regions for different periods. Here, Solow's index of total factor productivity for both- pre and post reform periods have been computed for the manufacturing sector of Tamil Nadu. The value of the total factor productivity has been presented in Table 71.

It is explained from Table 71 that Solow's index of total factor productivity slightly decreased during the mid eighties, thereafter it improved. There had been an increasing trend revealed by Solow's index of total factor productivity during the post reform periods (except 1995-96 and 98-99). The index of total factor productivity averaged 97 for pre reform period. It improved to 102 during the post reform period.

Comparing the pre reform period to the post reform period, the growth of total factor productivity increased in the post reform period more than the pre reform period at the rate of 0.86 to 3.04. It is observed that the economic reform led to the increase in productivity. This conclusion is in line with the results of Chaudhuri(2002), Unel(2003), TSL(2003) at all India level.

Table 71

Solow's Index of Total Factor Productivity in Tamil Nadu for Pre and Post Liberalisation Periods

Pre-Liberalisation			*Post-Liberalisation*		
Year	*Solow's*	*AAGR*	*Year*	*Solow's*	*AAGR*
1980-81	100.00	0.00	-	-	-
1981-82	101.90	1.90	-	-	-
1982-83	107.88	5.86	1991-92	100.00	0.00
1983-84	80.67	-25.22	1992-93	101.531	1.531
1984-85	89.63	11.10	1993-94	100.211	-1.300
1985-86	90.81	1.31	1994-95	103.363	3.145
1986-87	96.85	6.65	1995-96	99.435	-3.800
1987-88	98.03	1.23	1996-97	101.278	1.853
1988-89	95.05	-3.04	1997-98	112.639	11.218
1989-90	101.20	6.47	1998-99	85.042	-24.500
1990-91	103.57	2.34	1999-2000	115.782	36.146
X	96.87	0.86	X	102.142	3.037

Source: Computed from ASI Data.
AAGR-Annual Average Growth Rates.

Here the question emerged whether the *improvement in the total factor productivity is statistically significant or not?* To findout answer for this question the hypothesis is outlined that:

Null hypothesis: There is no significant difference between pre and post reform periods with respect to growth of total factor productivity.

Alternative hypothesis: There is a significant difference between pre and post reform periods with respect to growth of total factor productivity.

The independent sample 't' test is used to justify this hypothesis and the results of this calculation has been presented in Tables 72.

It is observed from this experiment that there is some difference in the growth of total factor productivity between pre and post reform periods, but it is not statistically significant as the value (.263) is obtained from this calculation.

Table 72

't'-test Result for Pre and Post Reform Periods (TFP)

Group Statistics

Year		*N*	*Mean Deviation*	*Std. Mean*	*Std. Error*
AAGR	Pre	11	.9173	9.2748	2.7965
	Post	9	1.4200	18.7019	6.2340

Independent Samples Test

		Levene's Test for Equality of Variances		*t-test for Equality of Means*						
									95% Confidence Interval of the Difference	
		F	*Sig.*	*t*	*df*	*Sig. (2-tailed)*	*Mean Difference*	*Std. Error Difference*	*Lower*	*Upper*
AAGR	Equal variance assumed	1.336	.263	-.078	18	.938	-.5027	6.4077	-13.9648	12.9593
	Equal variances not assumed			-.074	11.181	.943	-.5027	6.8325	-15.5112	14.5057

Hence, the null hypothesis that "there is no significant difference between pre and post reform periods with respect of growth of total factor productivity" has not got support from this test.

It means that even though the open door policy paved the way to the unleashing of license for new industries, inflow of foreign capital, technology, and labour, tax concession, and free market flow, its impact on the total factor productivity of Tamil Nadu is not substantial.

DISCUSSIONS [FACTOR WISE]

Four principal factors have been taken to analysis the growth, structural change, and productivity in the industrial economy of Tamil Nadu, those are:

(i) Productive Capital

(ii) Number of Persons Employed

(iii) Value of Output and

(iv) Value Added.

The performance of these principal characteristics has been discussed over the analyzed periods.

Productive Capital

Out of fifteen industry groups, the industry, which produces textiles and its related goods, occupies the first place with regard to productive capital in 1980-81, and it was replaced by chemical group in 1985-86, the position of chemical group had been maintained in 1990-91 also. But the food producing industry over took all the industrial groups and got the first place with its relative share of nearly 19 per cent. The chemical group again came to a predominant place with respect to productive capital in 1999-2000.

The changes in the investment on different types of industries might caused by expansion of internal and external markets, liberalization of finance, and rivalry condition of the economy. It is very obvious that after the globalization process the performance of chemical group in the manufacturing sector is considerable, which is reflected in the investment.

In the use-based groups the basic goods industry registered a dominant position up to 1995-96, thereafter it is replaced by capital goods in 1999-2000, with regard to productive capital. Similarly, in the input-based classification, the agro-based industry has maintained the first place over the study period with regard to productive capital. The reason behind the dominant position played by the agro-based industry is the favorable climatic condition and availability of raw materials; these are suitable to start the above said industries in Tamil Nadu. This accounted maximum amount of productive capital.

Considering the growth of productive capital, other manufacturing industry experienced the highest growth during the pre reform period and it is replaced by beverages, tobacco and tobacco producing industry in the post reform period. Owing to the expansion of population the demand for these commodities has been increased and it stimulates capital accumulation.

Among the use-based industry groups, the consumer non-durable registered the highest growth of nearly 17 per cent in the pre reform period and the intermediate group came to predominant place with regard to the growth of capital during the liberalized era. In the intermediate group, the agro-based industries such as spinning, sanforizing and cotton textiles and the non-agro based industries like photochemical have been accelerated in the recent periods.

In the input-based groups the metal based industry accounted for 9 per cent growth in the pre-reform period and it is replaced by chemical groups in the post reform period.

Totally, in the earlier phase the agro-based industries were dominating in the industrial economy of Tamil Nadu and it is replaced by the chemical based industry during the nineties with regard to productive capital. The prime causative factor for the dominant role played by the chemical-based industry is the increase of internal and external demand, starting of new chemical based industries, expansion of sub groups and atleast partially the influence of government policy.

Employment

With regard to employment, the textile industry has maintained the main role, despite minor fluctuations over the study period in the manufacturing groups of industrial economy of Tamil Nadu. The causative factors for the dominant role played by the textile industry are the favorable climatic condition, availability of raw materials, cheap labour and expansion of internal and external markets. The above cited factors influenced to start the textile based industries in Tamil Nadu and it absorbed the available workers.

In the use-based groups, the consumer non-durable goods contributed highest percentage of employment except in 1985-86, the intermediary group came to apex place with regard to its relative share in the generation of employment in 1985-86. In the consumer non-durable group the sub groups such as food products; drugs and medicines, matches and cosmetic items underwent perceptible growth over the study period.

In the input-based industry groups, the agro-based industry had got a sizable amount employment over the period of analyse. Because of the dominant role played by the textile and food producing industries, the agro-based industry contributed maximum amount of employment.

Viewing the growth performance of industrial economy of Tamil Nadu (with regard to employment), the chemical based industry registered maximum amount of growth among the fifteen industry groups during the pre-reform period and it is maintained in the post reform period also. The considerable growth achieved by the chemical based industry is mainly due to remarkable increase in starting chemical based industries in Tamil Nadu particularly in the southern districts. While considering the growth of twenty year period the different trend appeared that the 'other manufacturing industry' showed the highest growth. In the 'other manufacturing group' certain industries such as jewelleries and sports items have registered maximum growth during the recent periods. Due to this reason these industries witnessed a dominant role.

Within the use-based group, the consumer-non durable industry took the top place during the pre-reform period and it is overtaken by basic industry in the post reform period. In the first phase of nineties due to demand factor, fertilizer and cement industries expanded (which belonging to basic goods). It absorbed number of employees.

Chemical based industry has been performed well over the study period. In the input-based groups the metal group registered first place in the case of growth of employment during the pre-reform period and it is replaced by chemical groups during the post reform period. This trend is not only influenced by the demand for chemicals used by textiles, drugs and medicals, paints and varnish industry, but also due to extension of agricultural activities.

Output

The relative share of textiles, with regard to output has been in the top position over the study period, in the manufacturing economy of Tamil Nadu. The reason behind this is the performance of textile industry, the expansion of both internal and external markets, establishment of new industries, modernization of already existing industries and managerial skill.

While considering the output of use-based industry group, more or less all the groups of industries revealed a fluctuating trend over the study period. Up to the second phase of the eighties the intermediary goods contributed the highest percentage in the total output, thereafter, the consumer non-durable group came to first place and after 1995-96 the capital goods sector came to dominant place with its contributory share of 34 per cent in the total output. This fluctuating trend may be due to influence of exports. Here, Hoffmann's hypothesis is realized that the consumer goods industry develops first and the capital goods industry develops in the final stage.

In the input-based group, the agro-based industry had contributed maximum amount of output. The main role played by the agro-based industry with regard to output is mainly due to boosting up of textile and food producing industries. However, the contribution of agro-based industry declined over the study period indicating an economic transformation.

Considering the growth, out of fifteen industry groups, the other manufacturing industry registered the highest growth of 18 per cent in the pre-reform period. By contrast, the metal-based industry registered the highest growth during the post reform period. This appreciable growth of metal-based industry is due to improvement of computer based products during nineties. This industry (computer based) gained favorable government policy also.

In the use-based groups, the highest growth was recorded by consumer-non durable goods during the pre reform period and it is replaced by the intermediary goods in the post reform period. Owing to liberalization process, the intermediary group gained mechanization and technological upgradation in the nineties, which lead to improve the output of intermediary goods.

In the input-based groups, the metal-based industry revealed the maximum growth of nearly 9 per cent during the pre reform period. But during the post reform period the chemical based industry upsurged and came to the apex place. The supportive factor for the highest growth achieved by the chemical based industry may be due to phenomenal growth achieved by the sub groups, such as fertilizer, drugs and medicines, inedible oils and matches.

Value Added

While considering value added of different types of industries in the industrial economy of Tamil Nadu, the textile industry contributed the maximum amount of 25 per cent and it gripped in the same position up to 1995-96. In the industrial composition of Tamil Nadu, the chemical industry came to the first place in 1999-2000. Due to the expansion of demand of both agro and non-agro based activities, and increase in the number of factory this chemical based industries performed well.

The criterion (value added) in the use-based groups shows that the capital goods sector is in top place from the second half of the eighties. Though, its contribution has been fluctuating from 24 per cent to 34 per cent during the study period.

The input-based groups differed widely when compared to the use-based groups. In the input-based group, the contribution of agro-based industry has been holding the leading place up to first half of the nineties and it is replaced by the chemical-based industry in 1999-2000, with its contributory share of 37 per cent. This is not only due to the expansion of agro chemicals, but also due to the increase of variety of cosmetic items and chemical use by textiles.

While goingthrough the growth performance of different types of industry groups, the 'other manufacturing industry registered 18 per cent growth during the pre-reform period. But in the post reform period, the transport group witnessed acme growth of nearly 15 per cent. It is very transparent that the state Tamil Nadu is the home for major automobile companies. In recent years the production of passenger cars and two wheelers have increased (CII, 2000).

There are different trends appeared, while reviewing the growth of use-based and input-based groups. In the use-based groups, the consumer non-durable industry recorded 18 per cent growth in terms of value added during the pre-reform period. But in the post reform period covering 1991-92 to 1999-2000, the intermediary group came forward with its growth rate of 11 per cent. In the intermediary group cotton spinning, tyre and tubes and a number of chemical producing industries have performed well.

In the input-based industry groups, the industry producing chemical and its related commodities witnessed 16 per cent growth during the post-reform period. But in the previous phase (pre-reform period) the metal-based industry showed the highest growth of 8 per cent, due to expansion of transports, and medical surgical and scientific equipments.

In summing up, the agro and its related industries have been in the dominant position with regard to number of factories and particularly in the employment generation. In the industrial mix the textile group occupies the leading place with regard to number of factories, productive capital, employment generation, value of output and value added. Due to structural transformation of industrial economy, in 1999-2000, the chemical based industry alone came to top place with regard to productive capital and value added, at the same time all other characteristics are dominated by textile industry.

While analyzing the different aspects of industrial economy of Tamil Nadu, it is observed that its performance was poor (except some industries) during the study period.

The causative factors are lack of raw materials, fluctuation in the price of raw materials, erratic and poor supply of power, infrastructural bottleneck, poor quality of labour, unfavorable government policies and so on.

The industrial structure had somewhat diversified in favoring of modern based industries, particularly in chemicals. This structural transformation in the industrial economy of Tamil Nadu is mainly due to phenomenal growth recorded by the sub sector of the major industries and partially by the favor of government policies, as it leads to free flow of capital, technology, high quality of man power, advanced machineries and equipments, increase of private entrepreneurs, competition and expansion of exports.

In addition to this, our economists underlined that the demand factor, increase in per capita income, export expansion, import substitution, diversification of taste and preferences, different types of government policies, technological up gradation of existing industries, rate of economic growth, international integration, and development of technically educated entrepreneurs are the causative factor for structural transformation and sophistication of industrial economy.

CHAPTER 5

MAIN FINDINGS AND CONCLUSIONS

SUMMARY

The present work is an intensive investigation on the industrial economy of Tamil Nadu. The focus of this study is multi dimension- growth, structural change and productivity trend (both partial and total factor productivity).

Annual Survey of Industry (ASI) is the chief source of data for the present research, which is annually published by Central Statistical Organization (CSO), Calcutta. The CSO has been bringing out summary results of ASI for the entire factory sector comprising both the census and non census sector. This survey covers all the factories registered under the Factory Act, 1948. The census sector consists of establishment using power and employing 10 or more workers each and those not using power but employing 20 or more workers each on any day of the proceeding 12 months. In addition to this, Tamil Nadu- An Economic Appraisal, Industrial Profile of Tamil Nadu, Basic Industrial Statistics of Tamil Nadu, Population Census, Reserve Bank of India Bulletin, Basic Statistics on Indian Economy, and other published reports from various ministries of government of India and Tamil Nadu are the sources of data.

Two and three digit level data are available in ASI, which analysed for the period of 20 years starting from 1980-81 to 1999-2000. To understand the effects of New Industrial Policy on the industrial economy of Tamil Nadu, this period has been sub-divided into pre-reform period (1980-81 to 1990-91) and post-reform period (1991-92 to 1999-2000). The three digit level data have been grouped into functional and input-based classifications. This use-based group includes, basic, capital, intermediate, consumer durable and consumer non-durable goods. Similarly, the input-based group comprises three sub groups such as agro, metal and chemical based industries.

For the purpose of analyzing the data, simple statistical tools, such as percentage share, annual average growth rate, annual compound growth rate, trend analysis, correlation, 't' test, H.H Index, structural ratios, partial factor productivity and Solow's Index of total factor productivity have been used.

The present work revealed that the industrial structure was well diversified and sophisticated during the study period. The modern industry experienced highest growth then that of traditional industries, at the same time contribution of employment by the agro-based industries have maintained in the towering position. In the industrial composition, the textile group of industry occupied apex position with regard to contribution of value added in 1980-81, and it is replaced by chemical based industry in 1999-2000. It is to be noteworthy to mention that the industry producing textile contributed maximum share of employment till 1999-2000.

In the use and input based industry groups, capital and chemical groups came to significant places respectively with regard to percentage share of value added in 1999-2000. Where as, in terms of growth, the intermediary and chemical groups experienced perceptible growth during the post reform periods.

Productivity analysis yielded the result that, in the partial factor productivity, labour productivity has increased remarkably more than that of capital productivity. This result is looking alike for both pre and post reform periods. Total factor productivity has improved despite slight fluctuations, but this improvement is not statistically significant.

Thus it is clear form this study that the structural change is perceived in the industrial economy of Tamil Nadu. The traditional industries lost their shares over the period, by contrast the modern industries, gained noticeable progress. Even thought, various socio and economic factors played catalytic role to structural changes in the industrial economy of Tamil Nadu, the policy change must be a cause atleast partially for structural transformation, through free flow of capital, technological, labour, managerial skill and opportunity to global market.

ECONOMIC STRUCTURE

The structural transformation in the sectoral composition is perceptible in the state as well as in India. The share of primary sector in the Net State Domestic Product (NSDP), was 43.5 per cent in 1960-61, which slipped down to 35 per cent by 1970-71 and further it shrank to 25, 23, 18 percentages during 1980-81, 1990-91, 2001-02 respectively. But the share of secondary sector revealed the mixed fortune. It rose to 33.9 per cent by 1980-81 from 20.7 per cent and 26.9 by 1960-61and 1970-71 respectively. Thereafter, it decreased considerably while the tertiary sector had moved up steadily form 36 per cent to 50.2 per cent for the above-referred periods. Similar pattern is observed at all India level too. Owing to the changes in techniques of production, physical quality of labour, wide-spread information technology, application of Telecommunication in productive process through improved Human Resource Development, the economy has transformed from primary dominated one to service sector (DEAR, 2001-02).

The index of industrial productions is fluctuating form year to year for both the state and country. The mention should be made that in the analyzed periods India has revealed positive growth in all sub sectors. While Tamil Nadu shows negative growth for certain periods. The setback of index of industrial production is due to the deceleration of the sub sectors, such as electricity and manufacturing. The negative growth of these sub sectors pulled down the general index of industrial production in Tamil Nadu.

During 1988-89 to 1992-93 the mining sector has revealed an impressive growth of 10 per cent. While, it witnessed a negative growth rate of 0.62 per cent during 1998-99 to 2002-03. The growth rate of manufacturing and electricity has revealed a higher growth of 5.3 per cent and 10.5 per cent respectively during 1983-84 to 1987-88. Thereafter, its growth was slowed down considerably. The growth of general index of industrial production has also shown the same trend, which recorded 6 per cent growth during the above referred period and since then decreased noticeably. The deceleration in the manufacturing sector is due to slowing down of agricultural production. Low level of agricultural production, leading to fall in the production of agro-based industries.

It is to be mentioned that the index of industrial production of all the sub-sectors has been shown a strong growth during the pre-liberalisation periods. The same trend is observed at all India level also.

INDUSTRIAL STRUCTURE

In Tamil Nadu, the textile industry group is dominating in terms of its relative shares in productive capital followed by chemical and chemical products, transport equipment and parts and machinery and machine tools in the industrial economy in 1980-81. The textile group occupies the first place in respect of its relative share in employment also. The food product group, which occupies sixth position in its relative share of productive capital, stood second in terms of the employment generation. The relative share towards value added of the major industry groups viz. textiles, chemicals and chemical products, machinery and machine tools and transport equipment and parts was around 61.25 per cent in the same year.

In 1985-1986 the change in industrial structure was perceived by the relative role of chemical and chemical producing group, which has become dominant group in terms of its relative shears in productive capital alone. Till (1985-86) the textile industry occupied the predominant position in its relative roles of employment output and value added.

In 1990-1991 the chemical group was in the top position in terms of its share in investment. By contrast, in respect of relative shares in employment, output and value added the textile group maintains its top most position.

In 1995-96 the food producing industry over took all other industry group in terms of the relative share of productive capital. The textile group secured first place with a sea share (30%) of total employment, output, and value added also.

Again in 1999-2000 the chemical group emerged as a predominant one in terms of productive capital and it kept lion's share in terms of value added also. The textile industry dominated with regard to value added in 1980-81 but it was replaced by chemical based industries in the industrial economy of Tamil Nadu in 1999-2000. Hence, the hypothesis that *there has been broad spectrum of industrial diversification, with a bias on chemical and its related industries in the recent period in terms of value added* gained support form this analysis. In respect of employment, and value of output the textile group secured the first place due to its labour intensive nature. Among the fifteen industry groups, wood and wood producing industry is the meager group in terms of all the principle characteristics over the study period.

Owing to internal and external demand, freeing up of finance, expansion of population, and changes in taste and preferences, the above mentioned industries are fighting together to catch up the first place in terms of capital and value added. But the industry producing textile and its related products maintained its dominant place with regard to employment generation and output. The availability of raw materials, cheap labour, favorable climatic condition, and internal and external demand are the basic reasons for the dominant role played by the textile industry.

In 1980-81, the principal ratio that the value added per factory was the highest in the industry producing transport equipments and spare parts and followed by machinery and machine tools, chemical and chemical products, and electrical equipments and parts. This ratio was relatively lower in the industry producing wood and wood products. At the same time, the industry producing rubber, plastics, petroleum and coal products was in the towering position with regard to value added per employee and they were followed by electrical equipments and parts, machinery and machine tools and chemical and chemical producing industries.

In 1999-2000, value added per factory was the highest in transport group and it was followed by rubber, plastics, petroleum and coal products, and other manufacturing industries. Usually, it is lower in the industry producing wood and wood products. At the same time, value added per employee was the highest in the industry producing rubber, plastic, petroleum and coal product and followed by transport equipments and parts producing industry, and electrical equipment and parts producing industries.

In the ratio analysis the following findings are arrived at (a) the structural ratios differ widely for different types of industries and periods. (b) The structured ratios relatively small during first phase and increased significantly during subsequent phases, registered marked increase (c) most of the structural ratios increased significantly during the post liberalization period when compared to the pre reform periods (d) the transport group is predominant industry in respect of value added per factory, output per factory, employment per factory and productive capital per factory for the study period of 1980-1981 to 1999-2000 (e) the capital per factory and capital per worker had increased substantially, particularly in the 1990's. There was a declining in employment generation during the post liberalization period. This conclusion confirms the results of Upendranadh and et.al (1994), Burange (1999), Deb (2001), and Thangamuthu, *et al.* (2004).

The industrial structure of Tamil Nadu economy has been fairly diversified during the period under study. The modern industries such as chemical and chemical products, basic metal and alloy products, transport equipments and parts and machinery and machine tools are experiencing acceleration more than that of traditional industries.

In the use based group, the relative share of number of factories of consumer-non durable goods had upsurged from 47 per cent to 50 per cent; expansion of market for this commodity influenced to emerge new industries. In the case of productive capital, the basic goods had a stagnant position in 1980-81 and 1985-86, there after decreased sharply, this may be due to the reduction in the number of factories. The share of capital goods had a fluctuating trend up to 1990-91, thereafter increased sharply, this is due to many branches of this sector witnessing modernization and expansion in the scale of production.

The relative share of employment of consumer non-durable good is the highest during the study period except for the year 1985-86, and the intermediary goods industry got the first place by providing maximum employment in 1985-86.

The contributing share of output by capital goods registered 23 per cent in 1980-81 and it increased to 25 per cent and 27 per cent respectively for the following two periods. Its contribution was more than 30 per cent by 1995-96 and 1999-2000. Owing to economic liberalization a heavy dose of capital has been accumulating and high technology has been employed. They improve the output.

It is realized in the industrial economy of Tamil Nadu that the capital goods industry dominated in this state in 1999-2000. But upto 1970, consumer goods industry was dominating in the industrial sector of the state (Vijayalakshmi, 1994) *this is in conformity with W.G. Hoffmann's hypothesis(1958) of the patterns of development of manufacturing industries. He addressed that, whatever be the relative amount of the factors of production, whatever be the relative amount of the factors, whatever be the stage of technology, the structure of the manufacturing sector of the economy has always followed a uniform pattern- the consumer goods industries develop first and the capital goods industries dominate in the second.*

There has been a steady decline in the intermediary goods in the case of percentage share of value added upto 1990-91. It improved to 17.8 per cent by 1999-2000. But, the percentage share of consumer-durable goods decreased over the analyzed periods.

Similarly, based on the criterion of the number of factories, agro-based group was dominating throughout the study period. The climatic condition of this state is suitable to start the agro based industries, particularly in some industrially developed districts.

There has been a remarkable change in the structure of industries in terms of input based classification. Based on the criterion of productive capital, industrial sector showed continuous changes during the study period. The percentage share of agro-based industries dominated in 1980-81 and that was replaced by chemical-based industries in 1999-2000. The appreciable performance of chemical based industries was attributed to starting up of many new industries and expansion of already existing industries in this state.

Of the total employment, the agro-based industries has got sizable amount of employment over the study periods, in the agro-based industries, food and food products, and cotton textiles have provided a major contributor of employment(CII, 2003). The chemical-based industries amplified its contribution from 17 per cent by 1980-81 to 20 per cent in 1985-86, since then it shrunk for the following two phases and upsurged to nearly 22 per cent in 1999-2000. The reason behind was that during the second phase of nineties emerging up of new industries with a sizable new employee. The agro-based industrial group is the largest single group in terms of output. However, the output of agro-based industry dwindled from 1980-81 to 1999-2000. The use of chemicals in all the productions increased sharply, in particular the chemical use in agriculture, medical field and textile industries. This is due to the above mentioned reasons that output of chemical-based industries recorded a maximum amount of 34 per cent growth in 1999-2000 from 24 per cent in 1990-91.

Considering value added, agro-based industries, played a major role upto 1995-96, there after the chemical-based industry emerged as an important industry. The manufacturing sector of the state experienced a progressive structural change in favor of chemical based industries. The proportion of value added in chemical-based industry ranged between 19 and 23 per cent during 1980-81 to 1995-96 against 36 per cent in 199-2000. This considerable progresses made by chemical based industry was due to the contribution of the industries producing basic chemicals, fertilizers, pharmaceuticals, medicinal chemicals, cosmetic items, and manufacture of other chemicals such as matches and photochemical.

While comparing the pre reform to the post reform period, it is observed that textile industry is the largest group of industry in terms number of factories, employment, value of output and value added in the pre reform period. While, with regard to productive capital alone the industry producing chemical and its sub group is in a leading place. The prime reason for the distinguishing performance of the chemical based industry is due to increase in the number of factories (in 1980-81 the number of industries producing chemical and chemical products is 783 and it increased to 1227 in 1990-91). The increase in the number of factories leads to accumulation of huge amount of capital.

Based on the criterion of productive capital, employment, value of output and value added, textile group of industry was the foremost group in the period of post liberalization period also. The basic reasons for the dominant role played by the textile industry are that the favorable climatic condition, availability of raw materials, cheep labour and internal and external demand.

INDUSTRIAL GROWTH

With regard to growth, the non-metallic mineral industry stood first in terms of number of factories. In the case of investment, output, and value added the 'other manufacturing industry' registered the highest growth during the entire study period.

Considering growth rate of agro and non agro based industries, the growth of number of factories, productive capital and employment are nearly the same for both agro and non-agro related industries. Surprisingly, the growth rate of output of agro-related industries is slightly higher than that of non-agro related industries. But in respect of value added the non-agro related industries revealed dramatic growth. This growth is aided by the sudden growth achieved by chemical and chemical producing industries, transport equipment and parts and metal producing industries.

In the industrial economy of Tamil Nadu the rate of growth of employment had been shrinking more than that of the growth of capital investment, leading to a rise in capital intensity, which validates the hypothesis that *the capital investment in the factory sector has grown much faster than that of employment leading to rising capital intensity.* This trend may be due to the result of the changing industrial structure in favour of heavy industrial goods freeing up of capital market and attractive industrial climate.

During the pre-liberalization period the other manufacturing category of industries registered the highest growth rate in respect of productive capital value of output and value added. At the same time, the chemical group achieved first place in respect of employment growth. During the post liberalization period, the other manufacturing industry registered first place in respect to growth of number of factories and employment. The industries producing beverages, tobacco and tobacco products registered a predominant growth in capital. From this analysis of compound growth rate it is realized that the other manufacturing industries underwent phenomenal growth in respect of value added in the pre reform periods and it was replaced by transport group industries during the post reform period.

While comparing the growth rates of use based group between pre and post reform periods, it is observed that the capital good industry experienced higher growth during the pre reform period and it is replaced by the basic goods during the post reform periods. There has been a marked increase in the growth of productive capital of consumer non-durable goods in the pre reform periods and it is replaced by the intermediary goods during the post reform periods. This sector has assumed much importance in the state because cotton ginning, spinning and weaving are the important sources of income for many persons of the state, hence, there is a phenomenal increase in the investment of cotton yarn in the post reform period.

Heavy investment in the consumer non-durable industries in the pre reform period has led to increase certain amount of employment generation in this group. But during the post reform period the industry producing basic goods revealed more than 16 per cent growth in terms of employment. It may be due to the expansion of chemical and chemical based industries in this state during the post reform periods (the chemical and chemical based industries alone generated 136130 persons in 1980 to 81 and it increased to 280257 in 1999-2000).

Out of these use-based industry groups, consumer non-durable group revealed phenomenal growth of both output and value added during the pre reform period and it is replaced by the intermediate goods during the post reform period. It could be due to the improvement of investment and expansion of capacity in these industries.

In the input-base industries, the metal based industry has revealed nearly 3 per cent growth during the pre reform period and it is replaced by the chemical based industries during the post reform periods. Owing to expansion of demand for fertilizers, pharmaceutical chemicals, cosmetic items the number of chemical industry increased during the post reform period.

Owing to the structural transformation the growth of investment of agro-based industry was dwindled during the post-reform period but its growth was high during the pre-reform period. Due to improvement of number of industries in the chemical based industries (pharmaceutical chemicals and matches) the capital growth of this industry group revealed perceptible growth during the post reform period. With regard to employment, no one group has revealed appreciable growth during the pre reform period. But the chemical based industry expressed an extraordinary growth of nearly 16 per cent during the post reform period. The improvement in the number of industries has absorbed the number of worker during the post reform period. While viewing the entire manufacturing sector of Tamil Nadu, the decelerating trend is evident in the employment generation.

Considering output, it is observed that the agro based industry revealed a down turned trend from pre reform period to the post reform period, in the agro-based industries the industry producing wood and wood products also lost their share over the period. At the same time, the chemical based industry showed a tremendous growth in the post reform period when compared to the pre reform period.

The metal based industry revealed higher growth of value added during pre reform period and it is replaced by chemical based industries during the liberalized regime. This considerable progresses was due to the increase in the internal and external demand of industries producing basic chemicals, fertilizers, pharmaceuticals, cosmetic, and manufacture of other chemicals such as matches and photochemical.

While comparing the pre reform period to the post reform period, in agro-based industries, the productive capital and employment increased its growth from pre liberalization period to the post liberalization period. The value of output registered a stagnant position and all other characteristics decreased for the above mentioned period. Based on the non-agro based industries, productive capital and value of output increased at a snile's phase and the value added had increased nearly 4 per cent growth form pre to post reform period. Conversely, the number of factories revealed sharp decline.

Based on the growth of agro and non agro based industries it is observed that there is statistically certain significant difference in the growth of agro based industries between pre and post reform periods and this trend is not appeared in the non agro based industries. Hence, the proposed hypothesis, that *the output growth of agro-based industries has no significant difference between the pre and post reform periods* is partially accepted.

PRODUCTIVITY TREND

Considering the ASI data, the reform process had encouraged the partial factor productivity of both labour and capital. Solow's index of total factor productivity for both- pre and post reform periods have been computed for the manufacturing sector of Tamil Nadu. There had been an increasing trend revealed by Solow's index of total factor productivity during the post reform periods, the growth of total factor productivity also increased in the post reform period compared to the pre reform period. The independent 't' test result that there is difference in the growth of total factor productivity between pre and post reform periods, which does not justify the hypothesis that *there is no significant difference between pre and post liberalization periods, with respect to growth of total factor productivity.*

EFFECT OF NEW INDUSTRIAL POLICY

During the pre-liberalization period the industries producing rubber, plastics, petroleum and coal products registered the highest growth rate in respect of number of factories, productive capital, employment and value added. The other manufacturing industries had the highest growth rate with respect to output. There had been a negative growth rate in employment with respect to food products wood and wood products, chemical and chemical products and basic metal product.

During the post liberalization period (1991-92 to 1999-2000) the other manufacturing industry registered first place in respect to growth of number of factories. In terms of investment, beverages, tobacco and tobacco related industries, metal producing industries, and transport equipment and parts producing industries revealed significant growth. Due to increase of demand for the above said commodities these industries observed the huge amount of capital. At the same time, employment growth is not appreciable. The 'other manufacturing industries' underwent phenomenal growth in respect of value added in the pre reform periods and it was replaced by transport group industries during the post reform period. In addition, the inter-industry difference with respect to growth does exist. Similar result was obtained by Balakrishana, P. & M. Sureshbabu (2003) in the two digit groups at all India level during 1973-74 to 1999-2000.

With regard to the value added the industries producing wood and wood products, chemical and chemical products machinery and machine tools, electrical equipments and parts and transport equipment and parts are exhibited statistically not significant difference between the per and the post liberalization period. All the remaining industries revealed significant difference between pre and post liberalization period.

CONCLUSIONS

Industrial scenario of Tamil Nadu is like a Kaleidoscope, which reveals different picture. In 1980-81, among the industry groups, the industry producing textiles and its related goods contributed lion's shares with regard to productive capita,l employment, value of output and value added in the industrial mix. Interestingly, in the industrial composition of Tamil Nadu, the structural transformation is perceived, that the industry producing chemical and chemical products came to predominant place in terms of productive capital and value added in 1999-2000. Mention should be made that still the textile group occupies the apex place with regard to employment generation and output. The other important industries are transport equipment and parts, rubber, plastics, petroleum and coal products, and machinery and machine tools, in the case of vale added.

At the same time, value added per factory, and value added per employee have had increased noticeably in the industries producing transport equipment and parts, chemical and chemical products, rubber, plastic, petroleum and coal and other manufacturing industries.

In the input-based groups intermediary goods accounted for the highest by percentage shares in 1980-81, and it was replaced by capital groups in 1999-2000. In the input-based groups, agro-based industry was in dominant place upto the first half of nineties and it was replaced by chemical based industry in 1999-2000.

With the globalization of the economy and implementation of liberal industrial policy reforms, the overall industrial environment at the national and state level has become vibrant due to the spurt in direct foreign investment flow, technological imports and managerial improvement. In the industrial composition of Tamil Nadu, during the pre reform period, textile group revealed top place with regard to all the principal characteristics except productive capital. During the post reform period also, this same group of industry occupied the predominant place in all the principal characteristics. With regard to growth, other manufacturing industry witnessed perceptible growth in the case of value added during the pre reform period and the transport group of industry came to top place during the post reform period in the industrial mix of Tamil Nadu.

In the functional groups, consumer non-durable goods producing industry registered highest growth during the pre reform period and it was replaced by intermediary group during the liberalized regime. Where as, in the input-based groups metal-based industry accounted for the highest growth and it was overtaken by chemical based industries for the above mentioned periods.

In regard to productivity, the labour productivity has gained momentum than that of capital productivity. Also this trend is resemblance in both pre and post reform periods. Solow's index of total factor productivity witnessed a fluctuating trend, and it was improved during the post reform period when compared to pre reform period, but it is not statistically significant increase.

It is to be mentioned that the deceleration in the employment generation of overall industrial economy of Tamil Nadu during the reformed regime is a matter for serious concern and there is clearly a need to arrest this deceleration.

POLICY IMPLICATIONS

The prime shortfall of the ASI data is that it will take more than three years to publish the data, current year data are not available. Hence, the concerned authorities should take necessary action to provide with the data to study the current scenario of industrial Economy.

Analysis on ownership pattern, technological change and international integration will give meaningful result; hence the CSO has to supply data on the above mentioned characteristics.

At present, modern and high-tech industries are playing vital role in the contribution of income, hence the concerned authority should take necessary step to provide such kinds of data.

The growth and structural changes of industrial economy are encompassed by the quality and growth performance of sub sectors such as power, transport, communication, managerial skill and availability of educated manpower. In the case of Tamil Nadu, there is a gap between the growth of industrial and above mentioned sub sectors. The central and state government should take necessary steps with suitable policy to overcome this situation.

It is necessary to mention that (despite some fluctuations) the plan wise financial allocation for industrial and its related activities has been decreasing. This trend has a direct bearing on the growth and sophistication of industrial economy. Hence, the central and state governments should rationalize the allocation of funds.

The industrial and agricultural sectors are strongly correlated with each others. To harvest the full benefit of industrial economy some segments in agricultural sector need to be taken care as this sector provide necessary inputs for industrial sector.

Employment generation is one of the important factors of the world, particularly in the third world countries like India. There has been a sluggishness trend in the manufacturing economy of both India and Tamil Nadu. The policy makers should carefully frame with considering the employment generation.

Export is an essential factor for growth and structural changes of industrial economy, it is well observed at national and international level by scholars like Chennery. Considering the available statistics on trade, it is found that the growth of exports is poor in relation to imports. Hence, export should be improved further by framing more export friendly policy.

Growth and structural changes of industrial economy are linked with political power, political certainty, and government policies. All these thinks are carefully worked out to balanced and sustainable industrial development in this state. In addition, shortage of fuels, materials, and disturbed industrial relation are matter of concerns for the industrial development. Intervention of government is necessary, though the economy is market oriented one.

BIBLIOGRAPHY

ACD (1999), *"Asian Development Outlook"*, Oxford University Press, Hong Kong, p. 33.

Aggarwal A. K. and Ganesh Kumar N. (1991), "Indian Manufacturing Industry, Verdoorn's Law Revised", *The Indian Economic Journal*, Vol. 39. No. 2, p. 66-81.

Ahluwalia, I. J. (1990), "Productivity Trends in Indian Industry: Concerns for the Nineties", *Productivity*, Vol. 31, No 1, p. 1 to 17.

Ahluwalia(1991), *"Productivity and Growth in Indian Manufacturing"*, Oxford University Press, Delhi.

Ahluwalia, I. J. (1998), *"The Contribution of planning to Industrialization", in the State Development Planning and Liberalization in Indian"*, in T. J. Byres (ed). Oxford University Press, New Delhi, p. 254-295.

Alice Albin (1990), "Manufacturing Sector in Kerala-Comparative Study of Its Growth and Structurs", *Economic and Political Weakly*, Vol. XXV, No. 37, p. 2060.

Anyanwu, C. M. (2000), *"Productivity in the Nigerian Manufacturing Industry"*, Research Department, Central Bank of Nigeria, p. 124-175.

Attri, V. N. (1991), "Industrialisation in India: Export-Oriented Approach", *The Indian Economic Journal*, Vol. 38, No. 3, p. 19-36.

Ashoka Mody and Fang-Yi Wang (1997), "Explaining Industrial Growth in Coastal China: Economic Reforms and What Else?" *The World Bank Economic Review*, Vol. 11, No. 2, p. 293-234.

Balakrishnan, R. (1959), *"Measurement of Productivity in Indian Industies"*, University of Madras Pub, Chennai.

Balakrishna, P. & Suresh Babu (2003), "Growth and Distribution in Indian Industry in the Nineties", *Economic and Political Weekly*, Vol. XXXVII, No. 38, p. 3997-4004.

Bean, L. H. (1957), *"International Industrialization and Per Capita Income,"* Studies in Income and Wealth, Vol. II, p. 10-15.

Benjamin, R. E. (1987), *"Industrial Development in Tamil Nadu,"* in Studies in Industrial Economy of Indian, in V.S Mahajan (ed), Deep & Deep Pub., New Delhi, Vol. 2, p. 800-810.

Bhalotra, S. R. (1998), "The Puzzle of Jobless Growth in Indian Manufacturing", *Oxford Bulletin of Economic and Statistics,* Vol. 60, No. 1, p. 5-32, Cited by Panda.

Bhagavan Reddy (1988), "Industrialization and Employment in Indian", *Southern Economic.* Vol. 1, p. 9-12.

Bhagavan, M. R. (1987), *"Caital Goods Sector in India: Past and Present Trends and Future Prospects,"* in Studies in Industrial Economic of India, in V. S. Mahajan (ed), Deep & Deep, N. Delhi, Vol. 2, p. 473.

Bhagwati and Desai (1970), *"India: Planning for Industrialization and Trade Policy since 1951"*, Oxford University Press, London.

Bhandara, S. S. (2001), *"Indian Industry in the Post-Liberalization Era: Some critical Issues"*, Forum of Free Enterprise, Peninsula house, Mumbai, p. 1-20.

Bharathan, K. (1980), *"Changes in the Composition of Industries in Tamil Nadu: 1960 to 1970-A Study of Factory Sector"*, Unpublished M.Phil Dissertation, University of Madras.

Bhatia, G. P. (1990), "Productivity in the Manufacturing Sector of India, the UK and US-Estimates and Comparison", *The Indian Economic Journal,* Vol. 38, No. 2, p. 124-130.

Bhatia, G. K. (1999), *" The Impact of New Economic Policy on Output and Employment no Manufacturing Sector-A Case Study of Punjab"*, in V.S Mahajan (ed), Political Economy of Reforms and Liberalization–Achievements and Failures of Various Sectors, Deep and Deep, New Delhi.

Bhuwaneswan (1991), *"Industrialization Process", in Tamil Nadu Economy–Some Selected, Aspects"*, in Yasodha Shanmgasundaram, Rajalakshmi & Bhuvaneswari (ed), Ethiraj Research Centre, The Ethiraj College for Women, Madras, p. 63-77.

Brahmananda, P. R. (1982), *"Productivity in the Indian Economy: Rising Inputs for Falling Output"*, Himalaya Pub, Delhi.

Burange, L. G. (1999), "International Growth and Structure–Manufacturing Sector in Maharashtra", *Economic and Political Weekly,* Vol. XXXIV, No. 9, p. M. 39–M. 47.

Carbaugh (2000), *"International Economics"*, South-Western College Pub., Cincinnati, Ohio, p. 216 -217.

Census of India (1981), Series-20, *"General Economic Tables"*, Tamil Nadu, Part III, A&B(i).

Census of India (1991), *"Primary Census Abstract for General Population"*, Series. 23, Part-II,-B (i), p. 55-56.

Chandrasekher, K. (1987), "Declining Industrial Growth in Tamil Nadu", *Southern Economic,* p. 9-11.

Chandrasekar, C. P. (2001), *"Industrial Development-50 Years of Crossing a Bridge of Dreams: India & China"*, in G. D. Deshpande and Alka Achary (ed), Tulika Pub., New Delhi, p. 68-87.

Chandraseker, C. P. (2002), *" Industry and Finance"*, in Delhi Science Forum, the Indian Economy 2001-2001: An Altermative Survey, Prajasakthi (pnb)Hyderabad.

Chaudhare, M. R. (1989), "Industrial Development in India During the Planning Era", *Geographical Review of India,* Vol. 51,No. 3, p. 6-16.

Chadhuri, S. (2002), "Economic Reform and Industrial Structure in India", *Economic and Political Weakly,* Vol. XXXVI, No. 2, p. 155-162.

Chenery, H. B. (1980), "Interaction BEtweenIndustrialization and Export's", *American Economic Review,* Vol. 70, No. 2, p. 281-87.

Chen, E. K. Y. (1997), *"Factor Inputs, Total Factor Productivity and Economic Growth: The Asian Case"*, The Developing Economics, XV (i), 121–143–Cited in Mohd Den Bin Jantan & Rizaudin Bin Sahlan (2002).

Chenery, H.B. & Clark, Paul, G. (1967), *" Inter-Industry Economics"*, John-wiley & Sone, New York.

Chin Chankar, P. Y. (1969), *"Wage and Productivity in Indian Industries"*, Vora & Co Pub. Bambay.

Clark, Cal (1989), *"Taiwan's Development: Implications for Contending Political Economy Paradigms"*, Westport, Conn: Greenwood Press, p. 202.

CMIE (2004), *"Monthly Review of the Indian Economy"*, Mumbai, p. 2.

Colin Clark (1957), *"Conditions of Economic Progress"*, Mac Millen, London.

Colin Clark (1960), *"The Distribution of Labour Between Industries"*, The Condition of Economic Progress, Macmillan, London.

Das, H. C. L. (2001), *"Impact of Liberalization on Industrial Development in India"*, in Industrialization-New Challenges, in G. S. Batra and R. C. Dangwal (ed) Deep & Deep Pub., New Delhi, p. 1-27.

Das, D. K. (2004), "Manufacturing Productivity Under Varying Trade Regimes-1980-2000", *Economic and Political Weekly,* Vol. XXXIV, No. 5, p. 423-432.

Dawling, M. and Summers, P. M. (1998), "Total Factor Productivity and Economic Growth-Issue for Asia", *The Economic Record,* Vol. 74, (225), Pp. 170 – 185, -Cited in Mohd Dan Bin Jntan & Rizaudin Bin Sahlan (2002).

DEAR (1999–2000), *"Tamil Nadu-An Economic Appraisal"*, Govt. of Tamil Nadu, Chennai, p. 74.

Deepika Goel (2003), "Impact of Infrastructure on Productivity: Cas of Indian Registered Manufacturing", *Indian Economic Review,* Vol. XXX VIII, No. 1, p. 95–113.

Deepak Nayyar (1994), *"Industrial Development in Indian–Some Reflection on Growth and Stagnation"* in Industrial Growth and Stagnation–The Debate in India, Deepak Nayyar (ed) Oxford University Press, Bombay, p. 219-241.

Devine, P. J., Lee, N. Jones, R. M. Tyson, W. J. (1985), *"An Introduction to Industrial Economy"*, George Allen & Unwin, London, p. 31-32.

Dhal S. C. (1996), *"Structural Change in the Indian Economy in the 1980s and Some Reflections on Early 1990s"*, Occasional Papers, Reserve Bank Of India, Mumbai.

Dhanajayan, R. S. (1985), "Growth of Tamil Nadu Economy-A Perspective", *Southern Economics,* p. 12-13.

Dhingra, I. C. (2003), *"The Indian Economy-Environment and Policy"*, Sultan Cand & Sons, New Delhi, p. 152-153.

Dorth, M. C., Cormick & Poul Over Pedersen (1999), "Globalization and Regionalization of Kenya's Foreign Trade and Production", Centre for Development Research, Working Paper, Subseries on *Globalization and Economic Restruction in Africa,* No:VI, Denmaric, p. 8–26.

Economic Survey (2001-02), *"Pattern of Industrial Growth"*, Ministry of Finance, Economic Division, Govt of India. New Delhi, p. 145.

Economic Times (1984), *"Statistical Surrey of the Indian Economy"*, Vikas Pub. New Delhi, p. 72-75.

EPW (2003), "Domestic Product of States of India–1960-61 to 2000-2001", *Economic and Political Weekly*, Research Foundation, Mumbai, p. 30.

Evelyn Devadason (2004), "Labour Market Responses to Trade and Trade Structure: A Ponel Study of the Malaysian Manufacturing", *The Indian Journal of Labour Economics,* Vol. 47, No. 1, p. 81-91.

Fenske (1968), *"Productivity Measures at the Work Centre"*, Productivity, National Productivity Councile, New Delhi, Vol. 19, No. 3.

Ferguson, P. R. (1988), *"Industrial Economics: Issues and Perspectives"*, Mac Millan Edu. Ltd., London, p. 7-8.

Ghuman, B. S. (2000), *"Liberalization and Regional Pattern of Industrialization: The Indian Experience"*, in Dilip Dutta (ed), Economic Liberalization and Institutional Reforms in South Asia-Recent Experience and Furture Prospects, Atlantic Pub., New Delhi, p. 111-129.

George Rosen (1988), *"Industrial Change in India 1970-2000: Present State of Indian Manufactures and Out look of the Same"*, Allied Pub. Ahmedabad, p. 79–82.

Gillis, M., Perkins, D. H., Roemer, M. and Snodgrass, D. R. (1987), *"Economics of Development"*, W. W. Norton & Company, New York, London, p. 546-547.

Golder, B. N. (1985), "Technical Efficiency of Small Scale Units", *Arthvijanan,* Vol. 2, No. 3.

Goldar, B. N. and Anita Kumari (2002), *"Import Lberalisation and Productivity Growth in Indian Manufacturing Industries in the 1990s"*, Working Paper, E/219/2002, Institute of Economic Growth, Delhi, Cited by Panda.

Golder, B. (2004), "Indian Manufacturing: Productivity Trends in Pre and Post Reform Periods", *Economic and Political Weekly,* Vol. XXXXIX, No. 20, p. 5033-5043.

Gople lal Jain (1999), *"Economic Growth and Development in Indian and other Developing Countries"*, Mangal Deep Pub. Jaipur, p. 107-108.

Gopalm Singh (1995), *"A Geography of India"*, Atma Ram & Sons Pub. Delhi, p. 322-323.

Gorelal Yadava (1982), *"Induistrialisation of Bihar-Some Major constraints and Possible solutions"*, in D. M. Nanjundappa & R. K Sinha (ed), Sterling Pub., New Delhi, p. 232-243.

GoI (1980), *"A Handbook for Extension Service: Rural Industrial Development"*, Hyderabad, P.1.

GoI (1984), *"Statistical Survey of the Indian Economy"*, Vikas Pub., New Delhi, p. 72-75.

GoT (2003), *"Tamil Nagu-Human Development Report"*, Social Science Press, Delhi, p. 6.

Hansda, S. K. (2001), *"Sustainability of Service Lead Growth: An Input Output Analysis of the Indian Economy"*, RBI Occational Papers, Vol. 22, No. 1, 2&3, p. 82.

Hashim, S. R. (1991), "Forty Years of Indian Economy : Structure and Dimensions of Growth", *Indian Economic Journal,* Vol. 38, No. 3, p. 1-18.

Hoffman, W. G. (1958), *"The Growth of Industrial Economics"*, Oxford University Press, Bomby,

Howard Park (2000), *"Industrial Policy: Growth Elixir or Poison?"*, World Bank Research Observer, Vol. 15, No. 1, p.47-64.

Hughes, JRT (1968), "Industrialization - Economic Aspects", in Devid L. Sills (ed), *International Encyclopedia of the Social Sciences,* Macmillan, Vol. 7,p. 253.

Hussain, Syed Vazith (2004), "Performance of Small Scale Industries in Indian and Challenges Ahead", *Indian Journal of Industrial Relations,* Vol. 39, No. 3, p. 319-401.

ILO (1954), *"Higher Productivity in Manufacturing Industries"*, Geneva.

Indian Tax Foundation (2001), *"Indian Industry: Growth and Reform-1947-2002"*, Research Wing, New Delhi.

Jayasree, De (1993), *"Industrial Pattern of Gujarat" in N.K.P Sinha & M.B. Shingh (ed), Perspective on Industrial Development in Indian"*, Rawat Pub., New Delhi, p. 155-160.

Jeemol Unni. N. Lalitha & Uma Rani (2001), "Economic Reforms and Productivity Trend in Indian Manufacturing", *Economic and Political Weekly,* Vol. XXXVI, No. 42, p. 3914-3922.

John, K. Chang (1969), *"Industrial Development in Pre-Communities Chin-A Quantitative Analysis"*, Edinburgh University Press, North America, p. 74-80.

Joshi, S. (2004), "Tertiary Sector- Driven Growth in Indian-Impact an Employment and Poverty", *Economic and Political Weekly,* Vol. XXXiX, No. 37, p. 4175-4178.

Kaldor, N. (1963), *"Capital Accumulation and Economic Growth in the Theory of Capital"*, Machillan London

Kaintha, G. S. & Bawa, R. S. (1985), *"Economic Development and Structural Changes- An Empirical Investigation"*, Inter-Indian Pub, New Delhi.

Kalipada Deb (2004), *"Development and Disparities"*, Rawat Pub. New Delhi, p. 124-128.

Kannan, R. (2004), *"Rangarajan's Selected Essays on Indian Economy"*, Academic Foundation, New Delhi, Vol. 1, p. 330-354.

Karunia, L. (2001), *"Industrial Structural Change in Indonesia: A Study on Manufacturing Industry in the 1980s"*, Institute Pertanian, Bogor, Indonesia.

Kendric John, W. (1961), *" Productivity Trends in the United States"*, National Bureau of Economic Research, Princeton.

Kevin Allen & Andrew Stevenson (1974), *"An Introduction to the Italian Economy"*, Martin Robertson & Co. Ltd. London, p. 78-83.

Khan, M. Y. (1980), *"Trends in Industrial Production: 1951-77"*, RBI Occasional Papers, Vol. 1, No. 1, pp .71-103.

Kishor Sharma (2000), *"Liberalization and Structural Changes: Evidence from Nepal's Manufacturing"*, Economic Growth Centre, Yale University, Centre Discussion Paper.

Kulwindwe Kaur (1982), "Industrial Sector of Haryana: 1966-78", *Margin,* Vol. 14, No. 1, p. 68-73.

Kulkarni, K. G., Qixiang Sun (2004), *"Outward Looking Policies and Economic Development: A Case of Taiwan since 1952"*, Global Business Review, International Management Institute, Sage Pub. New Delhi, p. 1-13.

Kumaraswamy, S. V. (1993), *"Geography of Tamil Nadu"*, Sakthi Abirami Pub, Kumbakonam,

Kurien, C. T. & Josef Jemes (1979), *"Economic Change in Tamil Nadu – 1960-1970: A Regionally and Functionally Disaggregated Analysis"*, Allied Pub, Madras.

Kuznets, Simon (1966), *"Modern Economic Growth- Rate, Structure and Spread"*, Yale University Press, London, p. 153.

Lomas, K. S. (1959), "Production and Productivity Movement in the U.K. since 1900", *Journal of Royal Statistical Society*, Vol. 122, Part. 2, Part. 2, p. 185-210.

Maddison, A. (1955), *"Output, Employment and Productivity in British Manufacturing in the Late Half Century"*, Bulletin of Oxford Institute of Statistics, Part-17, p. 363-368.

Mahajan, V. S. (1986), *"Indian Economy and Regional Development"*, Deep & Deep Pub. New Delhi, p. 152-156.

Majumdar, R. C. and Chopra, P. W. (1996), *"Main Currents of Indian History"*, Sterling Pub., New Delhi, p. 224-225.

Malgavkar (1988), *"Industrial Policy and Prospects 2001.AD"*, Oxford & IBM Pub., New Delhi, p. 14-22.

Manmohan Singh (1986), *"Industry"*, in J. N. Mongia (ed), Indian's Economic Development Strategies 1951-2000) A.D", Allied Pub. New Delhi, p. 75–76.

Kehta, F. A. (1976), *"Indian Industry Looking Ahead"*, Summary Proceeding and Paper, Pub. Industrial Credit and Investment Corporation, Bombay.

Meire, G. M. (1995), *"Leading Issues in Economic Development"*, Oxford University Press, New Delhi, p. 329-375.

MIDS (1988), *"Tamil Nadu Economy–Performance and Issues"*, Oxford & IBI Pub., New Delhi.

Mieko Nishimizu and Sherman Robinson (1986), *"Productive Growth in Manufacturing"*, in Industrialization and Growth–A Comparative Study, Hollis Chenerry, Sherman Robinson, and Moshe Syrquin (ed). A World Bank Research Publication. Oxford University Press, New York. p. 283-308.

Mohamed Peer (1993), *"Social Effects of Industrialization"*, in Gangadhara Rao. Modeyard Heggade and Yadapadithaya.P.S. (ed)., Indian Economy–Trends, Problems and Prospects, Kanishka Pub. Delhi, p. 158-170.

Mohendra Pratap Singh (1977), *"Import Policy and Pattern of Industrialisation–A Case Study of Indian"*, The Economic Studies in D. N. , Mukherjea (ed), Vol. 17, No. 7, p. 361-369.

Mohd Dan Bin Jantan & Rizaudin Bin Shaln (2002), *"Total Factor Productivity: An Empirical Study for Selected Districts in Malaysia"*, School of Economics, University of Utara, Malaysia, 06010 Sintok, Kedah.

Mullen, J. K. & William, M. (1990), "Explaining Total Factor Productivity Differentials in Urban Manufacturing", *Journal of Urban Economic*, Vol. 28, p. 103–123, Cited in Mohd Den Bin Jantan & Rizaudin Bin Sahlan (2002).

Mukerjee, K. L. (1984), "Spacial Incentives for Prestige and Pioneer Industries", *Commerce*, Vol. 148, No. 3820, p. 40-44.

Munirathna Naidu (1983), "Structural Changes in Industrialization of Andhra Pradesh–Strategy in the 80s", *Southern Economist*, Nov. 1-15, p. 19 to 23.

Murray, D. Bryce (1960), *"Industrial Development–A Guide for Accelerating Economic Growth"*, Copyright @ (1960) by the Mc Graw–Hill Book Company, London, p. 3.

Nagaraj, R. (1990), "Growth Rate of Indian's GDP, 1950-51 to 1987-88, Examination of Alternative Hypothesis", *Economic and Political Weekly*, Vol. 15, No. 2, p. 1675-76.

Nagaraj, R. (2003), "Industrial Policy and Performance Since 1980: Which way Now?", *Economic and Political Weekly*, Vol. XXVII, No. 35, p. 3707-3715.

Narayansawamy, M. (1987), "Economic Change in Tamil Nadu", *Economic and Political Weekly*, Vol. XVI, No. 49, p. 1991-1994.

National Council of Applied Economic Research (1958), *"Techno–Economic Survey of Madras"*, New Delhi, p. 2.

Nicholson, R. J. and Guptha, S. (1960), "Output and Productivity Changes in British Manufacturing Industry 1948-54: A study from Census of Production Date", *Journal of Royal Statistical Society*, Vol. 123, Part-4, p. 427-459.

Papola, T. S. (1981), *"Spatial Diversification of Industries–A Study in Uttar Pradesh"*, Allied Pub., New Delhi.

Panda, Hrushukesh (2004), "Technological Change and Growth of Employment in the Organized Manufacturing Industries in India", *Journal of Indian School of Political Economy*, Vol. XVI, No. 1, January-March, p. 185-204.

Pawara, C. T. & Shinde, S. D. (1993), *"Industrialisaton in Maharashtra: An Overview"*, in N. P. K. Sinha & M. B. Singh (ed) Perspective on Industrial Development in Indian: Rawat Pub. New Delhi, p. 51-58

Perumal Swamy, S. (1985), *"Economic Development of Tamil Nadu"*, Chand & Company, New Delhi, p. 10.

Prakash Chandra Adhikary (1997), "A Short Description of Bangladesh's Agriculture and Industry During the First Fifteen Years 1971-85 of her Liberation", *Journal of the Institute of Asian Studies, Institutes of Asian Studies*, Chennai, Vol. XV, No. 1 p. 26-33.

Prakash, B. A. (1999), *"Economic Reforms and the Performance of Kerala's Economy"*, in B.A Prakash(ed), Kerala's Economic Development-Issues and Problems, Sage Pub., New Delhi, p. 27-46.

Rajeswari,V. (1989), *"Growth & Diversification of Industries"*, in Industrial Development of Andhar Pradesh in J. Mahender Reddy, Yahava Reddy, Upodhyay, and Raghuram.C.H.(ed), Streling Pub, Banglore, p. 122–135.

Ramanjaneyulu, M. (2005), *"Growth of Manufacturing Sectors in India"*, in N. Narayana (ed), Economic Development Issues and Policies, Serili Pub., New Delhi, p. 229-242.

Ramesh, A. & Tiwari, P. S. (1983), *"Basic Resource Atlasof Tamil Nadu"*, University of Madras, Chennai. P. 20.

Rangarjan, C. (2000), "Economic Reforms in Indian-Some Issues and Concerns", *The Asian Economic Review*, Vol. 2, No. 1, p. 1-5.

Rangarjan, C. & Kannan, R. (1994), "Capital Output Ratios in the Indian Economy (1950-51 to 1989-90)", *The Indian Economic Journal*, Vol. 42, No. 1, p. 1-16.

Rao, V. (1987), *"Economic Development of India"*, Chugh Pub., Allahabad.

Rao, A. V. V. S. K. (1989), *"Industrialization: A District wise Analysis"*, in J. Mahender Reddy, M. Yadava Reddy, S. K. Upadhyay and C. H., Raguram (ed), Industrial Development of Andhra Pradesh, Sterling Pub., Bangalore, p. 177-187.

Rashmi Banga (2004), "Impart of Japanese and US FDI on Productivity Growth–A Firm-Level Analysis", *Economic and Political Weekly*, Vol. XXXXIX, No. 5, p. 453-460.

Rastogi, P. N. (1986), "The Culture of Productivity", *Journal of Industrial Relation"*, Vol. 22, No. 2.

RBI (1975), *Bulletin*, September, RBI, Mumbai.

RBI (1977), *Bulletin*, February, RBI, Mumbai.

RBI (1998-99), *"Report on Currency and Finance"*, Department of Economic Analysis and Policy of the Reserve Bank of Indian, Mumbai, p. IV-1.

RBI (2000), *"Report on Currency and Finance"*, Mumbai-Cited by Seem Joshi.

RBI (2001), *"Hand Book of Statistics on Indian Economy"*, Deba Prasad Rath (Pub.) for RBI Mumbai, p. 43.

Roy, K. C. (1986), *"Foreign Aid and Indian Development–A Study from the View Point of Peace and Development with Particular Reference to the First Three Plans"*, Gujarat Vidyapith Pub., Ahmedabad, p. 129-130.

Russel, W. Fenske (1968), "Productivity Measures at the Work Center", National Productivity Councile, *Journal of Productivity*, Vol. IX, No. 3, p. 224.

Sadasiva Reddy (1983), "Role of Small Scale Industries in Indian's Economic Development", *Southern Economist,* Vol. 22, No. 2, p. 37-38.

Sastry, D. V. S & Kelkar, U. R. (1987), *"Regional Disparities in Industrial Development"*, Occasional Papers, Reserve Bank of Indian, Vol.8, No. 3, p. 266-275.

Scumpeter (1969), *"The Theory of Economic Development"*, Oxford University Press, London.

Sebasrian, J. (1989), "Structural Transformation Towards Stagnation: A Overiew- Kerala Economy", *Productivity,* Vol. 29, No. 4, p. 445-451.

Shanthi, K. (1981), *"Industrial Change in Tamil Nadu- A Case Study of Productivity Trends in Major Industries in Tamil Nadu"*, Ph.D Thesis, University of Madras.

Sharmd, N. K. (1988), *"Industrial Economics"*, Surabhi Pub., Jaipur.

Shirokov, G. K. (1973), *"Industrialization of India"*, Progress Pub., Moscow, p. 1-2.

Syed Vazith Hussain (2003), *"Small Scale Industries in the New Millennium"*, Sarup & Sone Pub., New Delhi, p. 23.

Siddharthan, N. S. and Lal, K. (2004), "Liberalization, MNC and Productivity of Indian Enterprises", *Economic and Political Weekly,* Vol. XXXIX, No. 5, p. 448-452.

Siddarthan, N. S. (2004), "Globalization: Productivity Efficiency and Growth-An Overview", *Economic and Political Weekly,* Vol. XXXIX, No. 5, p. 420-422.

Sinha, D. K. (1988), *"Economics of Industrialization in India"*, Deep & Deep Pub., New Delhi.

Sivasubramanian, S. (2004), *"The Sources of Economic Growth in Indian, 1950-51 to 1999-2000"*, Oxford University Press, New Delhi, p. 248-255.

Somra, S. S. (1999), *"State and Industrial development: An Alternative Paradigm"*, in G. Palanithurai (ed), Contemporary Issues in Development Dynamics, Kanishka Pub., New Delhi, p. 163-174.

Srivastava, D. C. (1986), *"Evaluation of Industrial Policy for the Development of Backward Regions I India-Case Study of Gujarat"*, Sardar Patel University Pub–Gujarat.

Subramanian, M. S. (1992), "Productivity Growth in Cotton Textiles Industry in Tamil Nadu", *Indian Journal of Industrial Relations*, Vol. 27, No. 4, p. 383–389.

Subrahmanian, K. K. (1990), "Development Paradox in Kerala-Analysis of Industrial Stagnation", *Economic and Industrial Relations*, Vol. XXV, No. 37, p. 2057.

Subrahmanian, K. K. (2006), "Economic Growth in the Regime of Reform: Kerala's Experience", *Economic and Political Weekly*, Vol: XLI, No. 10, p. 885-890.

Sundrum, R. M. (1984), *"Development Economics, A Framework for Analysis and Policy"*, John Wiley & Sons, New York, p. 44.

Suranjit, K. Saha (1991), "Role of Industrialization to development of Sub-Saharan Africa-A Critique of World Bank's Approach", *Economic and Political Weakly*, Vol. XXVI, No. 48, p. 2757.

Surandra, J. Patel (1970), *"Rates of Industrial Growth in the Last Century, 1860-1986"*, in V. B. Singh (ed), Patterns of Economic Development-A Study of the Economic Development of the U.K. the Japan, the USSR and China, Allied Pub, Bombay.

Sutcliffe, R. G. (1971), *"Industry and Underdevelopment"*, Addison Wesley Pub., London.

Tewari, R. T. (1988), "Inter-Regional Pattern of Industrialisation in India: 1971-87", *The Indian Economic Journal*, Vol. 36. No. 2, p. 1-23.

Thambi, M. M. (1999), *"Economic Liberalization and Industrial Development in Kerala: Challenges to New Investment"*, in B.A Prakash (ed), Kerala's Economic Development Issues and Problems, Sage Pub. New Delhi.

Thangamuthu, C. (1973), *"Industrialization of Tamil Nadu-Since 1951-A Structural Analysis"*, M. Lit. Thesis, University of Madras.

Thangamuthu, C. (1983), "Industrial Structure and Change in Tamil Nadu", *Southern Economist*, Vol. 23, p. 18-20.

Thangamuth, C. (2002), *"Trends and Issues in Industrial Development of Tamil Nadu"*, in Tamil Nadu Economy-Trend and Prospects, University of Madras, p. 256.

Thangamuthu, C. & Sankaran, A. (2004), "Industrial Sector Reform: Trends Towards Inter Regional Convergence or Divergence?", *Productivity*, Vol. 45, No. 5, p. 27-32.

Thirlwall, A. P. (1994), *"Growth and Development-With Speical Reference to Developing Economics"*, Mac Millan (Pub.), London.

Thomas, J. J. (2004), *"A Review of Indian Manufacturing"*, Indian Development Report, Oxford University Press, New Delhi, p. 84-101.

Todaro, M. P. (1997), *"The Economy of India-Case Study"*, in Economic Development, Longman, London & New York.

Todaro, M. P. & S. C. Smith (2004), *"Economic Development"*, Person Education, Delhi, p. 116.

Thampy, M. M. (1990), "Wage-Cost and Kerala's Industrial Stagnation-Study of Organized Small Scale Sector", *Economic and Political Weekly*, Vol. XXV, No. 37, p. 2077-2082.

Internet Sources

Foreign Trade Tamil Nadu. *www.tn.gov.deptst/tab30-09.*

Resources of Important Minerals in Tamil Nadu *www.tidco.com*

Profile of Tamil Nadu, *www. smallindustryindian.com*

Changing Structure of the Economy. *www.1.upinfo.com*

Economic growth and Structural Change *http://countrystudies:us/isrle.*

Structural Change and Industrial Slowdown *www.blonnet.com.*

Highlight of Economic Survey 2002-2003. *www.economywatch.com.*

APPENDICES

APPENDIX-I

Group	*Description*
20-21	Manufacture of Food Products
22	Manufacture of Beverages, Tobacco and Related Products.
23	Manufacture of cotton textiles, ginning, drawing and its Related Products
24	Manufacture of wool, silk & synthetic fibre
25	Manufacture of jute, hemp, mesta textiles
26	Manufacture of textiles products including weaving apparel etc.
27	Manufacture of Wood and Wood Products
28	Manufacture of Paper and Paper Products.
29	Manufacture of Leather and Leather Products.
30	Manufacture of Rubber, Plastic, Petroleum & Coal Products.
31	Manufacture of Chemical & Chemical Products.
32	Manufacture of Non- Metallic Mineral Products.
33	Manufacture of Basic Metal and Alloy Products.
34	Manufacture of Machinery & Machine Tools Products.
35-36	Manufacture of Electrical Equipments & Parts Products.
37	Manufacture of Transport Equipment & Parts.
38	Other Manufacturing Industries

APPENDIX-II

USE-BASED CLASSIFICATION

BASIC-GOODS

Group	*Class*	*Sub-Class*	*Description*
	1411	14220	Extraction of salt, [includes salt mining, crushing and
	2411		Manufacture of basic chemicals except fertilizers and nitrogen compounds.
	2412		Manufacture of fertilizers and nitrogen compounds
	2694		Manufacture of cement, lime and plaster
	2695		Manufacture of articles of concrete, cement and plaster

VISION 27: MANUFACTURE OF BASIC METALS

271	2710		Manufacture of Basic Iron &. Steel
272	2720		Manufacture of basic precious and non-ferrous metals
401	4010		Production, collection and distribution of electricity
402	4020	40200	Manufacture of gas, distribution of gaseous fuels through mains

CAPITAL- GOODS

	2813		Manufacture of steam generators, except central heating hot water boilers
	2893		Manufacture of cutlery, hand tools and general hardware

Group	*Class*	*Sub-Class*	*Description*
	2899		Manufacture of other fabricated metal products n.e.c.
	2911		Manufacture of engines and turbines, except aircraft, vehicle and cycle engines
	2919		Manufacture of other general purpose machinery
292			Manufacture of special purpose machinery
	2921		Manufacture of agricultural and forestry machinery
	2922		Manufacture of machine-tools
	2923	29230	Manufacture of 'machinery for metallurgy; converters, ingot moulds, ladles and casting machines; metal rolling mills and roils for such mills.
	2924		Manufacture of machinery for mining, quarrying and construction
	2925		Manufacture of machinery for food, beverage and tobacco processing
	2926		Manufacture of machinery for textile, apparel and leather production [This class includes manufacture of machines for preparing textile fibers, spinning machines, weaving machines (looms) auxiliary machinery, machinery for washing, bleaching. deying, dressing, finishing, sewing machines, machinery for preparing tanning, hides, skin or leather and machinery for making or repairing of foot wears etc,)
	2927		Manufacture of weapons and ammunition [includes tanks and other fighting vehicles; heavy weapons, artillery, mobile guns; small arms such as light machine, guns, rifles; air or gas guns and pistols; firearms which fire blank cartridges, signal flaies, captive bolts and other non-projected firing pistols etc.]

Group	*Class*	*Sub-Class*	*Description*
	2929		Manufacture of other special purpose machinery
293	2930		Manufacture of domestic appliances, n. e.c.

DIVISION 31: MANUFACTURE OF ELECTRICAL MACHINERY AND APPRATUS N.E.C.

311	3110		Manufacture of electric motors, generators and transformers.
312	3120	31200	Manufacture of electricity distribution and control apparatus; [electrical apparatus for switching or protecting electrical circuits (e.g. switches, fuses, voltage limiters, surge suppressors, junction boxes etc.) for a voltage exceeding 1000 volts; similar apparatus (including relays, sockets etc.) for a voltage not exceeding 1000 volts; boards, panels, consoles, cabinets and other bases equipped with two or more of the above apparatus for electricity control or distribution of electricity including power capacitors.]
314	3140		Manufacture of accumulators, primary cells and primary batteries

DIVISION 34: MANUFACTURE OF MOTOR VEHICLES. TRAILERS AND SEMI-TRAILERS

341	3410		Manufacture of motor vehicles.
343	3420		Manufacture of bodies (coach work) for motor vehicles; manufacture of trailers and semi-trailers
343	3430	34300	Manufacture of pans and accessories for motor vehicles and their engines [brakes, gear boxes, axles, roao wheels, suspension shock absorbers, radiators, silencers, exhaust pipes, clutches, steering wheels, steering columns and steering boxes and other parts and accessories n.e.c.]

DIVISION 35: MANUFACTURE OF OTHER TRANSPORT EQUIPMENT

Group	Class	Sub-Class	Description
351			Building and repair of ships & boats.
	3511		Building and repairing and ships [This class includes ship building and. Repairing (other than yachts and other vessels for pleasure or sports) and the construction and repair of floating structures, whether or not used in freight/passenger carriage]
359			Manufacture of transport equipment n.e.c.
	3591		Manufacture of motorcycles
	3592		Manufacture of bicycles and invalid carriages
	3599		Manufacture of other transport equipment n.e.c.

INTERMEDIARY-GOODS

1711		Preparation and spinninlg of textile fiber including weaving of textiles.
1911		Tanning and dressing of leather

DIVISION 20: MANUFACTURE OF WOOD AND OF PRODUCTS OF WOOD AND CORK, EXCEPT FURNITURE; MANUFACTURE OF ARTICLES OF STRAW AND PLATING MATERIALS

201	2010	Saw milling and planing, of wood
202		Manufacture of products of wood, cork, straw and plaiting materials
	2021	Manufacture of veneer sheets; manufacture of plywood, laminboard, .particle board and other panels and boards.
	2022	Manufacture of builders' carpentry and joinery
	2023	Manufacturing of wooden containers
	2101	Manufacture of pulp, paper and paper board

Group	*Class*	*Sub-Class*	*Description*
	2511		Manufacture of rubber tyres and tubes; retreating and rebuilding or rubber types
252	2520		Manufacture of plastic products
261	2610		Manufacture of glass and glass products
269			Manufacture non-metallic mineral products n.e.c.
	2691		Manufacture of.non-structural non-refractory ceramic ware
313	3130	31300	Manufacture of insulated wire and cable; [insulated (including enamelled or anodized) wire. cable (including coaxial cable) and other insulated conductors;' insulated strip as is used in large capacity machines or control equipment; and optical fiber cables]
314	3140		Manufacture of accumulators, primary cells and primary batteries

CONSUMER- DURABLE GOODS

2029			Manufacture of other products of wood, manufacture of articles of cork. straw and lanting materials

DIVISION 28: MANUFACTURE OF FABRICATED METAL PRODUCTS, EXCEPT MACHINERY AND EQUIPMENTS

281			Manufacture of structural metal products, tanks, reservoirs and steam generators
	2811		Manufacture of structural metal products
	2812		Manufacture of tanks, reservoirs and containers of metal [includes manufacture of containers of metal for compressed or liquified gas. Also includes manufacture of central heating boilers and radiators. Manufacture of reservoirs, tanks and similar \ containers of types normally installed as fixtures for storage or manufacturing use of metal,

Group	Class	Sub-Class	Description
			whether or not fitted with tops, closures, or lined with materials other than on, steel or aluminum]
	2919		Manufacture of other general purpose machinery
323	3230		Manufacture of television and radio receivers, sound or video recording or reproducing apparatus, and associated goods

DIVISION 33; MANUFACTURE OF MEDICAL, PRECISION AND OPTICAL INSTRUMENTS WATCHES AND CLOCKS

331			Manufacture of medical appliances and instruments and appliances for measuring, checking, lesting, navigating and other purposes except optical instruments
	3311		Manufacture of medical and surgical equipment and orthopedic appliances
	3312		Manufacture of instruments and appliances for measuring, checking, testing, navigating mid other purposes except industrial process control equipment
332	3320		Manufacture of optical instruments and photographic equipment
333	3330		Manufacture of watches and clocks

DIVISION 36: MANUFACTURE OF FURNITURE; MANUFACTURING N.E.C.

361	3610		Manufacture of furniture
369			Manufacture of n.e.c.
	3691		Manufacture of jewellery and related articles
	3693		Manufacture of sports goods
	3694		Manufacture of games and toys
502	5020	50200	Maintenance of repair of motor vehicles [including washing and polishing etc]

CONSUMER NON-DURABLE GOODS

DIVISION 15: MANUFACTURE OF FOOD PRODUCTS AND BEVERAGES

Group	*Class*	*Sub-Class*	*Description*
151			Production, processing and preservation of meat, fish, fruit vegetables, oils and fats.
	1511		Production, processing and preserving of meat and meat product.
	1512		Processing and preserving of fish and fish products [fishing and processing of [the catch aboard the fisher boats are classified in class 0500 whereas activities of vessels engaged only processing and preserving are classified under this class]
	1512		Cussing and preserving of fruit and vegetables
	1513		Manufacture of vegetable. and animal oils. and fats [Wet corn milling and production of corn oil is classified in Class 1532 and treatment of oils and fats by chemical processing is classified in Class .2429]
152	1520		Manufacture of dairy product [production of raw milk is classified in class 0121]
153			Manufacture of grain mill products, starches and starch products, and prepared animal feeds
	1531		Manufacture of grain mill products [Manufacture of potato flour and meal is classified in class 1513. Production of corn oil is classified in Class 1532]
	1532		Manufacture of starches and starch products
	1533		Manufacture of prepared animal feeds
154			Manufacture of other food products
	1541		Manufacture of bakery products

Group	Class	Sub-Class	Description
	1542		Manufacture of sugar [manufacture of glucose and other sugars made from starches is classified in class 1532]
	1543		Manufacture of Cocoa, chocolate and sugar confectionery
1544	15440		Manufacture of macaroni, noodles, conscious and similar farinaceous products
	1549		Manufacture of other food products n.e.c.
155			Manufacture of beverages
	1551		Distilling, rectifying and blending of spirits; ethyl alcohol production from fermented materials
	1552	15520	Manufacture of wines
	1553		Manufacture of malt liquors and malt
554			Manufacture of soft drinks; production of mineral waters.

DIVISION 16: MANUFACTURE OF TOBACCO PRODUCTS

160	1600		Manufacture of tobacco products [tobacco related products are also included while preliminary processing of tobacco leaves is classified in class 0111]
	1712		Finishing of" textile. (This class includes finishing of. textiles of Class 1711 by operations such as bleaching, dyeing, calendering, napping, shrinking or printing. No distinction is to be made between these activities carried out on a fee or contract basis, or by purchasing the material and selling the finished products).
181	1801		Manufacture of wearing apparel, except fur apparel, [this class includes manufacture of wearing apparel made of material not made in the same unit. Both regular and contract activities are included]
192	1920		Manufacture' of footwear

VISION 21: MANUFACTURE OF PAPER AND PAPER PRODUCTS

Group	*Class*	*Sub-Class*	*Description*
210			Manufacture of paper and paper product
	2101		Manufacture of pulp, paper and paper board
	2102		Manufacture of corrugated paper and paperboard and of containers
	2109		Manufacture of other articles of paper and paperboard
	2423		Manufacture of pharmaceuticals, medicinal chemicals and botanical products
	2424		Manufacture of soap and detergents, cleaning and polishing preparations, perfumes and toilet preparations
	2610		Manufacture of glass and glass products
	2691		Manufacture of.non-structural non-refractory ceramic ware
315	3150		Manufacture of electric lamps and lighting equipment.
	3699		Other manufacturing n.e.c.

APPENDIX- III

INPUT-BASED CLASSIFICATION OF INDUSTRIES

AGRO BASED INDUSTRIES

DIVISION 15: MANUFACTURE OF FOOD PRODUCTS AND BEVERAGES

Group	*Class*	*Sub-Class*	*Description*
151			Production, processing and preservation of meat, fish, fruit vegetables, oils and fats.
	1511		Production, processing and preserving of meat and meat product.
	1512		Processing and preserving of fish and fish products [fishing and processing of [the catch aboard the fisher boats are classified in class 0500 whereas activities of vessels engaged only processing and preserving are classified under this class]
	1513		Processing and preserving of fruit and vegetables
	1514		Manufacture of vegetable. and animal oils. and fats [Wet corn milling and production of corn oil is classified in Class 1532 and treatment of oils and fats by chemical processing is classified in Class .2429]
152	1520		Manufacture of dairy product [production of raw milk is classified in class 0121]

Group	*Class*	*Sub-Class*	*Description*
153			Manufacture of grain mill products, starches and starch products, and prepared animal feeds
	1531		Manufacture of grain mill products [Manufacture of potato flour and meal is classified in class 1513. Production of corn oil is classified in Class 1532]
	1532		Manufacture of starches and starch products
	1533		Manufacture of prepared animal feeds
154			Manufacture of other food products
	1541		Manufacture of bakery products
	1542		Manufacture of sugar [manufacture of glucose and other sugars made from starches is classified in class 1532]
	1543		Manufacture of Cocoa, chocolate and sugar confectionery
	1544	15440	Manufacture of macaroni, noodles, conscious and similar farinaceous products
	1549		Manufacture of other food products n.e.c.
155			Manufacture of beverages
	1551		Distilling, rectifying and blending of spirits; ethyl alcohol production from fermented materials
	1552	15520	Manufacture of wines
	1553		Manufacture of malt liquors and malt
	554		Manufacture of soft drinks; production of mineral waters.

DIVISION 16: MANUFACTURE OF TOBACCO PRODUCTS

160	1600		Manufacture of tobacco products [tobacco related products are also included while preliminary prqcessing of tobacco leaves is classified in class 0111].

DIVISION 17: MANUFACTURE OF TEXTILES

Group	Class	Sub-Class	Description
171	1711		Spinning, weaving and finishing of textiles. Preparation and spinning of textile fiber including weaving of textiles.
	1715		Finishing of" textile. (This class includes finishing of. textiles of Class 1711 by operations such as bleaching, dyeing, calendering, napping, shrinking or printing. No distinction is to be made between these activities carried out on a fee or contract basis, or by purchasing the material and selling the finished products).
172			Manufacture of other textiles
	1721		Manufacture of made-up textile articles, except apparel
	1723		Manufacture of cordage, rope, twine and netting
	1729		Manufacture of other textiles n.e.c.
173	1730		Manufacture of knitted and crocheted fabrics and articles

DIVISION 18: MANUFACTURE OF WEARING APPAREL; DRESSING AND DYEING OF FUR

181	1801		Manufacture of wearing apparel, except fur apparel, [this class includes manufacture of wearing apparel made of material not made in the same unit. Both regular and contract activities are included]
182	1820		Dressing and dyeing of fur; manufacture of articles of fur

DIVISION 19: TANNING AND DRESSING OF LEATHER; MANUFACTURE OF LUGGAGE, HANDBAGS SADDLERY, HARNESS AND FOOTWEAR

191			Tanning and dressing of leather, manufacture of luggage handbags, saddlery & harness.

Group	*Class*	*Sub-Class*	*Description*
	1911		Tanning and dressing of leather
192	1920		Manufacture' of footwear

DIVISION 20: MANUFACTURE OF WOOD AND OF PRODUCTS OF WOOD AND CORK, EXCEPT FURNITURE; MANUFACTURE OF ARTICLES OF STRAW AND PLATING MATERIALS

201	2010		Saw milling and planing, of wood
202			Manufacture of products of wood, cork, straw and plaiting materials
	2020		Manufacture of veneer sheets; manufacture of plywood, laminboard, particle board and other panels and boards.
	2022		Manufacture of builders' carpentry and joinery
	2023		Manufacturing of wooden containers
	2029		Manufacture of other products of wood, manufacture of articles of cork straw and lanting materials

VISION 21: MANUFACTURE OF PAPER AND PAPER PRODUCTS

210			Manufacture of paper and paper product
	2101		Manufacture of pulp, paper and paper board

DIVISION 23: MANUFACTURE OF COKE, REFINED PETROLEUM PRODUCTS AND NUCLEAR FUEL

231	2310		Manufacture of coke oven products [This class includes the operation of coke ovens chiefly for the production of coke or semicoke from hard coal and lignite, retort carbon and residual products such as coal tar or pitch. Agglomeration of coke. Distillation of coal tar is classified in class 2411,]

DIVISION 25: MANUFACTURE OF RUBBER AND PLASTIC PRODUCTS

251			Manufacture of rubber products
	2511		Manufacture of rubber tyres and tubes; retreading and rebuilding or rubber types

Group	Class	Sub-Class	Description
	2519		Manufacture of other rubber products
252	2520		Manufacture of plastic products

METAL- BASED

DIVISION 28: MANUFACTURE OF FABRICATED METAL PRODUCTS, EXCEPT MACHINERY AND EQUIPMENTS

281			Manufacture of structural metal products, tanks, reservoirs and steam generators
	2811		Manufacture of structural metal products
	2812		Manufacture of tanks, reservoirs and containers of metal [includes manufacture of containers of metal for compressed or liquified gas. Also includes manufacture of central heating boilers and radiators. Manufacture of reservoirs, tanks and similar \ containers of types normally installed as fixtures for storage or manufacturing use of metal, whether or not fitted with tops, closures, or lined with materials other than on, steel or aluminium]
		2813	Manufacture of steam generators, except central heating hot water boilers
289			Manufacture of other fabricated metal products; metal working service activities
	2891	28910	Forging pressing, stamping and roll-forming of metal; powder metallurgy
	2892	28920	Treatment and coating of metals; general mechanical, engineering on a fee orcontract basis
	2893		Manufacture of cutlery, hand tools and general hardware
	2899		Manufacture of other fabricated metal products n.e.c.

Group	*Class*	*Sub-Class*	*Description*
DIVISION: 29 MANUFACTURE OF MACHINERY AND EQUIPMENT, N.E.C			
291			Manufacture of general purpose machinery
	2911		Manufacture of engines and turbines, except aircraft, vehicle and cycle engines
	2914		Manufacture of ovens, furnaces and furnace burners
	2919		Manufacture of other general purpose machinery
292			Manufacture of special purpose machinery
	2921		Manufacture of agricultural and forestry machinery
	2922		Manufacture of machine-tools
	2923	29230	Manufacture of 'machinery for metallurgy; converters, ingot moulds, ladles and casting machines; metal rolling mills and roils for such mills.
	2924		Manufacture of machinery for mining, quarrying and construction
	2925		Manufacture of machinery for food, beverage and tobacco processing
	2926		Manufacture of machinery for textile, apparel and leather production. [This class includes manufacture of machines for preparing textile fibers, spinning machines, weaving machines (looms) auxiliary machinery, machinery for washing, bleaching. deying, dressing, finishing, sewing machines, machinery for preparing tanning, hides, skin or leather and machinery for making or repairing of foot wears etc,)
	2927	29270	Manufacture of weapons and ammunition [includes tanks and other fighting vehicles; heavy weapons, artillery, mobile guns; small arms such as light

Group	*Class*	*Sub-Class*	*Description*
			machine, guns, rifles; air or gas guns and pistols; firearms which fire blank cartridges, signal flaies, captive bolts and other non-projected firing pistols etc.]
	2929		Manufacture of other special purpose machinery
293	2930		Manufacture of domestic appliances, n. e.c.

DIVISION 30: MANUFACTURE OF OFFICE, ACCOUNTING AND COMPUTING MACHINERY

300	3000		Manufacture of office, accounting and computing machinery

DIVISION 31: MANUFACTURE OF ELECTRICAL MACHINERY AND APPRATUS N.E.C.

311	3110		Manufacture of electric motors, generators and transformers.
312	3120	31200	Manufacture of electricity distribution and control apparatus; [electrical apparatus for switching or protecting electrical circuits (e.g. switches, fuses, voltage limiters, surge suppressors, junction boxes etc.) for a voltage exceeding 1000 volts; similar apparatus (including relays, sockets etc.) for a voltage not exceeding 1000 volts; boards, panels, consoles, cabinets and other bases cquipped with two or more of the above apparatus for electricity control or distribution of electricity including power capacitors.]
313	3130	31300	Manufacture of insulated wire and cable; [insulated (including enamelled or anodized) wire. cable (including coaxial cable) and other insulated conductors;' insulated strip as is used in large capacity machines or control equipment; and optical fiber cables]
314	3140		Manufacture of accumulators, primary cells and primary batteries

Group	*Class*	*Sub-Class*	*Description*
335	3150		Manufacture of electric lamps and lighting equipment .
319	3190		Manufacture of other, electrical equipment n.e.c,

DIVISION 32: MANUFACTURE OF RADIO, TELEVISION AND COMMUNICATION EQUIPMENT AND APPARATUS

312	3210		Manufacture of electronic valves and tubes and other electronic components
322	3220		Manufacture of television and radio transmitters and apparatus for line telephony and line telegraphy
323	3230		Manufacture of television and radio receivers, sound or video recording or reproducing apparatus, and associated goods.

DIVISION 33: MANUFACTURE OF MEDICAL, PRECISION AND OPTICAL INSTRUMENTS WATCHES AND CLOCKS

331			Manufacture of medical appliances and instruments and appliances for measuring, checking, lesting, navigating and other purposes except optical instruments
	3311		Manufacture of medical and surgical equipment and orthopedic appliances
	3312		Manufacture of instruments and appliances for measuring, checking, testing, navigating mid other purposes except industrial process control equipment
332	3320		Manufacture of optical instruments and photographic equipment
333	3330		Manufacture of watches and clocks

DIVISION 34: MANUFACTURE OF MOTOR VEHICLES. TRAILERS AND SEMI-TRAILERS

341	3410	Manufacture of motor vehicles.	

Group	*Class*	*Sub-Class*	*Description*
343	3420		Manufacture of bodies (coach work) for motor vehicles; manufacture of trailers and semi-trailers
343	3430	34300	Manufacture of pans and accessories for motor vehicles and their engines [brakes, gear boxes, axles, roao wheels, suspension shock absorbers, radiators, silencers, exhaust pipes, clutches, steering wheels, steering columns and steering boxes and other parts and accessories n.e.c.]

DIVISION 35: MANUFACTURE OF OTHER TRANSPORT EQUIPMENT

315			Building and repair of ships & boats.
	3511		Building and repairing and ships [This class includes ship building and. Repairing (other than yachts and other vessels for pleasure or sports) and the construction and repair of floating structures, whether or not used in freight/passenger carriage]
352	3520		Manufacture of railway and tramway locomotives and rolling stock .
353	3530		Manufacture of aircraft and spacecraft
359			Manufacture of transport equipment n.e.c.
	3591		Manufacture of motorcycles
	3592		Manufacture of bicycles and invalid carriages
	3599		Manufacture of other transport equipment n.e.c.

CHEMICAL-BASED

232	2320		Manufacture of refined petroleum products
233	2330	23300	Processing of nuclear fuel [includes extraction of uranium metal from pitchblende or other uranium bearing

Group	*Class*	*Sub-Class*	*Description*
			ores; manufacture of alloys, dispersions or raixtuies of natural uranium or its compounds; manufacture of enriched uranium and its compounds; plutonium and its compounds; uranium depleted in U 235 and its compounds; other radioactive elements, isotopes or compounds; and, non-irradiated fuel elements for use in nuclear reactors]

DIVISION 24: MANUFACTURE OF CHEMICALS AND CHEMICAL PRODUCTS

241			Manufacture of basic chemicals
	2411		Manufacture of basic chemicals except fertilizers and nitrogen compounds.
	2412		Manufacture of fertilizers and nitrogen compounds
	2413		Manufacture of plastics in primary forms and of synthetic rubber,
242			Manufacture of other chemical products
	2421		Manufacture of pesticides and other agro chemical products
	4422		Manufacture of paints, varnishes and similar coatings, printing ink and mastics
	4423		Manufacture of pharmaceuticals, medicinal chemicals and botnical products
	4424		Manufacture of soap and detergents, cleaning and polishing preparations, perfumes and toilet preparations
	2429		Manufacture of other chemical product n.e.c.
243	2430		Manufacture of man-made fibers [This class includes manufacture of artificial or synthetic filament and non-filament fibers.]
314	3140		Manufacture of accumulators, primary cells and primary batteries

INDEX

E

F

G

H

I